306.4830941 TA

D0275907

Foo*bal and Fa

7

197

7

7

Sport, Politics and Culture
A series of books from Leicester University Press

Series editors: Stephen Wagg and John Williams
Department of Sociology, Universtiy of Leicester

Forthcoming titles:

G. Jarvis & G. Walker	*Scottish sport in the making of a nation*
N.Blain; R. Boyle & H. O'Donnell	*Sport and the mass media: national and European identities*
J. Bale	*Sport and landscape*
J. Sugden & A. Bairner	*Irish sport and the politics of partition*

Football and its Fans

Supporters and their relations with the game, 1885–1985

ROGAN TAYLOR

OXSTALLS LEARNING CENTRE
UNIVERSITY OF GLOUCESTERSHIRE
Oxstalls Lane
Gloucester GL2 9HW
Tel: 01242 715100

LEICESTER UNIVERSITY PRESS

LEICESTER, LONDON AND NEW YORK

DISTRIBUTED EXCLUSIVELY IN THE USA AND CANADA BY ST. MARTIN'S PRESS

© Rogan Taylor 1992

First published in Great Britain in 1992 by Leicester University Press
(a division of Pinter Publishers)

All rights reserved. No part of this publication may be reproduced, stored
in a retrieval system, or transmitted in any form or by any means, electronic,
mechanical, photocopying, recording or otherwise, without the prior permission of the
Leicester University Press.

Editorial offices
Fielding Johnson Building, University of Leicester, University Road,
Leicester, LE1 7RH, England

Trade and other enquiries
25 Floral Street, London, WC2E 9DS, England
and St. Martin's Press, Inc.
175 Fifth Avenue, New York, NY 10010, USA

British Library cataloguing in publication data
A CIP catalogue record for this book is available from the British Library.

ISBN 0-7185-1463 7 (pbk)

Typeset by Florencetype, Kewstoke, Avon
Printed and bound by Biddles Ltd of Guildford and Kings Lynn

LEARNING CENTRE
CHELTENHAM & GLOUCESTER
COLLEGE OF HIGHER EDUCATION

3701867987

306 4830941 H2

Inv. N7088168

*To Trevor and Jenni Hicks
in memory of their daughters,
Sarah and Vicki; and to
everyone else who lost loved
ones at Hillsborough on April 15th, 1989.*

CONTENTS

ACKNOWLEDGEMENTS

My primary debt of gratitude belongs to the Centre for Football Research at Leicester University and to the commitment of the Football Trust which enables its work to continue. My thanks go directly to the staff at the Centre, Professor Eric Dunning, Patrick Murphy, Janet Tiernan, Ivan Waddington and especially, John Williams. Thanks, too go to Stephen Wagg.

I am grateful for the assistance provided by current and past Officers of the NFFSC, in particular President Archie Gooch, who provided me with as complete a record as exists of Federation AGM's since 1948, and Chairman, Tony Kershaw. Many other football supporters spanning four generations, have contributed also and I thank them too.

Finally, I would like to acknowledge the efforts of the Centre's typist, Ann Ketnor, who must know this book by heart!

Rogan Taylor
Spring 1992

FIRST HALF

'Early Days' (1885–1939)

We are more than what we seem –
Men on the terraces, soaking wet.
We have glimpsed part of our golden dream.

[From *Men on the Terraces* by Gordon Jeffrey]

1
OPENING ACCOUNTS

Of course, I shall be there. Do you know what I tell my mates? Why, that football is the grandest thing that ever came out for the likes of me . . . I'd sooner miss the old woman's best Sunday dinner than a match on Saturday. (A football supporter, 1910)[1]

In 1985 English football reached its nadir. The steady decline in annual attendances since 1948 touched rock bottom at around 17 million. Scores of supporters died at football matches at Birmingham City, in the fire at Bradford and at the European Cup Final in Brussels, following crowd disturbances amongst Liverpool fans. Television companies refused to deal with the game. Its public image on and off the park was in tatters. Most of all, in the public's eyes football fans themselves were hopeless cases; stupid, violent and beyond the pale.

The immediate causes of football's problems seemed obvious: chronic hooliganism and poor administration, in deadly combination. Whatever complex issues might lie behind such easy phrases, one thing appeared unmistakable – the *relationship* between football and its fans was in terminal decline. It had failed. Some questions naturally arose. What was the history of supporters' relations with the game? How had they organised themselves traditionally, and to what purpose? What had happened over the past hundred years of professional football between those who sought to represent supporters' interests and those who owned the clubs and ran the game?

Any attempt to throw light on these questions must start at the beginning. It is impossible to understand the way that football's fans have been perceived – and the way they saw themselves – without some recognition of the peculiar history of the modern game and the social context of its emergence as a professional sport. It is only comparatively recently that serious attempts have been made to investigate such topics.[2] When it comes to the history of supporters themselves, the cupboard is almost bare.

It is common knowledge that the modern forms of football – both rugby and association games – were mediated into existence through the public schools of England. What is less well known is that the process of defining and codifying football was itself part of a specific attempt by public schoolmasters to *gain control* of the pupils nominally in their charge.[3] Public schools like Eton and Winchester had been founded originally for 'pauperes et indigents' to train them as clerics, but their statutes also permitted fee-paying pupils. Rugby and Shrewsbury, in contrast, were originally local grammer schools. By the last quarter of the eighteenth century, however, most public schools had become institutions which catered, almost exclusively, to the upper class and aristocracy. Yet the masters who taught in these schools remained members of much less privileged social circles, and disciplinary problems became endemic as the sons of aristocrats resented and refused to accept 'lower personages' in authority over them. There were sporadic outright revolts amongst the pupils of public schools throughout the late eighteenth and early nine-teenth centuries. Local soldiery were often required to fix bayonets and establish order.[4] The 'fagging' systems which developed in the public schools reflected the ferocious autonomy of the upper-class schoolboys. Refusing to be ordered or disciplined by their masters, they established their own forms of hierarchical control. The greater ruled the lesser; the strong subjugated the weak.

Just when older versions of 'folk' football were in decline – a result of complex social processes which detached the game from its traditional, cultural anchorages – football drew a new lease of life from its popularity in the public schools.[5] The 'top boys' (prefects) made the game compulsory, for it was on the football field(s) that the power relations between them-selves and their 'fags' were dramatically enacted. Up to two hundred poor souls were required to 'defend the line' or 'keep goal', whilst the preroga-tive of attacking remained solely with the prefects who smashed into the opposing line of 'fags' at will.[6]

When pressures rose to reform the public schools, the 'fagging' system became the central target of the reformers. Without at least some control over 'fagging', the schoolmasters could hardly organise a proper education for their pupils. Pressure to reform at Rugby School was particularly intense because it was a less 'aristocratic' establishment, filled with the sons of upper-middle-class parents, the latter who wanted their male progeny properly educated for the tasks of administering a growing British Empire. It was at Rugby, consequently, that the masters first succeeded in gaining a purchase on the prefect-fagging system, in part by instituting an indirect control over football: the rules of the game were written down. Though the prefects retained control of all sports, 'games' were to become a central part of the *official* life of the school, turning disordered autonomy into ordered hierarchy. Football became the field on which discipline, team spirit and an agreement to 'play by the rules' (of society) could be fostered and encouraged. The game was formalised and 'prefects' were appointed, for the first time, by the staff of the school.

When pupils from different public schools came together at university, there was no common set of rules by which they could play one another. Each public school had developed its own rules for the game and differences were wide, from the ready handling of the ball at Rugby to the required kicking of it at Harrow. (It was Eton, however, who first barred handling the ball and required it to be kicked between two posts and under a crossbar.) It is possible that the 'aristocratic' school boys at Eton and Harrow prohibited the handling of the ball in an attempt 'to put the upstart Rugby in its place'.[7] There were some attempts prior to 1863 to standardise a set of rules (involving committees of 'Old Boys' from Eton, Rugby, Harrow and Marlborough) but they had failed.[8] The graduates at Cambridge, however, in 1863, produced a set of rules which were subsequently used at the inaugural meetings of the 'Football Association' in London to defeat the Rugby faction.[9] Thus the most *aristocratic* version of the game became 'association football' – the version which forbade the use of the hands and thereby imposed greater 'control' (of self) and a higher level of skill to control the ball, on its players. This was the game that, by the turn of the century, had become the passion of so many ordinary folk of industrial Britain. Somewhere along the line, the game of the aristocrats and the well-to-do got plundered by the working class of Glasgow, Lancashire and the West Midlands.

This is not the place to investigate the process, 'both problematic and significant', whereby an ancient 'folk' game was formalised and transmitted by the sons of gentlemen to the industrial workers of Britain.[10] We do know it happened, and that recognising this process is the key to understanding the strange relationship that has characterised football fans and the game ever since. The developing attitude of those who owned football clubs, and those who administered the sport, towards the burgeoning crowds who came to watch, seems to betray some deep and lasting *embarrassment* that the aristocratic public school game left in their charge had been clutched so passionately to the hearts of less advantaged people. As their amateur, Corinthian vision of football dissolved into a fiery reality of private limited companies competing against each other with professional players, the upper class 'gents' who had midwifed the game swiftly abandoned the progeny on the nearest doorstep. Football was left 'in the custody of the lower middle class . . . a fractious alliance between clerks and self made businessmen',[11] to struggle manfully for its lost 'respectability', like an orphan child in a Victorian melodrama. This dramatic subtext helps explain with some clarity the *style* with which the game has been administered; the atmosphere in boardrooms amongst committees of solid citizens who behave as if the local landed gentry stood at their shoulders, watching every move. As Stephen Wagg aptly puts it, football administrators found themselves 'left to run their affairs the way they imagined their betters would have wanted.'[12] The same came to be true of the vast majority of football Supporters' Clubs, as they proliferated throughout the following fifty years.

But what of the first football spectators? Who were they? The original folk game, of course, might range over miles across the fields between pubs and villages or tumble through the narrow streets of towns. Any 'spectating' would have required almost as much involvement as *playing*. There were no real limits on the number of players and running alongside the action could, one imagines, easily involve actually playing the game. Once the limit of eleven players was established by the FA in 1863, and the game was restricted to a designated area, 'passive' spectating became possible – though somehow football spectators always remained in a highly participatory role, which could spill over in a variety of crowd disorders or just plain vigorous enthusiasm.[13]

The first football clubs were often simply *clubs* with 'members' who joined to get involved. Proliferating rapidly via a network of ex-public schoolboy groups, churches and chapels, pubs and workplaces, even individual streets, these early clubs were formed to run football teams and arrange matches. The first 'supporters' would have been *the members who were not playing* and, eventually, players who no longer played, friends and relatives of players and even, presumably, any local passing trade. The original 'membership fee' was often the equivalent of a 'season-ticket', but guaranteeing not only access but also a democratic involvement in the running of the club. Literally thousands of local teams flourished between 1870–1900, often based on no more than friendship or locality. Though difficult to prove, it seems that 'there are no major reasons why the bulk of those teams should not have been working class in origin and run by working class men . . .'[14]

The *commercialisation* of football, interestingly, came before its *professionalisation*.[15] Indeed, the one led to the other. Spectators who paid for the privilege of watching sports were not a complete novelty of course. They were around in the eighteenth century, paying entrance fees for prize fights, cricket matches and race-meetings. But a survey in 1830 failed to show any examples of regular sporting occasions tailored to working-class spectators.[16] The peculiar power of the intrinsic excitement of a football match, coupled with a team's ability to represent the people of a quite particular locality, soon led to an intense interest in the game.[17] This potent amalgamation of enthusiasm and identification which football could provide, combined with increases in real wages for workers in the 1870s and 1880s (plus a Saturday half holiday), lit the blue touchpaper for the explosion of the game's popularity.[18] In the first season of the Football League, 1888–89, average attendances in the First Division reached 4,600; by 1913–14 they averaged 23,100.[19]

The composition of those early football crowds in the last quarter of the nineteenth century could vary considerably, depending on the kind of game (Cup, League or 'friendly') and where it was played. It would be wrong to assume that an undifferentiated wedge of working-class men ubiquitously sustained the game in this period. In the 1880s, for example, 'a significant proportion of a good many football crowds was made up of the better off or middle classes.'[20] Women spectators were present too, sometimes in their thousands, and Preston North End was forced to abandon the, often standard, 'Ladies Free' concession in 1885, at a match at which some 2,000 female fans turned up. It is difficult to guess how many of these might have been working-class women but probably not too many given the traditional constraints upon their time and available money. If working-class women were present – as no doubt some were – they were probably young and unmarried, or older, beyond child-rearing age.[21] Exceptions to such rules, however, are clearly manifest in a referee's account of the personal abuse he received at a match in 1884 in which Preston was involved:

> After the affair was over I was tackled by a flock of infuriated beings in petticoats supposed to be women, who without doubt were in some cases mothers, if I may judge from the innocent babes suckling at their breasts. They brandished their umbrellas and shook their fists in my face . . . Before I got away from the mob another being – again a female – struck me on the back . . . and invited the dirty-nosed little rascals who spoil every football match they go to, to crush me . . .[22]

As Hutchinson points out, the descriptions of crowds 'vary considerably depending on the prejudices of the writer.'[23] One such, Charles Edwardes, writing in 1892, noted that it was 'quite odd' to see at League matches that 'football fever' extended to many old people and women. They crammed into the excursion trains, along with crowds of young men, to travel up to 100 miles for a match. When they got there, according to Edwardes, the language was blue: 'The multitude flock to the field in their workaday dirt, and their workaday adjectives very loose on their tongues.'[24] Edwardes was amazed to see so many of 'the fair sex' so keen to watch football, not just from the stands, but in amongst the crowd, taking 'their chance in the crush which often precedes entrance into the field: and, to do them justice, they do not seem to mind these crushes.'[25] Ominously, Edwardes reports: 'Nowadays more spectators than players die of football.'[26]

As crowds grew bigger – and crushing became more frequent and intense – probably fewer women attended matches and the proportion of middle-class spectators also diminished.[27] As the professional game developed, especially in the industrial north and midlands, crowds increasingly became more densely working class, both skilled and unskilled. By the inter-war period, 1920–39, 'representatives of all sections of working men more or less in proportion' were watching the game.[28] London and the south of England had, it seems, provided most of the early 'middle-class' element in football crowds. Almost all the public schools were, of course, located in the south from where, with the exceptions of Sheffield FC and Queens Park, Glasgow, the amateur game first emerged. The FA Challenge Cup competition, dominated in its first decade by amateur, 'Old Boy' teams, probably retained a middle-class audience for longest, as would prestigious International matches – and may still do so.

As we have noted, the prejudices of the writers could show strongly in their descriptions of football spectators. The old-guard defenders of an upper-class amateur, Corinthian ideal of the game could vent their spleen at the take-over of football by the industrial workers of the north by depicting the crowds as dirty, fickle and degenerate. The very word 'supporter' was used pejoratively to indicate the woefully common lack of good sportsmanship demonstrated by those who wanted one particular side to win.[29] 'Fan' of course, is short for 'fanatic'; a word defined in the OED as 'someone filled with excessive and mistaken enthusiasm, especially in religion'.

Football had been carried, often with missionary zeal, into working-class communities by ex-public schoolboys and 'muscular Christians' convinced of the game's value in promoting a healthy physique, the spirit of team-work and an alternative to gambling and drinking. Some even saw the game as a field on which class divisions could be blurred and diminished.[30] For them, the game was about *playing* not watching. But it rapidly turned into much more than that. Football was too potentially exciting for many to ignore and, anyway, everyone could not play, and even those that did, quite regularly, might also want to watch. They might want to drink and gamble on the result as well.

For the industrial workers of Britain – and eventually for almost anyone at all – football matches at their best became real festivals – ritual opportunities for delight and dramatic encounters which might reach high intensity. In the social setting of industrial, Victorian cities, replete with burgeoning populations sucked in from old rural England, the football festival began to work at a more profound level of experience than most ex-public schoolboys might have expected. As Richard Holt's approach emphasises, the sense of community, cohesion and enthusiasm, experienced by spectators at professional matches,

offered a second identity . . . a means by which men could come to terms with the reality of the late Victorian city and clarify their relationship to it . . . As three o'clock approached . . . the workers briefly took possession of the city.[31]

A profound sense of place and of one's identity in relation to it is not, traditionally, an exclusively social experience; it can include an individual, 'religious' dimension as well. Regular, enthusiastic festivals which encourage, then intensify, strong emotions can also promote powerful links between a specific location (the football ground) and those who ritually assemble there.[32] Professional football emerged with an umbilical attachment to, often quite small, placentas of territory – districts within cities. But it is not essentially about 'place' – it is about the *prospect of victory and the heightened sensations of those who watch* which can get channelled into feelings about identity and place.

Some people maintained that professional football was having an 'improving' effect on working people. Perhaps tendentiously, the founder of the Football League, William McGregor, in 1907, called attention to 'the steady increase in the respectability of the gate . . . their wives have told me that after . . . (their menfolk) . . . have taken to football, they have been more careful in regard to personal appearance, and have indeed changed for the better in many ways.'[33] Hutchinson makes reference to the frequency – especially after 1890 – of references to the 'respectable' nature of football crowds and the possibility that they were 'improving'.[34] No doubt it depended very much on which matches one looked at and where they were played. At Cup Finals and Internationals, 'many commentators noted a considerable degree of social mixing . . .' between horny-handed working men from Sheffield, 'hard as their native steel . . . a great contrast to the London crowd who are nearly all of what is considered superior social standing.'[35]

Do such commentators perhaps protest too much? Might not their keenness to emphasise the 'respectability' of football supporters – and the blurring of class differences at football matches – speak more of some deep perturbation they felt about the upper-class game's rapid descent 'below stairs'? Other writers had no compunction in their attacks on football and its crowds, some of which could rise to a crescendo of snobbery; 'the worst feature of professional football is its sordid nature . . . That the tendency of it all is towards brutality cannot be doubted.'[36] When the enthusiasm of supporters for mid-week matches prevented their attendance at work, more criticism followed.[37] In addition, football fans were charged with 'spectatorism' – a condition of passivity suited only to milksops unable to play the game. Supporters were accused of watching *instead* of playing – and thereby allowing themselves to deteriorate physically, at great threat to the British Empire which needed a fighting-fit army to defend its interests.[38] For the worst of the snobs:

> Professional football is doing more harm every year. It has already spread from the North to the South . . . The system is bad for the players and worse for the spectators . . . (who) . . . are injured physically and morally . . . the physique of

the manufacturing population is bad enough already . . . Gentlemen can now only play Association football with each other, for they cannot risk plunging into the moral slough.[39]

Recent research indicates that sports spectators are more likely than anyone else to engage actively in sport.[40] It may not have been true in the late nineteenth century, but commonsense tells us that the 'physique of the manufacturing population' of Victorian Britain had more to do with housing, diet and health care than with occasionally kicking a ball around or not. The overt disparagement of football's supporters – and the disguised versions that sought to 'respectablise' them – both had their roots in the earlier association of the game with the Corinthian ideals of an English upper class. (Much deeper cultural roots of the condemnation of 'spectators' trail back through the Puritans to the Christian Fathers of Rome.) But, surprisingly, football and its fans got little support from where one might have expected some: organisations that sought to *represent* ordinary working people – like trade unions and radical political groups. Vamplew suggests that working-class aspirations to 'respectability' – often channelled through trade union activity or radical politics – could itself place working people's organisations in direct opposition to football, and he cites the Unionists in Derby who attempted to stop a football game.[41] Football's links with drink and gambling – and occasional mob violence – also distanced it from workers' organisations seeking to 'educate' their fellows to better things and provide 'rational recreation'. Other, Marxist-oriented criticisms of sport and its spectators have emphasised its 'dehumanising' effect and the role it serves as part of the 'bread and circuses' that distract the proletariat from its real tasks.

> The rage and anger which should be directed against the ruling class is turned instead against the opposing team; the loyalty and emotional involvement which should be part of one's class consciousness is wasted on the home team.[42]

Thus, from the Church Fathers of second-century Rome via the nineteenth-century upper-class amateurs of Imperial England to neo-Marxist theoreticians of the twentieth century, few had a good word to say for 'spectators' of mass entertainments. The relationship between those who watched and those who administered football over the first hundred years of the game must be set in this context.

The commercialisation and subsequent professionalisation of football was fuelled by the desire of many people to watch the game and to see their team win. The rise of large urban populations – and some 'venture capital' from entrepreneurs – set the stage for football's expansion. In the early days, matches could be promoted by publicans, not seeking to charge for admission, but hoping to sell beer and snacks.[43] Facilities at football venues grew only slowly, and even changing-rooms at first were rare (except where the pitch was also used for cricket).[44] Often the first 'improvements' were simply attempts to ensure that spectators paid to watch. Consequently, if hills overlooked the pitch, as at the Cup replay between Bolton and Notts County in 1884, four or five thousand supporters might gather in the farmer's field best placed for viewing (though the farmer charged half-price for admission!).[45] In the 1880s small stands began to appear at some grounds, along with earth mounds or carts and wagons for spectators to stand on.[46] Soon, wide discrepancies were apparent between the grounds of rich clubs like Everton and other, less well financed clubs. Fans paid from 3d for the pleasure of a match, rising to an almost standard 6d for League football by the 1890s. International matches – and other big games – usually cost double.[47]

The safety and comfort of the mass of football's supporters does not seem to have featured prominently on the game's agenda, yet, '. . . the major crowd problem between 1890 and 1914 was overcrowding'.[48] Large iron fences were installed as early as 1887, at Sheffield Wednesday's Olive Mount ground, to prevent pitch-invasions which themselves were often the result of packing supporters too densely in enclosed spaces.[49] Police and club officials on hand were less concerned to prevent injury to fans than to prevent damage to property, if trouble broke out. 'This appears to have been the major role of the police at football matches throughout the period'[50] – a role largely uncriticised by the press, with the occasional exception like that in *The Athletic Journal* of 1888 which described the constabulary at one match as 'a pack of idiots . . . (who) . . . pushed and kicked about seemingly enjoying the struggle'. Press reports which grossly exaggerated problems at football matches were not unknown, like the headline, 'Military Called Out', which referred to a match at Villa Park in 1888 where too few police were on hand to deal with an over-full ground and 'two soldiers in uniform who happened to be at the game were mounted on cab horses and brought on to the field.'[51]

Spurned by political activists and occasionally harangued by 'snobs', the early supporters themselves, whether 'respectable' or not, had no organisations of their own through which their concerns might be expressed. Any dialogue between fans and their football clubs had to take place largely (as we shall see) through 'letters to the Editor' of local papers, and occasional public meetings and demonstrations. There was, of course, no dialogue between ordinary supporters and the Football League or the Football Association. What fans thought of these administrative bodies can only be guessed. The FA certainly came in for some stinging attacks from supporters during the summer of 1909 when the Player's Union (PU) threatened a strike. One letter from that period written to PU representative, Mr Bloomfield, congratulated the players on their 'gallant stand against the autocracy and hypocrisy of the Football Association'. The letter continued: 'It would be no bad job if the FA was smashed tomorrow.'[52]

The transformation of football clubs into private limited companies often worked to seal off the original supporters – once 'members' – from any significant involvement in their clubs' affairs. Ironically, it was often the fans' desire and insistence on seeing a winning team competing at League level that provoked the transformation. Even a club like the Woolwich Arsenal – born amongst factory workers in 1886, and run by a committee of working men elected by members – was unable to stave off company status. Rent increases for their ground forced the issue of 4,000 shares at £1 in 1893. Most of the initial shareholders were factory workers but rising debt (and longer shifts brought about by the Boer War) forced the club into the hands of local businessmen by the turn of the century.[53]

Some share-issues priced shares clearly out of reach of ordinary supporters, as at Sheffield Utd where £20 was the minimum required. When share prices were kept low to encourage wide ownership (5/- at Dartford and Southport; 10/- at Accrington Stanley) often too few local supporters took up the chance.[54] Even where shares were initially reasonably spread amongst working people, in time the bulk of shares seemed to concentrate in the hands of a few local well-to-do men.[55] Mason's survey of the shareholders of forty-seven football clubs (1886–1913) revealed most as distinctly middle class, yet there was still a large 'sprinkling' of others of lower social standing.[56] The problem – in terms of their exerting any real influence – was that most of the latter took up only one or two shares as *an expression of their support*: a continuation of their 'membership' of a sporting club they may have joined years before.[57]

In Scotland, when football clubs first adopted company status, they usually offered their previous 'members' 'either free proprietary shares or full or partial paid-up ordinary shares . . . as compensation for goodwill and the takeover of club assets'.[58] As around 80 per cent of the Scottish male members were manual workers – and the aggregate price of shares in Scotland was lower anyway than in England – probably more of the working class north of the border took up shares, but even there, they did not buy *many* shares. As Vamplew puts it:

> Perhaps many still saw the soccer club as a voluntary association rather than as a capitalistic enterprise. To them, shareholding probably was more consumption than investment . . . an extension of their involvement as members or as fans . . .[59]

South of the border – though data are more scarce – it seems that clubs were even more readily dominated by local proprietors and employers, and there was a significantly lower proportion of working-class participation.[60] In Tischler's survey of seventy-three club boards (1888–1914), he found that the occupations of 'builder' and the 'alcohol and tobacco trade' featured strongly – businesses which were, of course, able to benefit indirectly from their involvement with football clubs.[61] Both in England and Scotland, club directors usually sealed off their clubs from any 'outside' interference by keeping their proprietary ratio of share ownership well over 50 per cent; by maintaining the right to veto share transfers and allowing proxy votes (more easily 'sown up' by existing directors).[62] One affluent man often controlled the club in reality, by privately 'funding' the purchase of shares through friends, relatives and even employees.[63]

The earliest organisations run by supporters were called 'Brake Clubs'. Emerging first in Scotland, their organisers arranged travel to football matches from the 1880s onwards. The first Supporters' Clubs appear after the turn of the century, though many collapsed with the onset of the First World War. What historical evidence there is gives a picture of these clubs as mostly model organisations of respectability, manned, and very occasionally womanned, by a selection of local worthies.[64] Councillors, aldermen and mayors feature prominently on supporters' committees along with the occasional JP and MP. In photographs dating from 1913 to 1935, they appear comfortable, middle-aged and older, not unlike the members of the boards of their football clubs. Many of these early supporters' clubs (and those that followed) were probably formed at the instigation of their football clubs. (There is evidence to indicate that over half the clubs still active in 1965 were formed originally in such a way.[65]) This is not to suggest that ordinary supporters themselves were not often involved in attempts to form their own organisations, independently of their football clubs. But supporters seeking to *represent* themselves to their football clubs often faced fierce resistance.

NOTES

1. *Athletic News*, 5 September 1910, p. 1.
2. See, for example, E. Dunning, 'The development of modern football' in *The Sociology of Sport* (ed. Dunning), London, 1975; T. Mason, *Association Football and English Society, 1863–1915*, London, 1980, Harvester; W. Vamplew, *Pay Up and Play the Game*, Cambridge, 1988; J. Walvin, *The People's Game*, London, 1975.
3. For a detailed account of this process, see Dunning, op. cit., p. 134ff.
4. As at Winchester in 1818; see Dunning, ibid., p. 136.
5. S. Tischler, *Footballers and Businessmen*, New York, 1981, p. 13.
6. Dunning, op. cit., p. 136.
7. Dunning, op. cit., p. 146.
8. See Tischler, op. cit., p. 23ff.
9. See *The Official History of the Football Association*, London, 1953.
10. See Tischler, ibid., p. 34.

11. S. Wagg, *The Football World*, London, 1984, p. 6.
12. Wagg, ibid., p. 7.
13. See Dunning, Murphy and Williams, *The Roots of Football Hooliganism*, London, 1988, chap. 3.
14. Mason, op. cit., p. 32.
15. See Tischler, op. cit. p. 44.
16. Vamplew, op. cit., p. 43.
17. The importance of 'place' has been emphasised by R. Holt, 'Working class football and the city: the problem of continuity', *British Journal of Sports History*, 1986, vol. III, p. 5.
18. See Vamplew, op. cit., p. 50.
19. Vamplew, ibid., p. 53ff. See also Mason, op. cit., pp. 138–9.
20. Mason, op. cit., p. 152.
21. This is certainly the pattern today according to a survey of Rangers fans. It revealed that female supporters were twice as likely as males to be under the age of 21. Many are then lost to the game until middle age. *Seven Years on: Glasgow Rangers and Rangers Supporters, 1983–90*, Centre for Football Research, Leicester University, 1990.
22. Quoted in Mason, op. cit., p. 162.
23. J. Hutchinson, 'Some aspects of football crowds before 1914', from a conference on the Working Class and Leisure, 1975, University of Sussex, Paper 13.
24. C. Edwardes, 'The new football mania', *The Nineteenth Century*, October 1892, p. 627.
25. Edwardes, ibid., p. 628.
26. Edwardes, ibid., p. 630.
27. See Mason, op. cit., pp. 152–3.
28. See Mason, ibid., p. 157.
29. See Mason, ibid., p. 230. See also Holt, op. cit., p. 11.
30. See Hutchinson, op. cit., p. 5ff.
31. Holt, op. cit., p. 12.
32. J. Beale in his essay, 'British football and a sense of place', deals in more detail with this topic. See *British Football and Social Change*, ed. S. Wagg and J. Williams, Leicester, 1991.
33. Quoted in Hutchinson, op. cit., p. 8.
34. Hutchinson, ibid., p. 5.
35. Hutchinson, ibid., p. 6.
36. E. Ensor, 'The football madness', *Contemporary Review*, 1898, vol. LXXIV, pp. 756–8.
37. See Tischler, op. cit., p. 126ff.
38. See Tischler, ibid., p. 129.
39. Ensor, op. cit., p. 760.
40. See A. Guttman, 'On the alleged dehumanization of the sports spectators', *Journal of Popular Culture*, 1980, vol. XIV, pp. 275–82.
41. Vamplew, op. cit., p. 46. For a review of left-wing sports organisations' attitudes to professional football during the inter-war period, see R. Taylor, 'Walking alone together' in Wagg and Williams, op. cit.
42. Guttman, op. cit., p. 276.

43. Vamplew, op. cit., p. 15.
44. Mason, op. cit., p. 139.
45. See Mason, ibid., p. 167, note 3.
46. See Mason, ibid., p. 140.
47. See Mason, ibid., p. 149ff.
48. Hutchinson, op. cit., p. 12. In 1895, the Football League suggested railing in supporters, see W. Vamplew, 'Ungentlemanly conduct: the control of soccer crowd behaviour in England 1888–1914', in *The Search for Wealth and Stability*, ed. T.C. Smout, London, 1979, p. 139ff.
49. Hutchinson, ibid., p. 12.
50. Hutchinson, ibid., p. 13.
51. Hutchinson, ibid., p. 14.
52. Undated letter in current PFA Archives.
53. See Mason, op. cit., p. 35.
54. See Mason, ibid., p. 39. The most recent share-issue, at Newcastle in October 1990, required a minimum purchase of £100. It failed to attract sufficient interest and the share-issue was abandoned.
55. See Mason, ibid., p. 41.
56. See Mason, ibid., p. 38.
57. See Mason, ibid., p. 38.
58. Vamplew, op. cit., p. 155.
59. Vamplew, ibid., p. 159.
60. Vamplew, ibid., p. 161ff.
61. Tischler, op. cit., p. 76 (twenty-one different builders sat on Everton's Board before 1914).
62. Vamplew, op. cit., p. 169.
63. Tischler, op. cit., p. 74ff.
64. See R. Taylor, op. cit.
65. See National Federation AGM Minutes, 1965, p. 61.

2

AN OBJECT LESSON: LEICESTER FOSSE/CITY 1900–1948

After supporting the team through good times and bad times, we are told to mind our own affairs. (Leicester City supporter, 1924)[1]

Leicester Fosse FC was formed in 1884. Its members paid 9d to join and they elected a committee to run the club's affairs. Within a few years, there were sixty-five members producing three football teams. Despite struggling under the shadow of a strong local enthusiasm for rugby, the football club soon 'professionalised' with the signing of Harry Webb in 1888, at 2/6d a week plus travelling expenses. The drift towards professionalism intensified with Fosse's entry into the Midland League in 1891 and into the Second Division of the Football League in 1894.

The rise of Fosse's footballing status and its commitment to fulfil fixtures increased the financial pressures on the club's elected committee. Following entry into the League, the committee began actively to seek members from amongst 'the influential gentlemen of the town'[2] particularly to help with the perennial problem of finding supplementary employment for players. New rules were passed ensuring that anyone who wished to stand for election 'would be required to provide a guarantee to the bank'.[3] Within a short time, complaints were being made (in the local press) that the committee had become aloof towards the ordinary members and was acting dictatorially.

Most criticism from supporters during this early period centred on the team's performance and its failure to win honours. It often took the form of barracking players and writing vehement letters to the local paper, the *Leicester Mercury*. These latter, of course, tended to be written by supporters who readily put pen to paper, a 'more respectable, articulate and . . . highly committed group.'[4] The distance between club members/supporters and the committee continued to widen as debts mounted and more well off 'gentlemen' were recruited to stand as guarantors for the club. Limited Liability status was sought in 1897 and a share capital of £3,000 raised. Some ordinary members of Leicester Fosse became small shareholders.

As the argument developed between the newly-formed Board of the Football Club and the more voluble supporters (and small shareholders), much of it centred upon the *lack of football knowledge* which the fans attributed to Board members. The club's committee – now the Board of Directors – had traditionally selected the team and decided which players to employ. For many supporters, 'business acumen' seemed of limited value unless used in tandem with a firm grasp of the game and a good eye for a skilful player. Supporters and local commentators urged the Board to spend more money on good players – to break the cycle of debt which was already characterising the Club's affairs. The directors often replied by insisting that they were too busy keeping the Club afloat to think much about football.[5] One suspects that this basic 'dialogue' between supporters and directors has been rehearsed many times and at many football clubs throughout the history of the English professional game. In paraphrase, these are its bare essentials:

Supporters: You don't spend enough money – and when you do, you don't spend it wisely!
(Directors have little football knowledge.)

Directors: Don't talk to us about money. It's hell running this Club. Where were you when the shares were floated? Supporters know little of the *real* problems facing us.
(Supporters have little business knowledge.)

Supporters: You are too secretive and elitist. We never know what's going on, so how could we know the 'real' problems?
(There is no democracy in the running of the Club.)

Directors: Its our money and our business. You've no right to know what's going on.
(What's 'democracy' got to do with it?)

At Leicester Fosse, an 'expensive' new team was produced to push for promotion in 1900. It played poorly and gates dropped. The local press called on fans to get behind the Board; supporters were admonished for their lack of enthusiasm. At public meetings in 1901 and 1902, supporters were urged by directors to buy season tickets and raise 'a working man's subscription', to form 'a financial committee outside the directorate'; to provide the Club with 'the wherewithal for securing the services of (capable) players.'[6]

These suggestions were taken up. The leading fund-raisers amongst the supporters were probably existing small shareholders and they attempted to maintain control of the funds through a supporters' executive committee. The Club was pressed to consider greater participation by supporters and, on 3 February 1906, the Fosse's Secretary wrote to the *Mercury* approving occasional meetings between directors and supporters. There is, however, no record of any meetings and the fund-raisers appear to have soon lost control of their contributions. The Club Chairman announced that summer wages for the players (a chronic seasonal problem) would easily soak up the £500 raised. The Directors launched another fund – the Million Farthing Fund – with a promise that any money raised would not be used to pay off old debts. Criticism from supporters continued in the local press, much of which expressed the feeling amongst Leicester's fans that the Board never took them into their confidence or explained their plans and strategies.[7]

Promotion to the First Division in 1908 was quickly followed by relegation in 1909. There were constant calls by the Club for fund-raising efforts by supporters. A share-issue of 1,500 was launched and an 'instalment plan' (10/- down and three monthly payments of 5/-) made available, yet less than 100 shares were taken up.[8] The trauma of relegation in 1909 forced the abandonment of team selection by committee and an 'expert' was appointed with full responsibility. The chronic financial crisis continued and eventually triggered an interesting and 'democratic' encounter between the Club and its fans. The urgent need for cash brought forward a Board proposal in 1909 for a 'surcharge' to be levied on the (always popular) Christmas Day match. A few weeks beforehand, fearing possible reactions from the crowd, a mass public meeting at the ground was convened following a (fortunately) highly entertaining game. The supporters were asked to approve a 3d surcharge and, rallying to the cause, the crowd vigorously supported the proposal and went on to volunteer a further surcharge for the Boxing Day match. The following day, the *Mercury* recorded in Churchillian tones:

> Never before . . . has there been such gratifying unity between management and supporters.[9]

Groups of Leicester fans continued to raise funds for their club. In 1910, a 'successful skating party' was organised 'in view of raising money to help the Club', along with egg and spoon races and a women's half mile race.[10] Criticism of the Board was by now endemic and a local journalist warned the Club: 'Reticence encourages neither generosity nor charity, nor warm support.'[11]

The Club's tendency to withhold information from supporters was often at the source of fans' complaints. Even attendance figures and transfer fees were undisclosed. Two letters published in the *Mercury* in 1913, bitter at the sale to rich Everton of two star players (a theme familiar in recent years too) included:

You (i.e. the Board) are so close in regard to information, one can only guess, and here is the trouble . . .
I am sure the supporters of the Club in general would appreciate it very much if the directors would take them into their confidence and publish the 'gates' for every match and the amount of transfers for players.[12]

A decade later, little seemed to have changed in the relations between supporters and (the renamed) Leicester City Club. In 1921, the idea of forming a Supporters' Club surfaced but soon sank. In 1924, two supporters wrote to the *Mercury* seeking to justify their desire for greater involvment and express their anger at the club's indifference:

Surely we supporters are entitled to some say in the government of the game we support, and surely it's not asking too much that those in authority should answer the critics?
We are terribly interested in the game and its welfare in Leicester, though the City directors don't seem alive to the fact . . . they veil themselves in mystery . . . we grope in the darkness . . .[13]

In response to such criticism, the City Chairman, Mr Rice, told a local reporter that he had no intention of being drawn into any correspondence with local supporters. This unlocked a flood of letters to the *Mercury*, some from fans who, while recognising they had no right to pick the team, felt insulted by 'the directors' arrogance and high handed manner.'[14] Amidst a welter of letters – and some calls for a boycott – the idea of a Supporters' Club had re-emerged in 1923 in proposals that outlined, as a main role, the representation of supporters 'to the directors' and demanded room on the Board for two members elected by 'the very large band of supporters'. One letter suggested:

The Club is, properly speaking, an institution of the town and not a kind of private trading company, conducted at the whim of the few men who are at the moment immediately interested.[15]

The Club spurned any such suggestion and the Supporters' Club failed to materialise. The problem for those keen to organise supporters at Leicester City – and perhaps also at a number of other clubs – centred upon an almost cyclic ebb and flow of enthusiasm amongst fans. It seems that the desire for a closer involvement by many fans, and their determination to achieve it, dropped away in inverse proportion to the Club's success on the pitch.[16] When the team was playing badly and the Club was in crisis, however, popular enthusiasm for a Supporters' Club would rise sharply. Consequently, it was not until City's relegation struggles in the early 1930s that the idea of forming a Supporters' Club resurfaced yet again. But again it failed to get off the ground.

Leicester City's Board was still actively opposing any kind of Supporters' Club at the start of 1939, but within the year the club's directors underwent a sudden conversion. This sea change was almost certainly brought on by the outbreak of war and the recognition by the club of the prospect of unpredictable and declining attendances. By 1939, it was clear that only 'scratch' games, 'guest appearances' and armed forces teams would be the order of the day. In such circumstances, the club desperately needed to cultivate supporters' interests.

The Club quickly announced that, as far as a Supporters' Club was concerned, they were 'wholly in favour of it' and even willing 'to receive its representatives once a month to consider suggestions'.[17] The Supporters' Club was duly inaugurated but the events of war soon overwhelmed it and the members agreed to let it lie in abeyance for the 'duration'.

At a public meeting in Leicester in 1946, the Supporters' Club was re-formed and a committee appointed. According to local journalist, Simon Dee, in the *Mercury*:

> Amongst other things decided by the Committee was to request a meeting between its representatives and the Leicester City directors for an exchange of views. It is hoped to organise trips . . . and to put in a request for Cup-tie tickets for its members.[18]

The supporters were keen to emphasise that they did not seek simply to criticise the Club or create disharmony, and the new supporters' Chairman described their brief as 'to arrange support for the club'. Nevertheless, the supporters wished to raise certain topics they felt were legitimately within their sphere, including:

(a) better 'marshalling in the ground';
(b) a band to play live music instead of (the same) records every week;
(c) action on 'improved sanitary arrangements';
(d) a scoreboard giving the half-time scores of other clubs.[19]

With these, hardly revolutionary, proposals in mind, the supporters sought a meeting with the Club's directors. Their request was refused. Some of the supporters appeared mystified that the long-sought-for 'recognition' offered by the club so readily in 1940 was no longer available. Rather pathetically, the Supporters' Club Chairman wondered out loud if it might be 'because we left the Club then (i.e. in 1940) that no recognition is forthcoming now.'[20]

It seems more likely that the club's attitude was cynically conditioned by circumstances. Their approval of a Supporters' Club in 1940 was a volte-face of their previous, long-held objection, and had been inspired by the impending cessation of ordinary, civilian life. But by 1947 the club was only too well aware that crowd attendances were rising to unprecedented levels, reaching their all-time height in England by 1948. In such circumstances, the usefulness of 'recognition' of the Supporters' Club and any dialogue with its representatives was less clear to the football club. There were certainly to be no 'privileges' extended to Supporters' Club members. In January 1947, prior to a Cup replay, members were told 'to stand in line with everyone else if they wanted tickets'.[21] A year later, the Board reaffirmed its rejection of any form of 'recognition' of the organised supporters, reverting to the argument first voiced over fifty years earlier that the Club was 'a limited company and the shareholders (had) put a board of directors in charge to run their business . . .'[22]

Some members of the Supporters' Club became increasingly disgruntled. At a meeting in 1948, some urged the committee to 'take off their gloves' and take on the Club. Others suggested that a more determined stand would attract more members. However, the Supporters' Club affiliated in 1947 with the National Federation of Football Supporters' Clubs and the supporters' Secretary at Leicester, Mr Parfitt, urged caution against any militancy 'in line with the policy of the Federation and its "rule": To Help Not Hinder.' The Supporters' Club remained in limbo: a bride awaiting the call of the groom. As Mr Parfitt put it in the *Mercury* later that year:

> We have, neither by word or deed, encroached on the business of the football club. Our business is to support them through thick and thin. We are not recognised by the club directorate but they know we are organised and prepared to help at a moment's notice.[23]

This stuttering relationship between Leicester's Football Club and its active supporters spanned over fifty years. It illustrates vividly the problems facing supporters who sought to organise *interdependently* of their football club, and the attitudes adopted by those who ran the club's affairs. With minor variations, these themes were probably common to many other clubs and their fans. At Leicester, the original Club was a simple democracy: one member, one vote, to elect a committee in charge. Early pressures to rise in football status and produce a winning team created financial difficulties which the introduction of 'influential gentlemen' from the town as guarantors of the Club attempted to solve. This development led to the first rift between the now 'ordinary' members (who can no longer stand for election) and those with credit at the bank. This rift is institutionalised when continuing financial problems lead to the club's application for private limited company status and the original committee becomes a Board of Directors.

Some 'ordinary' members take up the option to buy shares but not in sufficient numbers to influence the Club's affairs. In subsequent share-issues, supporters remain unattracted by the prospect of share-ownership.

The small shareholders and other supporters feel increasingly divorced from those responsible for running the club. A characteristic 'dialogue' develops wherein each party accuses the other of lack of knowledge about the vital issue: 'football' for the supporters, 'business' for the directors. The supporters' desire for involvement and active participation is often successfully redirected by the Club into fund-raising efforts but, even after raising money, the supporters have difficulty maintaining any control over the way it is spent. There are continual complaints from supporters over decades that the Board is unnecessarily secretive; the fans call for more 'openness'. Attempts to form a Supporters' Club are often frustrated by the Club's refusal to accord 'recognition' (i.e. relationship) to it and the waxing and waning of popular demand, in counterpoint, it seems, with the rise and fall of the team's success. The Football Club, it appears, accepts the idea of 'relationship' only in terms of fund-raising activities by supporters, yet insists nevertheless that it is a 'private business'. In contrast, some supporters insist that, primarily, the club is 'an institution of the town.'

If the Club's circumstances became acutely difficult, the Board might suddenly switch to acceptance of supporters' involvement, as it did in 1939 at Leicester. But when the war was over and crowds were assuredly growing, the re-formed Supporters' Club was spurned, despite the fact that its leaders expressed no wish to 'interfere' with the Club but wanted, perhaps justifiably, to talk to the Board about issues like safety, pre-match entertainment and toilet facilities. In response, the Club simply reverted to its status as a 'private company'.

The most spectacular example of the Leicester Board's acceptance of the principle of supporters' involvement occurred in 1909, when the crowd was directly requested to approve in advance a 3d surcharge on the Christmas Day match. On this occasion it seems, the Board adopted a fruitful strategy for gaining both financial and enthusiastic support from the mass of the Club's followers. It involved a willingness to be honest and open about the Club's situation, and a readiness to *risk* the outcome by putting the proposition to supporters. In the event it succeeded, but it was a strategy adopted only in the most acute financial crisis. Many supporters might have argued that, for the Board, it should have been an object lesson in how a club like Leicester Fosse might draw broad support from across its community.

NOTES

1. I am greatly indebted to Patrick Murphy at the Centre for Football Research at Leicester University for access to his primary research and his paper, 'Notes on the relationship between Directors and Supporters of Leicester Fosse and Leicester City F.C., 1894–1960' (as

yet unpublished), and also his collection of cuttings from the *Leicester Mercury*.

2. Murphy, op. cit., p. 5.
3. Murphy, ibid., p. 5.
4. As Murphy characterises them, ibid., p. 1.
5. See Murphy, ibid., pp. 8–9.
6. See Murphy, ibid., pp. 11–15.
7. See Murphy, ibid., pp. 18–19.
8. See Murphy, ibid., p. 25.
9. See Murphy, ibid., quoted on p. 25.
10. *Leicester Mercury*, 9 February 1910.
11. *Leicester Mercury*, 23 September 1911.
12. *Leicester Mercury*, 1 May 1913.
13. *Leicester Mercury*, 16 January 1924.
14. *Leicester Mercury*, 18 January 1924.
15. *Leicester Mercury*, 10 May 1923.
16. Murphy makes this suggestion, op. cit., pp. 5–6.
17. Murphy, op. cit., part II, quotation on p. 8.
18. *Leicester Mercury*, 20 November 1947.
19. *Leicester Mercury*, 15 January 1947.
20. Murphy, op. cit., p. 10.
21. *Leicester Mercury*, 28 January 1947.
22. *Leicester Mercury*, 29 July 1948.
23. *Leicester Mercury*, 1 October 1948.

3

THE FUND-RAISERS AND THEIR FOOTBALL CLUBS

That (football) clubs normally named themselves after a specific place seems too obvious to mention. (Richard Holt, 1986)

The supporters' clubs that flourished were generally those that willingly raised money for their football clubs while expecting little or nothing by way of 'glasnost' in return. Yet the history of supporters' contributions to their football clubs, over and above the money paid through the turnstiles, is almost certainly longer than the history of supporters' clubs (SCs) themselves. Amongst all but the very richest football clubs, it seems, supporters' fund-raising has been encouraged – and even relied upon – since before the professional game began.[1]

In the early 1880s, clubs counted on supporters to help run annual sports meetings, bazaars, prize draws and lotteries.[2] We know also from the remarks of W.H. Squires, Director of Leicester Fosse in 1904, that supporters 'In some towns I could mention . . . (had formed) . . . a finance committee . . .' to raise money for their clubs.[3] We have already seen how, at Leicester, money to purchase players was frequently begged by the club from its wider community of supporters and citizens. Historically, football's cash for transfer fees was very rarely 'a function solely of gate receipts but also of public appeals and philanthropic patrons . . .'[4]

It is difficult to estimate how many supporters' clubs emerged during the first thirty years of this century. But it seems likely that the vast majority of the many hundreds of League and bigger non-League football clubs spawned supporters' clubs at some stage.[5] By the late 1920s, the most successful are clearly well established in fund-raising roles and they used an admirable variety of schemes and activities to attract donations. In the long term, the most significant fund-raising activity proved to be the running of lotteries, especially in the post–Second World War period and until the

1960s, when football clubs themselves were finally allowed by the FA to run their own. Some lotteries were run by supporters in the inter-war years, though the legal situation was unclear (and local police attitudes appeared to play a decisive role).

In addition, supporters raised money for their football clubs by:

(a) running 'penny-on-the-ball' competitions and prize schemes;
(b) standing as guarantors of the FC's overdrafts (see Aldershot, below);
(c) organising whist drives, smoking concerts, Xmas draws, punch boards;
(d) holding New Year's balls, Saturday dances, darts tournaments;
(e) raising direct subscriptions ('passing the bucket');
(f) encouraging season-ticket sales by offering 'instalment plans';
(g) supplying and renting out cushions for the stands;
(h) running 'summer wages' appeals and seasonal fêtes;
(i) producing and selling match programmes.

As well as making cash donations, supporters' provided their football clubs with:

(a) equipment, goal posts, nets, etc.;
(b) ground improvements, including roofing and new stands;
(c) new dressing rooms;
(d) players' strips;
(e) stewards;
(f) reserve team running costs;
(g) laundry facilities;
(h) free labour (painting the stands, etc.);
(i) benefits for retiring players;
(j) loudspeaker systems;
(k) match entertainments (bands, etc.).

One of the most spectacular examples of supporter fund-raising was sustained at Luton Town between 1931–35. The defunct Supporters' Club of the pre-First World War period was revived in 1931, certainly with the full approval (and possibly at the instigation) of the Football Club.[6] It is clear that the 'recognition' accorded supporters by the Board was bound up with expectations of financial support. The Board Minutes of 13 April 1931 note that the Supporters' Club 'asked for a meeting with our Board of Directors, regarding their position with reference to the Twenty Thousand Shilling Fund and Loan Fund. It was decided and arranged that the Board meet the supporters' Committee at 7.30 at the ground offices.'

Clearly, the supporters were already running a number of schemes to raise money for the club, including a Loan Facility. But there was, as yet, no institutionalised relationship between the two bodies, and the supporters, consequently, had to request a meeting.

The liaison that developed between the supporters' committee and the Board rarely involved a full-scale meeting of both parties. The pattern that developed (one already established at many other clubs) was for the supporters' committee to include a Board member amongst its number. This 'one-way' system of liaison was understandably preferred by the football club boards. It meant that they were privy to everything discussed by the supporters' committee, but not vice versa. At Luton, those same Minutes of 13 April 1931 give insight into the way the Board could use such a strategic advantage to the detriment of supporters' interests.

According to the Minutes, enquiries had been made about the price of two of Luton Town's best players (Clark and Kingham) by a rival club. The Board resolved 'that as our supporters were raising a fund to pay Summer wages, we do not quote any prices but that the door be left open for future negotiation.'[7] It was probably the intention of the supporters' raising the summer wages to help *retain* their best players, one imagines. Yet the Board appeared to be using the time bought for them by the supporters' donations to *elevate the price of the players* in 'future negotiations'. Otherwise, why should 'the door be left open'? Without representation on the Board, the Luton fund-raisers could exert no control over the way the money they raised was used nor could they know the club's long-term strategy.

In 1933, Luton Town FC bought its ground at Kenilworth Road. The Supporters' Club erected a 'hut' on the ground 'accessible to all supporters'. That year the supporters raised £300 for the club, running a 'Stop Watch' competition and forming a 'Traders' Section' which offered local shops a framed certificate to display in their windows, priced at half a guinea.[8] Under the Presidency of Philip Wright, a director of Luton Town FC, the supporters' committee set about raising the funds to provide for a series of developments which greatly added to the value of the ground. The wooden step terracing along the length of the pitch opposite the Grand Stand was removed and replaced with concrete steps and a covered roof. It was called the 'Bobber's Stand' after the price fans paid for admission to the terraces.

Before we consider the amounts of money raised by Luton's supporters (and the other Supporters' Clubs mentioned below) during the 1930s, we should bear in mind the real value of those monies in modern terms. Today it costs over one hundred times the shilling Luton's fans paid to stand on the terraces. Football players' wages were around £4 a week in 1933 and the 'ordinary working man's wage' stood at about £2.50 to £3 a week. Consequently, to appreciate the size of Luton Town's supporters' contributions we need to multiply the figures by a factor of around fifty to represent them roughly in today's values.

The Luton supporters began by funding the excavation required underneath the Bobbers' Stand and by themselves helping to clear away tons of soil with spades and wheelbarrows. They raised the money to build the Bobbers' Stand and subsequently built a Supporters' Club premises inside it which included two bars, a cafeteria, snack bar, games room and a 'wash and brush up' facility for 'those members arriving on the ground from work.'[9] The bars were staffed by supporters and open seven days a week; the only licensed premises for miles around in an area where Quaker influence had actively discouraged the provision of public houses. After the 'Bobbers' Stand' opened in 1935, the supporters went on to provide the funds required to roof the Oak Road End and to build twelve tea bars throughout the ground.

> All this activity . . . cost close on £20,000 and in addition we handed over to the Football Club various amounts totalling £8,500.[10]

These represent huge sums of money – perhaps something approaching £1½ million in today's terms. And it did not stop there. By 1965–66, the supporters' committee (with another club director, Len Hawkins, now installed as both President and Chairman) quotes additional sums 'somewhere between £30,000 and £40,000 in cash . . . given to the Football Club'.[11] Three years later, the figure has risen 'in hard cash to around the £60,000 mark'.[12]

The supporters' committee, chaired by a club director, had little control over what was done with the cash donations, although there was at least one occasion 'when we raised money to buy a (specific) player'.[13] The Supporters' Club did receive an allocation of tickets for matches and special preference was given to members on 'big' match occasions. But one suspects that any other organisation which pumped such large sums of money – over a prolonged period – into a football club would have been offered, as a matter of course, some direct representation on the Board. The supporters as a group may have out-invested many individual directors – perhaps even all of them put together – but without achieving the representation accorded to one of the directors. Were the supporters satisfied with the existing arrangements? Were there voices amongst them calling for more direct representation? There is no evidence of it, but more detailed research in the local press might reveal some. Perhaps the supporters – particularly the 'respectable' chaps who manned the committee – simply trusted that the Board would run the Football Club in the best interests of the many thousands of individual fans who had put their shoulders to the wheelbarrows and dug deeply (and frequently) into their pockets. The club has certainly sought, ever since, to keep a 'guiding hand' on the committee which co-ordinated supporters' efforts. On the one major occasion when Luton's supporters needed an organisation to fight against a decision by the Board, they had to form a new body – the Luton

Town Supporters' Club, 1983 – which conducted a successful campaign to defeat the proposed move of the club to Milton Keynes. An official Luton Town Supporters' Club was re-formed in 1988 to complement the existing 'Bobbers' Stand and Football Supporters' Club'. The re-formed supporters' committee was apparently 'selected' by David Evans, then Chairman of the club, by his writing letters to particular individuals asking if they 'would like to come forward'.[14] When Bob Redhead, a 'ball-boy' at Luton Town in the early 1930s, subsequently a player for the 'A' team and eventually Secretary of the Supporters' Club from 1960–75, was asked: . . . Do you think the supporters should by now be accommodated with representation at executive level?, he replied:

> I think if the game embraced supporters and made them feel part of the organisation, they will respect it more . . . the game has failed in its relationship with supporters . . . they are looked upon as somebody who puts the money down on a Saturday . . . and a roof on the stand if necessary . . . that's what you're for, nothing else . . .[15]

During the 1930s, a time of economic depression and mass unemployment, the prodigious fund-raising of Luton Town's supporters was widely reflected in the work of other Supporters' Clubs throughout England. The pages of the few surviving copies of *The Supporter*, the official organ of the Supporters' Clubs' Federation – published in 1934 and 1935 – reveal a series of snapshot impressions of the current activities and donations from supporters' clubs ranging from Manchester Utd to Golders Green FC.

Chester City

> Extensive ground improvements . . . and the City Supporters' Club has been responsible for no little portion . . .

Aldershot Town

> . . . the financial help given to Aldershot Town F.C. amounted to £450 . . . The payment of £300 to the firm which erected the covered terracing was made in response to an urgent appeal by the Directors . . . six gentlemen stood security for the sum of £50 each in order to raise an overdraft on the Supporters' Club banking account and . . . only £188.5.11d remains to be cleared . . .

Golders Green

. . . purchase of a Sun Ray Lamp and Electric Leg Cradle for use of Golders Green F.C . . . part cost of presentation to International Player and commencement of ground improvements . . . The chief objects of the club . . . are the completion of the terracing and provision of covered accommodation on the popular side.

Leeds United

. . . one of the most powerful and energetic Supporters' Clubs in Great Britain . . . Provide stewards on the stands on match days; loan out cushions at a charge of one penny . . . a splendid source of revenue . . . the great objective for this season is the erection of covered accommodation on the 'popular' side of Elland Road ground for 25,000 spectators . . .

Wrexham

Since the (Supporters) Club's inception in 1926, very much hard work has been done and covered accommodation . . . erected at a cost of over £1500 . . .

Manchester United

A tremendous amount of spadework has been put in by the United Supporters' Club at Old Trafford and they are hopeful of brighter days there now.

Colwyn Bay

. . . in season 1933–4, they raised and handed over to the parent body the excellent sum of £253.15.3d . . . they undertook the running and financing of the Reserves . . . To relieve the Club of further responsibility . . . New goal nets were supplied . . . they ran the Café and paid for the washing of player's kit and paid for the bill-posting and printing of bills advertising matches.

Plymouth Argyle

. . . enthusiasts who banded themselves together for the purpose of rendering useful and profitable service to the Plymouth Argyle F.C . . . Three seasons ago the members . . . undertook to provide covered accommodation on the 'popular' side . . . The structure was built at a cost of £1,511 and was declared free of debt last year . . .

With an interesting example of local authority involvement, the passage continues: '. . . in an endeavour to alleviate the circumstances of some of the local unemployed, the City Council sanctioned an expenditure of £3,666 on ground Improvements being carried out, the only obligation being that the Football Club would be liable for additional rental of £150 per annum for ten years in respect of the charges. The Supporters' Club willingly came forward and relieved the Company (ie. the football club) of that responsibility . . .'

Northampton Town

. . . We have handed to our Board of Directors in cash and kind the value of £5,095 . . . last year we gave them £1000 and the previous year £700 . . .

Rhyl

Since the club was inaugurated we have given nearly £10,000 to the Rhyl Football Club besides providing the money for the erection of a covered shelter on the popular side of the ground . . .

Southend United

Cheques totalling £500 have been handed to the Football Club Directors and a further cheque of £200 is to be handed to the Chairman of the Football Club . . .

Brighton and Hove Albion

. . . raising funds for ground improvements . . . Last year they were able to clear off the debt remaining on the covered stand the total cost of which was £1,300 . . . selling season tickets on the instalment system . . . The idea was that the money should be paid and handed to the Club during the close season when it would be most useful . . .

Bournemouth and Boscombe

We were able to hand over to the Football Club nearly £300, made up of £200 in donations and £93 from the Summer Wages Appeal Fund . . . During the past twelve years the 'Cherries' have been helped to the extent of about £2,730 by the Supporters' Club.

Sheffield Wednesday

. . . installed a loud speaker set at the ground last winter . . .

At Swindon Town between 1931–33, severe financial difficulties prevailed. In an attempt to survive, the club launched a 'Shilling Fund' and
encouraged the Supporters' Club into an active role:

> The Supporters' Club and its fundraising activities brought the Club's struggle
> for survival to the heart of communal life. Within a month, 16,000 members had
> paid the 1/- subscription, at a time when unemployment was rising, from 794
> locally to a peak of 4,501 in 1933.[16]

Swindon supporters raised other monies in a breathtaking plethora of whist
drives, jumble sales, raffles, fairs and fêtes. The role of women supporters
(who rarely featured on the grave photographs of Supporters' Club committees) was publicly acclaimed. (The Swindon 'Ladies Committee' staged
81 dances and 145 whist drives in 1931–32 alone.) Together, and in
addition to their shillings, the supporters raised just under £1,000 to help
pull the club through. It was an example, not untypical in England, of the
effort a whole community could make, focused through the organised
supporters, to help sustain their football club as an *emblem* of their
communal life.

Inevitably, these snapshots of supporters' activities and fund-raising
feats are only a cross-section of the total. None the less, they provide a
useful indication of the scope of financial assistance clubs received via their
fans in that period. Some evidence appears in the September 1935 issue of
The Supporter, when the Wrexham SC (who were largely responsible for
putting the monthly paper together) published 'some statistics appertaining
to the work accomplished by merely twenty-two Supporters' Clubs'. These
figures had apparently been compiled from information published earlier
that year, in the April edition of *The Supporter* (of which no copy appears
to survive). They reveal that 'No less than £44,662 was raised and utilised
in the erection of seven grandstands, ten covered shelters providing cover
for over 70,000 spectators.'

Such remarkable and substantial sums of money raised by and through
supporters' organisations do not appear unique to the 1930s. Though we
know much less in detail about the earlier decades of fund-raising, it is
clear (as we will see) that supporters continued to provide high levels of
additional finance to their clubs throughout the late 1940s, 1950s and early
1960s. What is particularly remarkable about the fund-raising of the 1930s
is that it took place throughout a time of *acute unemployment* and against a
background of *steadily rising attendances* which eventually reached their
peak in 1948 when some 42 million attendances were registered for
Football League matches alone. In 1935, for example, 77,582 people

attended the Manchester City v. Arsenal match and, in Scotland, the all-time British record was set at Ibrox when 118,567 'Old Firm' supporters turned out for the derby match in 1937. The question inevitably arises: whatever happened to all those shillings collected from the millions of supporters attending matches? The money was not (except illegally) taken in profits. The shareholders of clubs were restricted by FA regulation to no more than 7.5 per cent profit on their investment. It is true that transfer fees were rising throughout that period (the money involved, of course, represents expenditure in one case, income in another, for a club), with Sunderland breaking the record with their purchase of Bob Kelly from Burnley for £6,550 in 1925; £7,500 paid for Jimmy Gibson by Aston Villa in 1927 and £14,000 for Bryn Jones by Arsenal in 1928. But players' wages were severely restricted and bore little relation to the players' real worth. There were no chief executive salaries to find, and other modern over-heads, like policing costs, were at a minimum. In the decades before 1914, the original development of grounds and subsequent improvements to them probably took care of most (if not all) of the money available from gate receipts, hence the frequent requests for public and private benevolence to provide cash for the transfer market.[17] But during the inter-war years, the grounds were often packed:

> Entrance fees were admittedly low, but so too were the clubs' overheads . . . Nor was the money invested in the football stadiums which remained in their early 20th century conditions (adequate by the standards of 1914 but crude and often dangerous by 1945). Indeed, it was only the decline in attendances in the 1950's which forced the management to look at their rusting girders, crumbling terraces and medieval lavatories.[18]

So where did all those shillings go? Did the money just lie around, unused and unmanaged until inflation and the rising costs of the post-war commercialisation of the game swallowed it up?

No doubt some of the money clubs took at the turnstiles was ploughed back into club and ground facilities but such improvements often favoured the directors themselves or the seated patrons. At Millwall, for example, when the team's good FA Cup run in 1937 was followed by promotion in 1938, substantial extra money flowed into the club. Some £60,000 was spent at the Den, largely on improvements which favoured the board members and the management. A 'luxurious' boardroom, bar, billiards room and palm court(!) were appointed alongside a new manager's office. Though Millwall supporters did get a roof over their heads in the 'Spion Kop', they paid an increased price for the privilege. Other facilities for ordinary fans remained rudimentary.[19]

As the extracts from editions of *The Supporter*, reproduced above, clearly show, putting a roof over the 'popular' ends of grounds was very often left to supporters themselves to finance entirely or contribute towards. Despite the sterling efforts of so many supporters' groups and clubs, many of those terraced areas behind the goal remain – nearly sixty years on – uncovered and primitive today. (Even at a club the stature of Newcastle United, such lamentable conditions still prevail at both ends.) The generally dilapidated state of so many English League grounds bears mute testimony to the failure – despite the enormous and voluntary contributions from supporters – of most clubs in the past to update and make more comfortable the 'popular' experience of watching football.

Not only did the supporters' fund-raising in the 1930s take place against a back drop of unemployment, it also occurred at a time when money was available to football from the Pools industry – substantial money too – if the Football League management had cared to collect it. Yet football clubs were always pleading poverty. After the First World War, attendances had surged initially and some football clubs had committed themselves to costly ground improvements. Within a few years, however, with a trade recession biting, attendances began to fall back (though were still higher than pre-war gates). Some clubs found themselves financially over-committed (and it may be that this was the period when Supporters' Clubs began actively to take over more responsibility for ground improvements). Clubs in the meantime had grown used to pleading their hard times, both to supporters and players. Yet, in 1934, just as Luton Town's fans were beginning their great fund-raising feats, a Liverpool solicitor, Watson Hartley proposed that the Football League copyright its fixtures list and sell it to the Pools companies. Nervous of any overt association between football and gambling (and unable, it seems, to drag itself out of its late Victorian mould) the League's management committee would not even discuss the idea.[20]

After the war, from the recommencement of the Football League in 1946 to the late 1960s, the pace of supporters' fund-raising, if anything, quickened. There were a handful of 'rich' clubs, like Everton, Arsenal, Manchester Utd, Aston Villa, Sunderland, and a clutch of other Lancashire clubs, who were unreliant on intermittent bouts of fund-raising by fans. The vast majority, however, were only too glad of such generosity.[21]

The running of lotteries by Supporters' Clubs became increasingly the most significant source of funds raised. There was certainly nothing new about lotteries operated by supporters to enrich football clubs – it had probably been a feature of football finance since the earliest days of the professional game. Football clubs themselves were unable to run their own lotteries by regulation of the FA – the other body traditionally concerned about any association of football with gambling. Supporters and their clubs had readily stepped into the breach, though the law was ambiguous about the legitimacy of this aspect of supporter fund-raising and it is clear that the old Betting and Gaming Act was interpreted differently up and down the country.[22]

With lotteries and similar schemes as the backbone of supporter fund-raising – and a huge variety of other techniques of raising donations employed – some supporters' contributions in the post-war period were stunning. At Oxford Utd, for example, the active supporters not only bought the football ground but also provided about £250,000 in cash to the club:

> They (i.e. the supporters) bought the ground for £10,000 around the end of the 1950's . . . its worth in the region of £4.5 million now . . . They gave it to the Club . . . who mortgaged it the very next week, I understand they were so short of money.[23]

Stockport County SC estimates some £100,000 given to the club between 1954–63.[24] Aldershot FC received £124,000 in donations from supporters in the fifteen years to 1967 and Ipswich Town got £42,000 similarly over a decade.[25] Bedford Town fans gifted £175,000 to their football club between 1950–65.[26] Sometimes houses were purchased by organised supporters and given to their club to house new players, as did the 'Ladies Section' of Torquay SC in 1948 with £1,000 raised by running social events.[27]

In the years 1957–69, Coventry City SC contributed substantial sums of money to their club. Unusually, there survives a more detailed account of how the money was spent, recently republished in the Coventry SC Diary, 1985:

> From 1957 to 1961 the Supporters' Club fulfilled an undertaking to pay for the Floodlighting Installation at a cost of:
> £13,300

> In 1961 and 1962 the amount subscribed for general purposes was . . .
> £8,336

> From 1962 to 1964 the amount subscribed for the pitch Levelling Operation was
> £14,123

> In 1964 and 1965 the Supporters' Club paid for the construction of the original Club premises in the Sky Blue Stand an amount of
> £27,587

> Between 1962 and 1969 the Supporters' Club paid in respect of admissions and season tickets for old age pensioners . . .
> £7,752

Between 1966 and 1970 the Supporters' Club paid for the construction of the Lounge and Games Room the sum of £13,600 previously financed by the Brewers . . .

£13,600

In 1965 the Supporters' Club undertook to be responsible for a special Sky Blue Stand overdraft at the Bank which amounted to £41,000 at the time. Between 1965 and 1971 the amount paid off this overdraft was

£32,385

Total Subscribed

£117,083

The amount owing to the bank in respect of the above special overdraft was £8,615 at 31st May, 1971 and it looks as though the Supporters' Club will be able to clear this during its current financial year. When this has been achieved I guess we take a deep breath and start all over again.

J.R. Mead

By 1950, Southampton SC had built and equipped a gymnasium, recreation and billiards room for the players, as well as contributing annually to 'help solve the summer wages problem'. The supporters bought the annual supply of footballs and 'when employment was bad in the town, they paid for their own unemployed members to see certain matches . . .' In 1951, £1,637 was raised to buy floodlighting which was expanded two years later at a cost to Southampton's supporters of a further £1,239. Shortly afterwards, they loaned the club £3,000 'to get us out of a credit squeeze jam' and provided £1,000 towards a transfer fee. According to the Vice-President of the Football Club:

. . . it is no exaggeration to say that without there unstinted aid, there have been times when the directors would have been hard-put to keep the Club going.[28]

At Southend Utd, by 1953, the Supporters' Club had 'bought and paid for a new Ground . . . costing something like £17,000.'[29] Walsall supporters estimate some £2 million contributed in the period 1947–89,[30] and at little Gainsborough Trinity, a breathtaking £60,000 was raised plus the purchase of the ground, new stands, boardrooms, dressing rooms and other facilities, before 1965.[31]

The Chester Report, in 1968, estimated that in the three years from 1963–66, around £4½ million was raised by the organised supporters of professional clubs alone (and the activity at many amateur and non-League clubs – as the Gainsborough Trinity example illustrates – was equally intense).[32] In 1967, the National Federation of Football Supporters' Clubs calculated from questionnaire replies from 179 Supporters' Clubs that their annual total contribution amounted to £484,023.[33]

We will consider in more detail later the changes, originating in the 1950s and developing rapidly during the following decade, that gradually reduced the scope of supporter fund-raising.[34] Suffice to say at this point that by the early 1970s, the grand era of Supporters' Clubs whose raison d'être involved sustaining the financial stability of their clubs was over, replaced by the age of the 'commercial manager' and the 'development association'.

To date some Supporters' Clubs still continue to make contributions to their football clubs, though on a much reduced scale. For example, Sunderland AFC Supporters' Association (formed at the instigation of the football club in 1965) occasionally sponsors a match, in addition to providing match balls and sponsorship for (currently two of) the players' kits. The money is raised from members' subscriptions, profits from the travel club and the profits from sales of souvenirs from a shop provided rent-free by the club, adjacent to Roker Park. Nottingham Forest SC has donated around £1,000 a year to its parent club for the last twenty years and five branches of the Supporters' Club sponsor eight of the first team players' kits. One particularly vigorous branch – at Heanor in Derbyshire – contributes about £1,000 every year towards sponsorship of the family enclosure. At Cardiff City, in the 1989–90 season, one of the club's two Supporters' Clubs donated around £2,000. It consisted of:

Programme advertising	£200
Players kit sponsorship	£110
Match ball sponsorship	£69
Cash donations	£500
St John's Ambulance fees	£100
Match sponsorship (v. Walsall)	£460
Various small donations	£250
Profits from programme fair	£150
Various raffle profits	£270[35]

Most recently, in the 1990–91 season, Sheffield Utd's supporters have been involved in raising a substantial portion of the £400,000 required for the purchase of Glyn Hodges from Crystal Palace. This took the form of participation in a sweepstake draw, run by the club for the express purpose of raising the transfer fee, with only a small prize on offer of £2,000.

At the smaller football clubs, supporters still continue the tradition of fund-raising to significant effect. At Bognor Regis Town, for example, the Supporters' Club (revived in the early 1970s) has a turnover of around £10,000. Over the last five years, the supporters have contributed between £1,000–£3,000 a year, raised through raffles, shop profits and an innovative scrics of 'race nights' at which films of horse-races are screened and members bet on the runners. In the recent past, the SC has been responsible for building a new stand, a toilet block and other general refurbishments, as well as sponsoring match balls and players' kits.[36] In Scotland, too, the further down the leagues one travels, the more significant the fund-raising of local supporters. In the Scottish Second Division, in the Highland League, and at 'junior' football level (which is not for youngsters but the equivalent of the English non-league game) the supporters' input is often crucial with funds frequently raised from the proceeds of social clubs run by supporters in connection to the Club.[37]

It seems unlikely that organised supporters will ever again raise such significant and substantial sums of money for professional clubs, though supporter fund-raising will probably remain important at non-League levels. Yet throughout eighty years of football's life in Britain (1885–1965), the organised fans certainly did contribute substantially, voluntarily, and often crucially, towards maintaining the broadly-based network of clubs which sustained the national game. Without that contribution – in potent combination with their enthusiasm – football could not have flourished so vigorously.

SUPPORTERS ON THE BOARD

How did football clubs respond traditionally to the supporters' organisations that were raising such large sums of money, especially during the period 1930–70? In general, they maintained a highly paternalistic relationship with supporters – as at Luton Town in the 1930s – characterised by a 'recognition' or 'goodwill' which depended upon continued contributions and no further 'interference' in the club's affairs.

There were, however, some football clubs that responded imaginatively to the financial (and emotional) links which supporters built; others that felt sufficiently embarrassed by the high levels of donations to offer Board representation. At Aldershot, where as we have seen, the Supporters' Club had raised £124,000 over the fifteen years to 1967:

> Liaison between us and the football board is that I, as Chairman of the Supporters' Club, have been elected to the football board as one of the directors . . . this is the sort of thing that needs to be done . . . with pressure from Supporters' Club to get representatives . . . on the football board.[38]

At Southampton, where the Supporters' Club was established in 1926 at the instigation of the football club, the supporters' Chairman was invited on to the Board. It followed a financial crisis in 1934 when supporters' contributions proved so vital that the then Chairman of the club, Major Sloane Stanley, felt,

> We could not go on accepting these donations unless they had a representative on our Board and . . . we invited (the Supporters' Club) Chairman M.C.E. Hoskins, to become a Director . . . that office he held up to his death.[39]

Wrexham's Supporters' Club, like Southampton's, was also founded in 1926. Its first president, Cyril Newman, had previously been the Town Clerk of Exeter, and the first Chairman, Mr E.A. Cross, MBE, JP, was an Alderman and Director of the National Chamber of Trade. The original Supporters' Club at Wrexham was one of many such groups who financed the roofing of the 'popular side' of their grounds. In 1934, the Wrexham supporters stated:

> Our relations with the Wrexham FC Board of Directors have always been of a most cordial nature . . . we have two able representatives on the Board . . . one of whom is Alderman Horace Blew . . . and the other is Councillor Edward Williams . . .[40]

At Rhyl FC where fans had raised the modern equivalent of half a million pounds in the early 1930s,

> . . . the Football Club directors appreciate our efforts to such a degree that they actually allow us to have a representative of five on the directorate . . .[41]

Similarly at Plymouth Argyle, again following substantial contributions from the Supporters' Club, in the early 1930s, the latter's Chairman, Mr T.R. Nicholls, was included on the football club board.[42]

Yet these examples of direct 'two way' liaison between organised supporters and their club Boards seem rare in the context of the many hundreds of Supporters' Clubs functioning and raising such large sums of money. Very few of these 'two way' relationships survived beyond the 1950s, it seems, though at Coventry City in 1960, 'the Club did draft one supporter as a representative . . . But he was useless . . . he never opened his mouth to the Club . . .'[43] More recently in 1982 Oxford Utd FC 'merged' with its Supporters' Club and three of the latter's committee took places on the Board. However, this followed the take-over of the club by Robert Maxwell and the real decision-making power was no longer in the boardroom.

The most typical pattern of supporter-club liaison throughout the period 1930–70 was that which operated at Luton Town. This was the 'one way' system which involved a Board member acting as president and/or Chairman of the Supporters' Club and its committee. There appear to be no examples of Supporters' Club members being given the opportunity even to elect which of the Board members should sit on their committee; presumably the Board itself decided the matter. There are numerous examples of this form of liaison amongst those Supporters' Clubs contributing to *The Supporter* editions of 1934 and 1935. At Sheffield Wednesday, the Secretary and the Chairman of the Football Club both sat on the supporters' committee.[44] At Blackpool in 1934, the Chairman of the supporters' club was appointed by the Board.[45] At Bournemouth and Boscombe, the Supporters' Club president was a director of the football club.[46] This favoured system of 'one way' liaison was clearly preferred by most football clubs because – as we saw at Luton Town in the 1930s – it kept the Board free to manoeuvre over issues which could be in direct opposition to the interests of the supporter fund-raisers.

The football clubs tended to see their Supporters' Clubs as essentially *a fund-raising arm of the club*, forced by circumstance (and FA regulations) to operate through a voluntary organisation of supporters. Hence the likelihood that around half of the latter were established at the instigation of the football clubs. We will discover later that when the opportunity arose in the 1960s for the clubs to run their own lotteries and schemes, they often took over existing Supporters' Clubs of long standing – assets and all – without compunction. Despite the proliferation of Supporters' Clubs, their combined, enormous membership, and their crucial financial contributions to their football clubs, no organisation had set its stall out simply to organise and represent the views of football fans. Those involved in the running of Supporters' Clubs – many of whom hailed from the ranks of local aldermen, councillors, justices of the peace and solicitors – appeared content to trust their football club's Boards to act with integrity. They saw their role in much the same perspective as their club directors; and so it is hardly surprising that, when they federated into a national organisation of Supporters' Clubs, they adopted a motto which could have been penned in any boardroom: 'To Help and Not To Hinder'.

NOTES

1. See M. Marples, *A History of Football*, London, 1954, pp. 215–16.
2. See T. Mason, *Association Football and English Society, 1863–1915*, Gt. Britain, 1981, p. 37.
3. Quoted on p. 15 of P. Murphy, 'Notes on the relationship between Directors and Supporters of Leicester Fosse and Leicester City FC, 1894–1960' (unpublished).
4. W. Vamplew, *Pay Up and Play the Game*, Cambridge, 1988, p. 17.
5. For an account of the emergence of some of the earliest SCs, see R.

Taylor, 'Walking alone together', in *British Football and Social Change*, ed. S. Wagg and J. Williams, Leicester, 1991.

6. Personal interview, Bob Redhead aged 72 years, Secretary of Luton Town SC, 1960–75, March 1990.
7. Luton Town FC Board Minutes, 1931, p. 304.
8. *Luton News* Football Handbook, 1933/34, pp. 21–2.
9. *Luton News* Football Handbook, 1951/52, p. 36.
10. *Luton News* Football Handbook, 1951/52, p. 36.
11. *Luton News* Football Handbook, 1965/66, p. 6.
12. *Luton News* Football Handbook, 1968/69, p. 1.
13. Bob Redhead interview, op. cit.
14. Bob Redhead interview, ibid.
15. Bob Redhead interview, ibid.
16. N. Fishwick, *English Football and Society 1910–1950*, Manchester, 1989, p. 43.
17. See above. See also Vamplew, op. cit., p. 86.
18. James Walvin, *The People's Game*, London, 1975, p. 147.
19. For an enlightening account of the history of Millwall supporters and club 1930–60, see Chris Downham, 'Dockers, lions and bushwackers', MA dissertation, University of Warwick, 1987.
20. See John Harding, *For the Good of the Game: The Official History of the Professional Players Association*, London, 1991, p. 191. Eventually the FL was persuaded to meet the pools' companies in 1936, but the negotiations were so completely mishandled that the League gained nothing but bad publicity from the encounter (see Harding, p. 193).
21. The Everton SC representative at the National Federation's 1965 AGM confided: 'We who support Everton, a club that has never needed our money and never needed anything from its Supporters Club . . .'. See AGM Conference Minutes, 1965, p. 48.
22. The law was eventually clarified in 1956 with a new Lotteries Act entering the Statute. Though the legislation was, at the time, vigorously supported by the Nat. Fed., who lobbied hard on its behalf, it proved the death knell for many Supporters' Clubs. See below, Chapter 8, 'Supporter-club relations'.
23. Personal Interview, Jim Hunt, Secretary Oxford Utd SC, 1969–76, March 1990.
24. Nat. Fed. AGM Minutes, 1963, p. 36.
25. Nat. Fed. AGM Minutes, 1967, pp. 68 and 70.
26. Nat. Fed. AGM Minutes, 1969, p. 81.
27. *Sport Weekly Magazine*, 21 August 1948, p. 15.
28. J.R. Sarjantson, 'A tribute to Supporters' Clubs', *F.A. News*, vol. VII, no. 2, September 1957.
29. Nat. Fed. AGM Minutes, 1953, p. 30.
30. *End to End*, the current Nat. Fed. quarterly publication, Xmas 1989.
31. Nat. Fed. AGM Minutes, 1965, p. 47.
32. The Chester Report, 1968, p. 31.
33. Nat. Fed. AGM Minutes, 1967, p. 69.
34. See below, Chapter 8, 'Supporter-Club Relations'.

35. From information supplied by Mr D.L. Lambert, Cardiff City SC.
36. From information supplied by Mr E.G. Brice, Chairman, Bognor Regis Town SC.
37. From information supplied by Martin Rose, Secretary of the Scottish Division of the Nat. Fed.
38. Nat. Fed. AGM Minutes, 1969, p. 31.
39. *F.A. News*, vol. VII, no. 2, September 1957.
40. *The Supporter*, vol. 1, no. 1, October 1934, p. 3.
41. *The Supporter*, vol. 1, no. 1, October 1934, p. 5.
42. *The Supporter*, vol. 1, no. 1, October 1934, p. 8.
43. Personal Interview. Jim Hamill, President, Coventry City SC, 1990.
44. *The Supporter*, vol. 2, no. 1, September 1935, p. 5.
45. *The Supporter*, vol. 1, no. 1, October 1934, p. 7.
46. *The Supporter*, vol. 2, no. 1, September 1935, p. 7.

4

THE RENEGADES AND THE RESPECTABLES

The real challenge to a board came only when the opposition was well-organised into 'share-holders associations' or 'supporters' clubs' . . . the latter became so as soon as they did anything other than supply passive support for the board . . .[1]

With few effective channels through which the vast majority of supporters might express their disapproval of those who ran their football clubs, most fans could only either 'vote with their feet' and stay away, or join a spontaneous post-match protest outside the boardroom or on the pitch. Though there were occasions when politically-inspired groups turned their attention to football – like the 'Soccer for Sixpence' campaign launched in 1929 by the London Labour Party's 'Sports Association'[2] – there appear surprisingly few examples prior to recent times of supporters themselves organising seriously in any form or in any roles other than those tacitly approved of by their football clubs.

There were, however, sporadic campaigns to organise boycotts of matches, like that at Manchester United in October 1930. A run of poor results led to a mass meeting of around 3,000 United supporters at Hulme Town Hall and a decision was made to boycott the visit of Arsenal the following day. The fans' leader, George Greenough, addressed the crowd and, on boycott-Saturday, it was he who 'stood on a soap-box outside Old Trafford and implored people not to go in.'[3] The boycott did have some impact – a mere 23,000 attendance at Old Trafford that day bore evidence of it – and, as the season progressed, gates dipped below 10,000.

George Greenough was a local taxi-driver, not at all in the mould of the local councillors and aldermen that so often founded supporters' clubs. He had formed the first Manchester United supporters' club in the mid-1920s. It may be that he came to represent a real threat to the club and some form of compromise emerged. In an intriguing reference to him in *The Supporter* of October 1934, he appears a highly 'respectable' figure, now on the staff of the Football Club:

> The Founder and President of (Manchester United Supporters' Club) is no less a personage than Mr. Geo. H. Greenough, who has travelled extensively in his lifetime in connection with the Football Club . . . he now holds an official post with the United Club . . . (the Supporters' Club) . . . holds some very interesting socials, whist drives, concerts and lectures, the latter being one of Mr. Greenough's pet hobbies . . .[4]

The tactic of boycotting matches, however, was rarely successful in either persuading sufficient numbers to join it or in exerting pressure on the club. To be effective, a boycott needed very substantial support and perhaps many fans were caught between their desire to support the *team* and their wish to censure the Board.

Football club Boards, most of the time, had little real trouble from opposition groups.[5] Dissidents found great difficulty in organising any serious tactical manoeuvres to disrupt the directorate. With only one-third of a Board up for election each year and any vacancies in the meantime filled by Board decision, it was not easy for any but the most affluent to gain a purchase on power. Elections to a Board were rarely even contested – defeats at elections were rarer still.[6]

Nevertheless there were those who tried. At Swindon Town in 1921, Mr T.C. Newman – a persistent critic of the Board – launched a supporters' club with the two aims of getting a roof to cover the 'popular' side of the ground and greater openness from the Board about the financial position of the club. In an attempt to gain election to the Board, he campaigned for a new share-issue (which would finance the roof over the terraces) but the Board held out and Newman was defeated.[7]

A few clubs refused to adopt private company status and were run in their original form, with members electing a committee to run their affairs. Oxford City was one such, though with the membership fee at a guinea in 1932, few 'ordinary' supporters could afford to take part. The Oxford City Supporters' Club was formed in 1931 under the 'approved' format of acting as a fund-raising body and stewarding force to stamp out barracking of players. It became a more militant organisation under the leadership of F.P. Thornton in 1932. Thornton orchestrated attempts at the 1932 and 1933 AGMs to involve supporters more directly in the club's affairs by reducing the membership fee to 5/- (1932) and 10/6d (1933). Both attempts failed. The Supporters' Club subsequently raised £20 and offered it to the committee in return for automatic representation for one of its members. The committee took umbrage and withdrew all 'recognition' of the Supporters' Club. A bitter feud developed with fans distributing leaflets, organising protest meetings and threatening boycotts, but the committee held out.

The problem for the Supporters' Club was:

> It could not get men onto the Committee without broadening the electorate, and it could not broaden the electorate without getting men onto the Committee . . . the lack of institutional power in Supporters' Clubs enabled the Club controllers to call their bluff . . .[8]

These comparatively rare examples of Supporters' Clubs organising in direct opposition to their football clubs illustrate the difficulties that faced any group of fans seeking to operate without the 'approval' or 'recognition' of their FCs. Enthusiasm for such attempts to represent the interests of supporters independently often foundered on the rise and fall of local issues (and the fortunes of the team). For those Supporters' Clubs prepared to operate from within the parameters defined as 'proper' by their football clubs, relationships could be established, providing no 'interference' in the club's affairs was attempted.

Fund-raising was the key to being allowed *any* participation in the life of the football club, apart from watching from the terraces or stands. It was the common effort to raise money by a variety of schemes that first drew individual Supporters' Clubs together to form a national organisation.

THE RISE OF THE NATIONAL FEDERATION OF FOOTBALL SUPPORTERS' CLUBS (1926–36)

> Northampton Town ('The Cobblers'), at the suggestion of their secretary during the months of September and October, 1926, sent out letters to various supporters' clubs inviting their opinion upon the formation of a federation. During the ensuing correspondence, it was learned that there was a small association in the North. After some careful consideration by the Cobbler's Executive, it was decided to call a preliminary meeting of those who were interested: this was held in London, on Saturday, January 22nd, 1927, at Lyons Restaurant, 2, Bridge Street, Westminster, the following clubs were represented: Northampton, Boscome, Brentford, Charlton Athletic and Plymouth Argyle . . . thus the Federation came into existence.[9]

The secretary of Northampton's Supporters' Club in 1926 was Tommy Hodgeson. It was his wife who had originally thought of the idea of forming a National Federation of Supporters' Clubs; a suggestion she made 'over a cup of coffee' after a match.[10] The list of the six original member clubs shows that all were from the south of England and, it seems, as the Federation developed in its early years, the organisation, became at least briefly (1931–34), a bipartite one with a Northern Division and Southern counterpart, each holding an Annual General Meeting. There may have been a prototype Federation of Supporters' Clubs earlier than 1926 according to a reference to 'a similar organisation . . . (that) . . . had died out',[11] and there is also the reference above to 'a small Association in the North' (presumably of Supporters' Clubs) – which probably evolved into the Federation's Northern Division.

The earliest document available which throws light on the fledgeling national organisation is a Notice of the Third AGM, to be held at Slater's Restaurant, High Holborn on 5 July 1930. This single sheet reveals that there were twenty-one clubs affiliated to the Federation at this time, half of which were amateur clubs (including Yeovil Petters United and Tunbridge Wells Rangers). All the affiliated clubs come from the southern half of the country, with Notts Forest at the northern outpost.

The first Chairman of the Federation was Councillor Talbot Nanson, Lord Mayor of Brighton. The President in 1930 was F.C. Parker Esq., a Councillor and Justice of the Peace from Northampton, and the Vice-President, A.J. Playdon, was also a Councillor from Bournemouth. Tommy Hodgeson was Joint Hon. Secretary. Thus the pattern we have noted earlier of a keen involvement in the supporters' organisations of local councillors, JPs and aldermen was quickly reflected in the officials of the new Federation.[12]

More detailed information about the Federation becomes available with the publication, in 1934, of the 'Official Organ' of the organisation, *The Supporter*.[13] The first edition of this monthly broadsheet newspaper featured on its front page an editorial column alongside an imposing photographic portrait of Councillor Parker, in three-quarter profile. Underneath the photograph, his 'President's Message' calls on Federation members to 'spread the spirit of goodwill amongst the followers of our great game'.

The National Officers of the Federation in 1934 no longer include the founder member, Tommy Hodgeson. There are now four Vice-Presidents, three of whom are Councillors, and also two Lord Mayors, Talbot Nanson and A.E. Wilkinson, JP (Mayor of Leeds and Chairman of the Federation's Northern Branch) are amongst the listed officers. In addition to the Hon. Secretary and Hon. Treasurer, an Hon. Solicitor, G.S. Godfree Esq., 'a member of the Income Tax Payers' Association', has been appointed to the Federation. At the bottom of the front page there is a group photograph of the delegates who attended the 1934 Annual Conference. Against a backdrop of the New Civic Hall in Leeds (the Conference venue), the Lord and Lady Mayoress of the City stand in the midst of fifty-five Federation members; all men and virtually all middle-aged or older. They have removed their trilby hats for the occasion and their double-breasted suits are neatly buttoned. They seem the very picture of lower middle-class English respectability in its mid-1930s mode.

The motto the Federation adopted (though its origins remain obscure) sums up the organisation's model aspiration: 'To Help and Not To Hinder' (often shortened to 'Help not Hinder'). This motto assumes a fundamental objection (probably voiced by some football clubs) to the very idea that supporters might organise themselves independently. The motto absorbs the fear that self-organised supporters will be nuisances and difficult to control (like children). It assures the 'parent' football clubs that the supporters involved will be 'good' and not seek to interfere. There is also an almost Victorian undertone to the motto – re-emphasised by the Kipling-esque sentiments of Tommy Hodgeson's thoughts on it:

> What a motto we have chosen for our National Federation; what a message to live up to! . . . Put it into our daily lives, see what a lot it means. What a sermon it is. Oh! If only it could be graven on all our buildings both national and local. What a lot it would do if it were ever in our thoughts and on our tongues.[14] (Perhaps the motto was Tommy Hodgeson's personal choice?)

The reassurance explicit in the motto is further elaborated in the stated Aims and Objects of the Federation, outlined on page two of *The Supporter*:

> It was hoped that Supporters' Clubs, by getting together and pooling ideas and interests, would be of more assistance to their Football Club, and at the same time, unity being strength, they would have more weight within the football world and also be held in more esteem by their own football club.

Thus the Federation set out its stall: the primary aim was to provide 'more assistance' to the clubs but it was also hoped that 'unity being strength' (a trade union-like phrase) the Supporters' Clubs together might develop some 'weight' and attract 'higher esteem' from their 'parent' bodies. The Federation was also concerned to encourage its member clubs to check 'unsportsmanlike' displays (presumably a reference to forms of crowd misbehaviour). In practical terms, it offered its membership the chance to exchange (fund-raising) ideas and it provided advice on income tax problems and other relevant issues. The membership fee stood at a guinea for Football League-associated clubs and half a guinea for others. No form of membership was available to individual supporters.

The bulk of the remaining columns in the first edition of *The Supporter* are made up of brief sketches from member clubs of their regular activities and achievements. In between, there is a column penned by Tom Crew ('International and Cup Final Referee') and one from 'A Convert' to the idea of Supporters' Clubs – clearly a club director – who describes his early suspicion of 'these supporter fellows' who might 'interfere', and his conversion following the establishment of 'a splendid branch in my own particular town'.[15]

The editorial team of *The Supporter* are keen to hear from correspondents in time for the following month's issue. They request information from member clubs about their relations with Boards of Directors, whether they hold any share capital in their clubs and whether they have any representation on the Boards. Some issues are opened for discussion, including the unpredictable legality of 'penny-on-the-ball' schemes; the sale of *The Supporter* at football grounds, and transport difficulties experienced by travelling fans. Perhaps most intriguingly, 'the vexed question of FA Cup Final tickets' is a topic invited for discussion.[16]

The Federation had certainly attempted to develop some dialogue with the Football Association as early as 1930. In the AGM Notice of that year, items six and seven on the agenda include:

6) Delegates to report on the interview with Sir F.J. Wall
7) Relationship and recognition by the Football Association

There survives no account of the 'interview' and one can only guess at its course, but we do know something of Sir Frederick Wall, Hon. Secretary of the FA from 1895 (until succeeded by Sir Stanley Rous in 1934). He was 'austere, top-hatted . . . an arch conservative', with little sympathy for the very idea of supporting one team above another. Indeed, he often declaimed to those within earshot that, before playing the Royal Engineers in the FA Cup, he 'had eaten a rump steak . . . so careless had he been of the result.'[17] In this, the FA Secretary reflected something of the mid-Victorian, amateur Corinthian vision of the game, to which professionalism and the desire to win were anathema. Just the word 'supporter' – a pejorative in times past – might have been a sufficient cause for dyspepsia. There was certainly no 'relationship and recognition' forthcoming from the FA. Despite Stanley Rous's willingness to accept a Vice-Presidency of the Federation in 1935, half a century would pass before any 'official' meeting took place between the supreme body in charge of the amateur and professional game in England and the Federation of Supporters' Clubs, with their members whose voluntary work was so crucial (especially for the amateur and smaller clubs) to the maintenance of a broadly-based national sport.

Perhaps one way the organisation might have exerted some pressure on the FA would have been to orchestrate a publicity campaign at national and local levels (where FA County Representatives – the most powerful group within the FA – operated). But, from its earliest days it seems, the Federation was unable to attract the kind of attention from the media (i.e. principally news/sports papers) that it thought appropriate. In 1935, H.P.

Lawrence (Hon. Secretary, Golders Green FC Supporters' Association) was complaining:

> Who has seen any interest taken in the movement (i.e. the Federation) in one of our national journals? Has anyone ever seen there a reference to the movement? Its objects and its importance? To all Sports Editors, it is nonexistent. It is not a question of amateur or professional; it is merely ignoring something which is of national sporting interest and of national sporting importance . . . no recognition is given to the movement . . .[18]

As it turned out, the Federation did receive publicity late in 1935 – but not of the kind it desired. By 1935 the organisation claimed a membership of 'eighty professional and amateur clubs from all parts of the country and a further fourteen clubs in Scotland.'[19] That year's AGM was held at Sheffield and considered a great success. *The Supporter* had been published (as far as one can gather) on a regular monthly basis and was entering its second year. The publication described itself as 'the only periodical which is prepared to publish full reports from Supporters' Clubs . . . whereas in the past (they) have been compelled to receive attacks from the press without hope of retaliation . . .'[20] It was in defence of one Supporters' Club – Portsmouth – that the Federation incurred the wrath of *The People* newspaper.

It appears that Portsmouth Supporters' Club was the subject of an 'attack' by *The People*, perhaps in the summer of 1935. We gather that the Editor of *The Supporter*, Jack Williams of Wrexham SC, produced a vigorous response, for we read in September 1935:

> The Portsmouth Supporters' Club is particularly grateful to Mr. Williams for the ready manner in which he defended the club when it was attacked in *The People*.[21]

Jack Williams's response apparently triggered a further riposte from *The People* on 3 November, only this time the attack was directed against the Federation itself, under the headline: 'Where Supporters' Money Goes'. The writer – Cecil Hadley, Sports Editor of *The People* – questioned the whole raison d'être of an organisation like the Federation. Hadley was an honorary member of Northampton Town's Supporters' Club (the founder-member club of the Federation, with Tommy Hodgeson still its Secretary) and he reflected upon the current campaign in Northampton to recruit 2,500 new members to the club:

> The subscription is only a shilling a head and there are at present 419 members, but what I do not like is that a large part of that sum goes to the National Federation of Supporters Clubs (sic). The exact figures . . . are subscriptions and donations, £26.17.6d and of this £17.2.5d goes to the National Federation,

part in donation, part in expenses. I ask those who gave their shilling, 'Did they intend to benefit Northampton Town or the National Federation? . . . I am an uncompromising opponent of the Federation, for which I cannot see the slightest necessity except as a vehicle for providing joy rides . . . (the Federation) is an excrescence for which, in my view, there is not the slightest excuse or reason . . .[22]

This attack upon the Federation was reproduced on page 6 of the November 1935 edition of *The Supporter* and subjected to 'A Spirited Reply' by Jack Williams. He reviewed the sterling work of fund-raising that Northampton Town's supporters had accomplished, which included £400 donated towards a recent transfer fee and the purchase of footballs, ground repairs, band fees and 'dressing room sundries' (to the value £19.17s). He goes on to state the Aims and Objects of the Federation and maintains that the gathering together of delegates from a large number of Supporters' Clubs was useful both for supporters and football clubs: 'Some . . . may have a profitable scheme which, with slight alterations, may be passed on . . .'. Thus, the 'joy-rides' to conferences that Hadley complains of are often of direct benefit to the football clubs represented. Williams concludes by quoting the Federation's motto and offering Hadley a right of reply in the next edition.

By 1935, the Federation had been in existence for eight years and had made some notable achievements. It had established, for the first time, a national organisation that included around eighty Supporters' Clubs in England and Wales and about fourteen in Scotland. It had also produced the first national publication written by supporters which gave space to air their grievances and describe their clubs' activities. The Federation's annual conferences were well attended and well organised, and its affairs were conducted with great propriety by (largely) a coterie of local councillors, aldermen and mayors. The Federation had made some headway as a resource offering legal advice – especially concerning the organisation of coach travel for parties – and was able to provide assistance to supporters launching new clubs.

But there were already signs of the difficulties which lay ahead. If the Federation were ever to become a body with 'more weight in the football world', it would need a more *public* role, reflected in the media of the day, than it had succeeded in establishing. The Federation's member clubs were clearly very proud of their fund-raising achievements – *but such activities took up all the time and energy of the available activists*. It left very little time for Federation affairs and little room for manoeuvre at a national, campaigning level; the real commitment of most member clubs was *local*. Even *The Supporter* proved unsustainable for more than two seasons 'so poor was the response of Supporters' Clubs in general that it was found impossible to continue so elaborate a publication.'[23] Perhaps most significantly (and ominously for the Federation), the Football Association showed no sign of giving ground in response to requests for 'relationship and recognition'. Though FA Secretary, Stanley Rous, accepted a Vice-Presidency of the Federation in 1935 – and became its Patron in 1965 – he did not attend one single Annual Conference until 1980.

NOTES

1. N. Fishwick, *English Football and Society 1910–1950*, Manchester, 1989, p. 33.
2. See R. Taylor, 'Walking alone together', in *British Football and Social Change*, ed. J. Williams and S. Wagg, Leicester, 1991, p. 11.
3. M. Crick and D. Smith, *Manchester Utd: The Betrayal of a Legend*, London, 1989, p. 9.
4. *The Supporter*, vol. 1, no. 1, October 1934, p. 3.
5. See Fishwick, op. cit., p. 32ff.
6. The recent history of Newcastle Utd FC illustrates how difficult, for even the most rich, taking over an unwilling Board still can be. Millionaire John Hall with his Magpie Group failed to gain a majority despite three years of calculated efforts.
7. See Fishwick, op. cit., p. 34.
8. See Fishwick, op. cit., p. 35.
9. *The Supporter*, vol. 1, no. 1, October 1934.
10. Tommy Hodgeson gives a brief account of this in the National Federation AGM Minutes, 1953, p. 17; and co-founder, Mr Onley, describes it in AGM Minutes, 1958, p. 18.
11. *The Supporter*, vol. 2, no. 1, September 1935, p. 5.
12. A pattern less true today, though the current Chairman of the Federation, Tony Kershaw, is a Councillor in Loughborough.
13. The writer has seen but four surviving copies of this monthly publication: October 1934; September, November and December 1935. I understand that it folded in 1936. See below, Chapter 10.
14. *The Supporter*, September 1935, p. 4.
15. *The Supporter*, September 1935, p. 4.
16. *The Supporter*, September 1935, p. 4.
17. See S. Wagg, *The Football World*, London, 1984, p. 32.
18. *The Supporter*, September 1935, p. 5.
19. *The Supporter*, September 1935, p. 2; see also November 1935, p. 6.
20. *The Supporter*, September 1935, p. 6.
21. *The Supporter*, September 1935, p. 6.
22. *The People*, 3 November 1935 (reproduced on p. 6 of *The Supporter*, November 1935.)
23. From an appeal for support by Federation Chairman, Talbot Nanson, in *The Supporter*, November 1935, p. 2.

SECOND HALF

Helping Not Hindering:
The National Federation of Football
Supporters' Clubs, 1945–1985

5

STRUCTURE AND MEMBERSHIP

. . . we were continually brainwashed into believing that age was a great asset by the persistent mutual admiration among the Executive Committees . . . One of the overriding impressions that we came away with was that so much of the business of the Conference was far divorced from what we had imagined football supporting was all about. (Two Chelsea fans in *Chelsea Blue*, August 1973)

The boom in football's popularity that followed the Second World War was reflected in a burgeoning membership of the Federation. Unfortunately, it is not possible to place an accurate figure on the total number of supporters who, through their membership of clubs affiliated to the Federation, were, at least notionally, represented. Nor is it possible to give exact numbers of the Supporters' Clubs who paid their Federation dues in the years following 1948.

In 1977, Federation Secretary, Tony Pullein, reflecting on the fifty years' history of the organisation, suggested that: 'During those boom years the membership . . . rose to over 500 clubs'.[1] In 1953, the Deputy Lord Mayor of Cardiff, addressing the Federation AGM, refers to 'some 400 clubs' in membership and, in 1987, reflecting on sixty years of Federation history, president Archie Gooch mentions 412 clubs.[2] But these figures all seem too high. The *Football Supporters' Gazette* – the post-war 'official organ' of the Federation – claimed 200 Supporters' Clubs in membership in 1948 (the year of peak attendances in the Football League and probably also the year of peak membership of the Federation).[3] The most accurate picture of membership is contained in a brief exchange recorded at the 1948 AGM. The Federation Treasurer, Mr Manley, quotes the figure of 155 member clubs. This figure is questioned from the floor and Mr Manley clarifies it by saying it refers to paid-up member clubs. The Federation Secretary, Leslie Davis, notes there are 215 clubs on his register, concluding 'a number of clubs . . . have not yet paid their dues'.[4] It seems, therefore, that at its height, the Federation's membership of affiliated Supporters' Clubs reached somewhere between 200–250 member clubs.

As to the make-up of this membership, it appears that supporters of *amateur/non–League football clubs* were in a preponderance. At the 1948 AGM, 131 Supporters' Clubs were represented of which over 120 appear to be without Football League status.[5] In 1953, of 89 delegates attending the AGM, over 50 represented amateur clubs.[6] In the opinion of the Worcester SC delegate, in 1953, the 'overwhelming majority' of supporters' clubs in the Federation are from amateur or non-League football.[7]

Some of the Supporters' Clubs from non-League football had surprisingly substantial numbers of individual members. For example, Colchester Utd – a non-League club until 1950 – claimed in 1948 to be the largest Supporters' Club in England.[8] Worcester Supporters' Club was known to include tens of thousands of members and Poole Town SC quoted 49,000 members in 1962![9] It is obvious that these figures go far beyond the actual *attendances* of supporters at their clubs' matches and they probably reflect the wide community involvement of local people in fund-raising and social events which benefitted their football clubs.

In the Football League, a club like Norwich City (in Division II in 1962) claimed a supporters' membership of around 7,000; Grimsby Town SC included 34,000.[10] (In the latter case, participation in the supporter–run weekly lotteries required one to be a member of the Supporters' Club.) The total number of supporters (and sympathisers) who belonged to clubs affiliated to the Federation at its height can only be guessed. In 1953 (with membership already in decline), Federation Chairman, Talbot Nanson, referred to 'nearly 500,000 rank and file supporters' represented by delegates at conference.[11] Whatever the true figure may have been, it is clear that, during the decade following 1945, the Federation offered a national focus for hundreds of thousands of supporters within their membership. However, it is also apparent that the vast majority of Supporters' Clubs involved were associated with amateur, non-League or 'smaller' professional teams. There is also some indication that the south of England provided a large portion of the member clubs. In 1956, during a debate about the representation of geographic areas on the Federation's Executive Committee, the Southern Area is described as having 'the proponderance of clubs' within the Federation. Clubs from outside this Area are suspicious 'that a certain section of the Southern Area are aiming at dictatorship, never mind monopoly . . .'[12]

In the 1930s, the Federation's structure had been based on *counties* – just like the Football Association. The Executive was made up of one delegate per ten clubs within a given county, plus four national officers. In total, it could prove a large and unwieldy number for a committee. In 1948, a new structure was proposed dividing England and Wales into four regional areas (which later grew into six). Each of the new areas could elect up to four representatives (one per ten clubs in membership within the area) who would join the national officers on the Executive.

The Federation remained, post-war, committed to the same vision of the role of a Supporters' Club that had been expressed pre-war. Despite its growing membership of Supporters' Clubs, many of which, as we have seen, were raising vital and substantial amounts of money for their football clubs, the Federation generated little enthusiasm for radical ideas or campaigns which might have given their members 'more weight in the football world'. Instead, the organisation resubscribed to the passive, child-parent model of relationship between supporters and their clubs. In the words of Secretary Leslie Davis, in 1948,

> 'The primary objective of every Supporters' Club is to create and foster enthusiasm in the parent Club; to encourage greater support at the matches and, by raising of funds, financially assist the football clubs . . .'[13]

Even the hint, dropped a decade before in the pages of *The Supporter*, that in combination ('unity being strength') football fans could exert some real pressure on clubs and administrators, had politely disappeared. The Federation had become as 'respectable' in word and deed as any of its most worthy founding fathers could have wanted. With Stanley Rous, the Secretary of the FA, as a Vice-President and (by 1953) Viscount Alexander, ex-First Lord of the Admiralty, Chancellor of the Duchy of Lancaster and Vice-President of both the FA and Chelsea FC, installed as Federation President, the organisation had the *appearance* of official recognition and status within the game, but without the substance. As Chairman, Talbot Nanson, described it, looking over the packed hall of delegates at the conference in 1948.

> Today everyone knows what a power – *a friendly power* – the Federation has become in the football world . . . [14]

And when, in 1956, the establishment of a Legal Aid Fund was proposed to help supporters in specific campaigns, it was rejected by the Executive with the words:

> We are not so much a fighting organisation as a helpful organisation.[15]

Unfortunately for many of the Federation's member clubs, when their very existence came under threat a few years later, being 'a friendly power' and 'a helpful organisation' in the football world would count for very little.

In 1948, membership of the Federation cost two guineas a year for Supporters' Clubs of professional clubs and one guinea for others. By 1954, a new headquarters for the organisation had been established in Pall Mall,

London. This eminently respectable address was in reality a dark and cramped room in the basement of a once-grand town house. (According to Federation 'legend', Leslie Davis went blind eventually, as a result of many years working in its gloomy light.) The organisation was run on a largely voluntary basis before 1956 and it attempted to offset its costs by running a ticket-business from the Pall Mall address, selling (as agents) '. . . Theatre, Circus, Amateur Cup and miscellaneous Match Tickets . . .'[16] It was clearly a busy (and, perhaps, profitable) operation to run on a voluntary basis and in 1956, Leslie Davis became a salaried Secretary at £688.10.6d per annum.

The atmosphere at the Federation's annual conferences throughout the post-war period – as recorded in the surviving Minutes – exudes a general air of self-conscious respectability and careful restraint. The year of 1948 signalled the Federation's 21st Anniversary and the then Patron, Lord Broadbridge, was on hand to celebrate it. Following 1953, the year of her Coronation, Queen Elizabeth II regularly received the loyal greetings of conference delegates, sent by telegram; her reply of thanks was read annually, on its arrival, to 'loud and prolonged cheering'.[17] The language of speakers at conference is pedantic and formal. Delegates speak of the 'honour' of a 'conference' when referring to little more than a social chat with a football administrator or aristocrat. In 1954, the recently elected Chairman, Ray Sonin, appeared on a BBC radio programme. His reflections on the occasion, given at the conference later that year, portray his gratification at such an (obviously rare) event:

> I think you will agree it was a high honour paid to the Federation that its Chairman should be asked to take part in a programme in which dignitaries of the local football club were present . . .[18]

By 1957 the Federation had elected a new Chairman, Dr Hancock, Harley Street practitioner and Director of QPR.[19] Dr Hancock, who was invited along to a conference by the Secretary, Leslie Davis, was, apparently, not actually a *member* of the Federation at the time of his election. According to later Secretary, Tony Pullein,

> . . . he had never been in the Federation actually . . . was elected Chairman – being such an eminent man – before he knew anything about the organisation at all. Being Chairman was the first he knew about it.[20]

Dr Hancock remained Federation Chairman until 1964 when he was elevated to a Vice-Presidency, and Deputy Chairman, Archie Gooch, took over the chairmanship of the Federation for the next decade. (It was in that year – and at the instigation of the departing Chairman, Dr Hancock – that special 'Badges of Office' were commissioned for senior Federation personnel, to be worn around their necks on chains like prototype Lord Mayors.[21])

Thus the Federation, as it reached its maturity and achieved its widest membership during the two decades after the Second World War, resembled closely the earlier models of successful supporters' organisations: eminently respectable; glad to be 'of service'; quite literally patronised by senior football administrators, and chaired by either a Lord Mayor or a football club director. Its active membership of officers and delegates were men (almost entirely) drawn very much from the same age group as those who owned the football clubs and who ran the game. The Mayor of Scarborough gives, unwittingly, a telling description of Federation delegates gathered at the 1965 conference. He urges them to enjoy the seaside town and adds:

> . . . bring your children along for their holidays or, perhaps, looking around, I ought to say your grandchildren . . .[22]

For the Federation, the age of its active members (i.e. those delegates who turned up for conferences) – and their prior commitment to running their Supporters' Clubs – made for a less than vigorous profile for the organisation at national level. Almost everyone involved in the Federation was already spending many evenings and most weekends organising supporters' club activities: travel, lotteries, stewarding, producing and selling programmes, operating turnstiles, running tea-bars. Some had no time even to *watch* the football matches – 'Many . . . see little or nothing of the games'[23] – which left them at a considerable disadvantage for representing spectators. The week-long commitments of these dedicated organisers left even less energy for promoting Federation affairs. This almost inevitable strain on the 'active' Federation membership bedevilled the success of any public campaign or media stimulation the Federation might attempt. As for the 'rank and file' members of the Supporters' Clubs affiliated, it seems likely that most knew nothing at all about the Federation which, nominally, represented them at national and regional levels. It remains true today, according to current Federation Chairman, Tony Kershaw:

> Many individual members of the Supporters' Clubs don't know about the Federation – and the service it provides . . . They may not tell their members much, if anything about the Federation.[24]

Though membership (i.e. member clubs) declined from its 1948 peak throughout the next decades, the number of delegates attending annual conferences usually represented just above or just below one hundred Supporters' Clubs. From the late 1960s, through to the present day, the number of delegates in attendance has steadily declined to a plateau of around forty and the percentage of non-League clubs represented shrank, as shown in the list below.

Conference year	Number of clubs represented	Percentage of non-League clubs
1948	131	80
1953	89	60
1954	113	65
1956	95	65
1958	100	65
1960	139	62
1961	127	65
1962	93	65
1963	94	65
1964	108	55
1965	110	60
1966	91	53
1967	75	52
1968	84	53
1969	75	53
1970	54	44
1971	71	55
1973	61	50
1974	60	45
1975	58	50
1976	55	40
1978	51	40
1979	54	55
1980	52	50
1981	54	45
1982	61	45
1983	47	45
1984	48	40
1985	46	40
1986	41	25
1987	45	30
1988	40	35

Throughout the 1960s and onwards, Federation members often complained from the floor of annual conferences about the apathy which dispirited the organisation. As the Northern Area Secretary put it in 1960:

I cannot understand why people join the Federation and then take no interest.[25]

More complaints surfaced the following year when, offering a rare opportunity for publicity, the *Daily Mail* attempted to survey the Federation's clubs for the basis of an article about supporter opinion. Questionnaires were sent to seventy-five member clubs, but so few returned that the paper shelved the idea.[26]

There were already fears for the Federation's 'health' expressed as early as 1956. Secretary Leslie Davis, responding to attacks on the Federation's weakness and accusations that it was 'going backwards' replied:

> If your neighbour is looking seedy, you don't tell him he is going to die; you pat
> him on the back . . . That's the type of encouragement we require . . .[27]

Some Federation officers were becoming painfully aware of the discrepancy between the manner and substance of Federation conferences, and the concerns of ordinary football supporters. Thus the Chairman, Ray Sonin, in 1956:

> . . . there is a tendency creeping into this Federation of bothering too much
> about procedure, geographical differences and other little problems . . . There
> have been pin pricks here, there and everywhere . . . I see on the Agenda today
> . . . that there is only one item which affects the ordinary rank and file
> supporter.[28]

When the Federation did attempt to stimulate changes that would benefit many ordinary fans, the Federation's impotence – its lack of weight with the media and in the football world – provoked occasional militant outbursts from the conference floor. In 1961, following failed attempts to get price reductions for older supporters (OAPs), the truculent Coventry representative, Jack Patience, suggested a remedy:

> We had a little advice last year from a small club who pointed out that we had
> thousands of pounds available each year as Supporters' Clubs and if football
> clubs wanted money, and most have spare space, it would be a good idea to
> purchase tickets. My club decided to do that . . . by negotiating for £1000 worth
> of season tickets for old age pensioners . . . We are saying to the clubs 'You
> want our money: OK. We want old age pensioners in!'[29]

Surprisingly, this speech is one of the very few made at Federation conferences which emphasised the *power* many Supporters' Clubs had over their 'parent' bodies in the latter's reliance on supporter fund-raising. For the Coventry representative it was simple: if you want free (or reduced price) access for OAPs, stop giving all the money you raise to your football club and, instead, buy the tickets and give them out yourself.

Very few Supporters' Clubs took up such a radical idea. The Federation's motto 'To Help and Not To Hinder' was applied primarily to *football clubs*, not football fans.

A few years later, in 1965, and against a background of collapsing supporter's clubs,[30] the Leyton Orient delegate renewed the call for a more determined stand by Federation representatives:

> We have got to do something in order that we can meet the F.A. and the parent clubs on a more or less equal footing. To endeavour to negotiate through weakness is futility itself . . . it has got to be done through the medium of strength . . . you have within your hands the power . . . unless we show strength, we are going nowhere at all.[31]

Of course, *individual membership* of the Federation was not available to football supporters (whether outside or inside the membership of their Supporters' Club). In 1962, the first shot was fired in what turned out to be a long-running and (to date) futile campaign within the Federation to allow individual supporters to join up.[32]

In a confused and confusing debate, the question of Associate Membership of the Federation was launched by the Chairman with the sentence: 'This word (i.e. "associate") should not be taken too literally; it was a word that was used for want of a better word.'[33] The stimulus for change had come from the parlous state of the Federation's finances.[34] The 1961 conference had instructed the Executive to look at ways of increasing the Federation's insufficient income. Several ideas had emerged, including

> . . . the possibility of forming an associate membership which could be open to all persons interested in soccer. It was suggested that a levy of 3d should be made on all members of Supporters' Clubs affiliated to the Federation.[35]

Unfortunately for the subsequent debate, these two very different ideas – that of levying Supporters' Club members and that of admitting 'all persons interested' – became readily confused. The prospect of actually representing supporters in general hardly broke the surface of the discussion. The first speaker – Vice-Chairman Archie Gooch – outlined the possibility of individual membership for 3d (the price of a newspaper at the time), available to Supporters' Club members *and* to 'any individual with an interest in soccer'. He listed the advantages of such a membership including: a card; a badge ('very small . . . as opposed to the usually large Supporters' Club badge'); a group insurance scheme; the interavailability of Supporters' Club premises to members; use of the ticket agency run by the Federation, perhaps even a handbook diary ('but we must be careful not to infringe on our Supporters' Clubs' activities'). Mr Gooch hoped that the 'approximated 400 clubs in membership' – a somewhat exaggerated figure

– might volunteer their committees as 'founder members', providing a base membership of around 4,000 people.

The prospect of a 3d per member *levy* on the affiliated Supporters' Clubs' members, though supported by some, was greeted with sanguine expectations by others. Archie Gooch himself thought a levy would be 'difficult to collect' and 'would lead to the resignations of quite a number of clubs'. Poole Town pointed out that, with its membership of 49,000, 'the club would have to pay over £500 to the Federation . . . its committee will ask whether they are going to get £500 worth of benefit'.

Returning to the idea of 'associate membership' for any supporter, the Leyton Orient representative asked what such might mean:

> I am at a loss to know. What would this body do that ordinary Supporters' Clubs cannot do? Nothing at all. What is the purpose of it?[36]

The Chairman responded with a plea to the conference not to take the words 'associate membership' too seriously: 'I did not intend the word to stick. It was only for the sake of a name'. It is, he insisted, *the financing of the Federation* that is urgently under discussion, 'because I do not want to become known as the beggar of Pall Mall who comes here every year asking for money.' Subsequent speakers, however, ignored this plea and derided the prospect of individual membership, fearing the threat it would imply to the very basis of the Federation:

> The management of this Federation is in this delegate conference, and in five or ten years' time, if this associate membership proposal is carried, they will over-rule this conference and be the governing factor in this Federation. This year alone we have lost about forty clubs.[37]

Another representative warned of the expectations of individual members:

> . . . they would want some rights of membership and representation at conference. This conference belongs to Supporters' Clubs . . .[38]

With that, this first of many debates on individual membership of the Federation petered out with no real conclusion.

The Federation's office in Pall Mall provided the 'ticket-agency' service which included tickets for international matches (bar those for England v. Scotland, which were forever in short supply). But the Federation had never formally sought to organise supporters of the England national team until, in 1963, England's manager, Walter Winterbottom, suggested the formation of a club for England fans. The Federation took up the suggestion and established the England Football Supporters Association (EFSA). Eight members of the Federation's Executive Committee agreed to form a steering committee to guide EFSA and tuck it under the Federation's wing.[39]

Tony Pullein became Secretary of the Federation in 1960–61 when Leslie Davis retired with failing eyesight. Pullein spotted a picture in the *Sporting Record* with a story about Davis's retirement and applied for the job. 'I was desperate to get involved in the football world in some way.'[40] In 1963, he became one of the founder members of EFSA and resigned as Federation Secretary in 1969, one year before the collapse of the England supporters' club. He told the story of EFSA's demise amidst accusations of financial mismanagement:

> It was a club to help organise travel for England team supporters. This chap Frank Adams got the franchise to organise travel to Mexico in 1970. We thought this was a good opportunity for Frank to get something worthwhile going . . . He formed an account and people paid in monthly sums of money to save up for the trip. What we didn't know at the time was that Frank had opened up another account for the England Supporters' Association and he was taking the money and using it for other investments and so on. Anyway, at some point I got a call from a newspaper saying Frank Adams had run off with the money. At the end of the day, he went to jail for five years, I think. I doubt whether Frank actually made any money out of it – there were other people involved.[41]

The complaints about apathy amongst the Federation's member clubs resurfaced in 1966. One of the major problems facing the organisation revolved around the widely differing concerns which occupied the variety of Supporters' Clubs involved. Fans who supported big League clubs had very different priorities from those watching Gainsborough Trinity or Corby Town. Attendance at Federation regional meetings was poor, as the Midlands Area representative pointed out:

> . . . there is such a wide divergence in types of club attached to the Federation that it is sometimes hard to find the common ground to create interest . . .[42]

Another, related, difficulty was posed for the Federation as football clubs increasingly took over traditional Supporters' Clubs, or simply ousted them from their club premises to set up their own 'official' versions.[43] Should these latter 'Supporters' Clubs' be allowed to affiliate? According to Federation Rules, any 'properly constituted' Supporters' Club might become a member – but interpretations of the crucial phrase differed, and many, old-established, but recently-ousted Supporters' Clubs were naturally set against the admittance of their usurpers. As the Federation had been set up, not primarily for the purpose of representing its member clubs but rather to *help their football clubs*, the organisation found itself in a cleft stick. The new 'official' clubs, established and run solely for the (financial) benefit of their football clubs, were clearly 'helping' (and some disgruntled old Supporters' Clubs were, by now, rather belatedly 'hindering'as best they could such developments). Yet part of the Federation felt that it owed a duty to those old campaigners who found themselves replaced. It is evident, however, that the Federation *did* accept 'official' Supporters' Clubs into affiliation to the detriment of the original clubs, and it clearly created constitutional difficulties.[44]

Mr Gooch informed the conference that the Federation Council had thought deeply on the problems posed by the rise of these 'new supporters' clubs'. He suggested consideration of a two-tier system of membership: one for the 'officially recognised' Supporters' Clubs affiliated; one for 'the clubs concentrating on social activities' (which, of course, many were required to do once their traditional, fund-raising schemes were taken over). In his dismissal of those who argued that 'puppet' Supporters' Clubs, formed by their football clubs, should not be allowed, in principle, to join the Federation, Mr Gooch described the argument, rightly in the context of the Federation's history, as

> . . . a ridiculous idea, for most Supporters' Clubs came into being because of a need on the part of a football club. Indeed, many Supporters' Clubs have the same officials as the football clubs they support . . .[45]

The years 1966–68 were particularly difficult for the Federation – a prelude to the collapse in membership which proceeded during the following decade. As we shall see, financial problems beset an organisation which was already in difficulties trying to steer a course through changing times and circumstances. Complaints about the efficiency of its administration were made angrily from the floor of the 1968 conference.[46] Though the question of individual membership had recently faded from conference debates, it is clear from a remark by the Aldershot representative that attempts to involve 'ordinary' football fans were proceeding:

> There is no wonder we are getting *a takeover bid from a man who wants to form a union of spectators*. I do not know why but it seems to me that he feels that no one is getting anywhere in this Federation and he is bringing up an opposition . . . this Federation is going downhill rapidly . . . I feel (we should form) not a union amongst ourselves but something in the Federation whereby every individual member feels that he belongs to the Federation as an individual as well as a club . . .[47]

Just precisely what this 'takeover bid' amounted to is difficult to discern. The Chairman at the time, Archie Gooch, cannot remember any *real* attempt to create an organisation to rival the Federation. He remembers occasional rumours that something was happening but no names were attached and nothing ever developed.[48]

Following Tony Pullein's resignation in 1969, the complaints about administrative inefficiency were given some substance when the incoming Secretary, the 63-year-old Jack Patience, long a stalwart of the Federation, discovered the confusion of records inhabiting the basement office in Pall Mall. He told the conference delegates it was 'chaos'; that no real membership list existed at all:

> To my dismay we did not even know *where* you lived. We did not know if you *did* live. According to the books, we are still wondering if some are alive today.[49]

The Federation had sought to offset its losses by running a variety of schemes and lotteries to raise money. The legal niceties of running these schemes led to further discussions on individual membership. The problem was, under the existing legislation, clubs could sell lottery tickets, etc., to 'members' only. Were the individual members of affiliated Supporters' Clubs also (in law) 'members' of the Federation? Following Jack Patience's speech, Chairman Gooch, interestingly, runs the concepts of *representing* individual supporters alongside that of selling them tickets in fund-raising competions:

> . . . if we are going to organise such competions as we have been doing; if we are going to represent the supporter; you see, we represent the Supporters' Clubs: we ought to be representing the supporter . . . future policy will have to be that any member of a Supporters' Club affiliated to the National Federation is a member of the National Federation . . . whether this is legally possible – that is something we have got to consider.[50]

As Federation membership began to tumble in the 1970s the membership issues gathered momentum. In 1971, the Midlands Area representative repeated his fears (last voiced in 1966) about

> . . . the wide differences existing in the make-up of Supporters' Clubs . . . Some operate purely as social clubs, others as fundraising organisations and (others) just existing to call themselves Supporters' Clubs without any real motivating force. This is probably the real reason for apathy . . . it becomes impossible to find common ground . . .[51]

A suggestion emerged to add the words 'and Associations' to the full title of the Federation (which would have yielded an even more unwieldy set of initials: NFFSCA). The point was to 'open the door wider' to different types of clubs joining. It came to nothing, perhaps not surprisingly, given the Midlands' complaint about the already difficult problem of finding common ground amongst existing members.[52] As to the prospect of individual membership, there were those who wondered how many supporters would be attracted into the Federation. Chairman Gooch pointed up the chronic weakness in the organisation's public profile since its earliest days:

> The Federation since 1927 lacked very considerably in public relations. There was no doubt in my mind that if you talked to a football follower in the street, and the same is true to some extent today, he does not know what the Federation stands for . . .[53]

This did not prevent the (by now, annual) renewed call for individual membership, this time from the Colchester representative, who regretted the fact that 'the ruling bodies . . . can truthfully say that we represent the views of only a tiny minority . . .'[54] The gathering of data about the Federation's actual membership continued with some difficulty for years after Jack Patience encountered the confusion at Pall Mall. The Secretary could not give the 1972 Conference any accurate figures because, as he explained, of 200 questionnaires sent out to plumb the membership, only 34 were returned from clubs with a combined individual membership of 48,120. He informed the conference that, whilst publicly quoting a 'total membership' figure of 700,000, he did not know what the real figure was.[55] In the meantime, a motion was passed to allow 'social clubs associated with football clubs' access to membership – though fears were expressed (somewhat unaccountably from an organisation once chaired by a Director of QPR) that club directors who sit on social club committees might 'infiltrate' the Federation. It was agreed that applicants would first be 'screened' by their Area committees and that membership will be on condition that 'a majority' of the applicant committees must be elected by club members.[56]

The average age of the Federation's officers remained in the 55–70 years range and delegates too tended to be late middle-aged men. This in itself caused some concern and, with the emergence of the (comparatively) young Vice-Chairman, Mr Southernwood, (in his early forties), in 1973, feelings were expressed that the Federation needed a more aggressive approach and a more determined attempt to link itself to the mass of 'ordinary' fans:

> I think that the Federation should become a little more abrasive without necessarily becoming militant . . . Very little is done, I feel, to obtain the views of what you might say is the organised body of supporters in the country.[57]

Mr Southernwood is keen to cast the Federation's net much wider and to attract some of the new breed of fans who are producing their own magazines:

> . . . we should begin to try to push forward and to promote conferences with

younger delegates if possible; the type of gentlemen who contribute to the Chelsea Magazine . . . we should begin to think in much wider terms and make conferences generally more interesting.[58]

Despite such interventions from Federation Officers, little was done to slow the demise of activity and membership of the organisation. In 1974, the Midlands and Northern Division representatives feared a 'slide into obscurity' for the Federation; the result of poor public relations, slow reactions to football issues of the day, chronic apathy and diminishing numbers. The Midlands Division once contained some 70 member clubs within its area; now a mere 27 survived.[59]

A resolution proposed that year by the Ipswich Town representative, Stanley Butler, marked the dire straits the Federation sought to negotiate. It called on the Federation to relinquish its sole attachment to *football*: to look to 'other sports' and their associated clubs and to set up a committee to investigate the prospects:

> Times have changed and football is big business . . . so commercialised that we in this Federation are being left behind like flotsam in its wake. We are at the present time too parochial . . . little pockets of complacency standing in the warmth of our past achievements, back to the days of the Charleston, back to the days when the directors of our local clubs needed us more than we needed them . . . we must cease looking backwards . . . the supporter's role has changed so much and the Federation's role so very little. We envisage a Federation in which . . . each individual member pays a Federation fee . . . a Federation which would embrace any sports club democratically run . . .[60]

This revolutionary proposal was underscored in the seconder's speech (Norwich City) which called for an alteration to the Federation's full title, 'in order to omit the word "football" '. Individual membership should be open to any supporter – 'a genuine supporter, of course, not one of the riff raff we hear so much about.'[61]

Frustration seethed through the ranks of Federation delegates as they considered their situation. They represented an organisation that, by 1974, had been in existence for nearly half a century; its member clubs had contributed to football on an enormous financial scale and with prodigious energy; it had comported itself with all the respectability of a Victorian governess; but what had been gained?

> I feel there should be a big demonstration . . . You must force the people who are responsible to recognise the Federation . . . the Football Association, the Football League and the Minister of Sport won't listen . . . they ignore you.[62]

Despite objections from the floor that the removal of the word 'football' from the Federation's title was unthinkable – and the practical problems of organising various supporters of rugby, speedway, ice hockey and cricket, looked substantial – the resolution was carried and a committee appointed to examine the prospects. In time, it came to nothing, but for the Federation, this was a humbling moment. The Spurs delegate summed it up:

> Who do we represent? Quite frankly, in my opinion, nobody . . . It is time we started to represent somebody.[63]

Soon to retire, the Chairman, Archie Gooch, in response, reminded delegates:

> We have never . . . had the publicity we deserve. We have never been recognised and have never been supported by the clubs in this Federation . . .[64]

As Mr Gooch relinquished the Chairmanship of the Federation, in 1975 (to become 'Senior Life President'), the Midlands' delegate called for more youth to come forward and invigorate the organisation. He complained that the FA and the Federation *looked* the same – a gerontocracy at work.[65] Incoming (and youngish) Chairman, Southernwood, faced a ticklish problem which regenerated the individual membership debate. Though now Chairman of the Federation, Mr Southernwood had 'lost' his Supporters' Club (Ipswich Town) which had recently ceased to exist. He was, therefore, no longer eligible for his post. Other Supporters' Clubs had offered him membership to maintain his eligibility, but Southernwood thought it ridiculous that he, an Ipswich Town fan, should have to join Colchester Utd's Supporters' Club in order to take part in Federation affairs. His predicament brought home forcibly the disadvantages of the Federation's current structure and the way it could, unwittingly, exclude even those who had long supported the organisation in word and deed. Consequently, the new Chairman argued for plain individual membership 'especially for those who just support football',[66] and he pointed to 'the complete dearth of new material' amongst the membership. The Federation's problems can only be overcome, he argued, when it can attract,

> . . . a new talent and new ideas . . . by opening up the membership to a far wider range of people . . . the evidence of the last ten years proved that there was no basis on which to conduct the future of the Federation.[67]

The new resolution to allow 'private members' was backed by the Executive. Nevertheless, strongly-felt arguments were raised from the floor in opposition. The Spurs delegate expressed concern at the prospect of a new, individual member coming in through the 'back door', rising to eminence in the Federation – even to the top table – but who 'would not be beneficial . . .'[68] The Hearts representative was worried about the devaluing effect on Supporters' Clubs that such a development might trigger. Southernwood returned to the fray to insist that there was, of course, no intention to devalue the Supporters' Clubs, but 'fundamental change' was vital and they must learn 'to think of football supporters as supporters and not necessarily as football supporters clubs in particular.'[69] (This latter was received with great disapproval from the assembly.) But Southernwood continued:

> . . . the hallowed shrine idea that the Federation seemed to have, that supporters' clubs were all powerful . . . (was simply unsubstantiated) . . . to continue as they had been doing for the past 10 to 15 years was merely to see the Federation dying a slow death.[70]

It went to a very close vote but the resolution was defeated 41–43. Prophetically, the Eastern Division representative warned that a national supporters' organisation would emerge, 'not next year, but possibly within ten years.' He was proved right. Just over nine years later, in Liverpool, the Football Supporters' Association (FSA) was launched offering direct membership to any individual with an interest in the game.

In 1977, the Federation celebrated its Golden Jubilee. Mr Gooch had become President and Tony Pullein returned to his former role of Secretary. Mr Southernwood resigned from the Chair (in the end refusing to join another Supporters' Club and, therefore, technically invalidating his eligibility for office, though many of his colleagues were prepared to ignore the discrepancy). In 1978, Chairman-elect, Mr Hunter, reported that recruitment of new members was 'still poor' but, paradoxically, he insisted that the football authorities feared the Federation gaining too much power. Looking to the future, he suspected that,

> In time all supporters will have to carry an identity card and there was nothing wrong with that if you are a good supporter . . .[71]

Tony Pullein sought to regenerate the individual membership debate through articles in the Federation Newsletter. He suggested that at clubs where no Supporters' Club existed, the Federation should recognise and admit 'supporters' sub-committees' to membership.[72] By the following year's conference, the Federation's financial position was improving considerably and the then Minister of Sport, Denis Howell, accepted a Vice-Presidency. The Minister actively sought to involve the Federation in discussion with the football authorities, but that year's debate on 'Who Are Supporters' Club Members?' highlighted a fundamental weakness in the make-up of the membership of some clubs 'represented' by the Federation.

As the Coventry City delegate revealed,

> My club has 3000 members . . . Half of these must be ladies and I should say 90% of the ladies don't go to football matches . . . 75% of the male members don't go . . . a lot of these people are not too interested in football.[73]

This revelation drew a stinging response from Stoke City (London) representative, Monica Hartland, herself a founder-member (the year previously) of the Association of Provincial Football Supporters' Clubs in London (APFSCIL) – a group of highly committed supporters who spent most Saturdays travelling the length and breadth of the country to follow their clubs. She commented on the Coventry City account:

> . . . whilst 99% of the club's supporters may spend their time playing Bingo, they would be first in the queue for Wembley tickets . . .

Federation Patron, the 85-year-old Sir Stanley Rous, attended his first conference in 1980. He heard Tony Pullein complain of continued apathy in the organisation and poor support for the fund-raising scheme from which the Federation benefited. A 'Supporter of the Year' competition had been received unenthusiastically by member clubs. That year, Federation President Archie Gooch accepted the Chairmanship of Bristol City FC.[74]

Concern about growing 'militancy' within Federation ranks sometimes lay, confusingly, cheek by jowl with complaints of 'apathy'. In the early 1980s some member clubs in the Northern Division – and also in Scotland – were causing the Executive to seek greater powers of control. In 1982, a resolution was proposed enabling the Executive to expel from the Federation any Division that broke carefully maintained rules of propriety, long a feature of the organisation. That this resolution was 'anti-militant' in intent is made plain by speaker, Jack Lambert, an octogenarian stalwart of the Federation from its earliest days:

> Someone has used the word 'militancy' . . . I've suffered in my long life from militancy . . . and I'm damned sure I would not allow any militants to enter or take over the Federation . . . this resolution was tabled just to safeguard the Federation against the militants who want to be bigger than this Federation.[75]

But radical voices were emerging. Scottish Divisional representative, Charlie Bent, in 1981–82, led legal action (on behalf of his Division) against the English FA, over the latter's refusal to sell tickets north of the border for the biannual England v. Scotland game at Wembley.[76] Under a relatively new 'portfolio' system of devolving responsibility from the Executive, Mr Bent had received the 'Future Policies' portfolio and, as he complained in the 'Conference Reflections' paper of 1982, it was proving a 'daunting prospect'. The problem was:

> . . . the dearth of existing policies. Looking back through Conference reports of the past decade, it is noticeable that not only have very few policies been decided upon, but hardly any clubs have put forward policy making resolutions. Since 1974, we have made only one policy decision at Conference . . . Sad to say, we have virtually no policies to speak of. Perhaps our lack of policies is attributable to the parochial outlook of some of our member clubs.

Finally, Charlie Bent reached the nub of the matter – the Federation's *motto* – and launched his attack:

> 'To Help – Not Hinder'. To help whom? Not to Hinder whom? I suspect that a fair number of Supporters' Clubs will reply – 'why, the Football Club, of course.' I would venture to suggest that our priority should be our members, their needs and rights as paying customers. We should be doing our utmost to help *them*, and making sure no one hinders them in their activities as responsible football supporters . . . the Federation should be – or strive to become – the 'Paying Customers' Union' – sounds a good motto![77]

The Scottish delegates put their ideas to the test at the 1983 conference. Hamilton (with Motherwell seconding) called for the abandonment of the old Federation motto and its replacement with 'The Voice of the Paying Customer'. Charlie Bent's arguments were rehearsed once again: 'What we want is to represent the fan.' The Motherwell delegate enlarged on the theme and urged the Federation, in effect, to become a 'consumer-watchdog', assuming,

> . . . a position where the media, when they are dealing with any item which affects supporters, automatically come to the Secretary . . .[78]

The proposal met stony ground on the floor of the conference. Even Monica Hartland – in the context of the Federation, a 'radical' woman and 'feminist' to boot[79] – could not support it, though she was prepared to go along with a change to something 'less over-aggressive'. Mrs Hartland was concerned that, appearing on all official notepaper, such a motto would be 'a smack in the eye' for the administrators at Lancaster Gate. She preferred something 'a little more dignified' like 'The Voice of the Genuine Enthusiast – an apt description of Monica herself.

Jack Patience of Coventry City agreed; and Manchester Utd's David Smith preferred the reassuring ring of the old motto, to this 'far more sinister sounding' new one. Finally the millenial prospect of 'opening the floodgates for militancy' was invoked once more, and the resolution soundly defeated at the vote.[80]

Later that day, another attempt to introduce individual membership was proposed by the Sunderland (London) representative, Ian Todd. Against a background of rumour that the Football League intended to set up a national Supporters' Club (which in the event did not appear), Mr Todd reminded the delegates of previous debates and the fears that had been expressed about 'devaluing' the membership of a Supporters' Club. Mr Todd told delegates that many football teams had no Supporters' Club for fans to join and that there were also many people who have no primary allegiance but who pick an attractive game each Saturday.

These people are no less football supporters than we are.

In order to avoid the possibility of a 'take-over bid' from members who joined as individuals, the resolution provided for a requirement of three years' membership before qualifying for election to Divisional committees and five years for the National Council. He concluded:

Most importantly, this is an opportunity for the Federation to establish itself here and now as the only national organisation representing all football fans . . . [81]

Manchester Utd's David Smith welcomed the 'vetting' procedures which would defend the Federation from 'individuals of doubtful pedigree (who) might be seated at the top table' and gave the resolution his support with the warning:

Today it is virtually a necessity in order that the Federation might survive. [82]

Nevertheless, the proposal was narrowly defeated once again. The deep-seated anxieties of those Supporters' Club officials present who feared the rise of individual voices, unrestrained by their membership of any local organisation, won the day. Those fears were potently expressed by an 'Unknown Delegate' who spoke vehemently against the motion, concluding:

I say if they want to join, let them join a Supporters' Club . . . and support any old team they like. [83]

At the vote, the resolution was lost 39–41.

One last attempt at raising individual membership was made, ironically, in 1985, just a few months before the emergence of the FSA in August. The disastrous events that year at the European Cup Final in the Heysel Stadium – with the deaths of 39 mostly Italian supporters, following crowd disturbances amongst Liverpool fans – came too late for serious consideration by the 1985 conference, though (rather surprisingly) the fire at Bradford City, and the death of a young supporter at Birmingham City, earlier that year, did not loom large in the debates either.

The membership proposal was similar to that in 1983 with an added proviso that only supporters who 'are not at the same time a member, or *eligible* for membership of any supporters club' affiliated to the Federation', could join. Clearly objections had been raised by Supporters' Clubs that supporters *within* their catchment areas could bypass them by joining the Federation directly. Despite another strong speech from Ian Todd, the resolution was lost, yet again by a margin of two votes: 37–39.[84]

The season following the Heysel disaster, 1985–86, saw attendances at League games in England reach an all-time low – the bottom of a much reduced barrel. No League football featured on television that year. The Popplewell Inquiry proceeded and talk of restructuring the Football League was heard. Almost immediately following the Heysel disaster, an organisation originating in Reading called 'Supporters United' was publicised. Two months later, the FSA proclaimed its existence and held its first public meeting in September 1985.

Emerging from Liverpool – and involving supporters of the Club whose fans bore some responsibility for the deaths at Heysel – the FSA naturally attracted considerable media attention, and it launched a vigorous campaign to recruit members on a national basis. A report from the Federation's Northern Division – which included the Liverpool and Everton Supporters' Clubs – was commissioned to investigate the emergence of the FSA and to inform the proposed debate: 'Does the rise of the FSA present a threat?'

It was quickly apparent that what irked many members of the Federation was the ready access to national publicity that the fledgeling FSA enjoyed. It touched a sore spot with Federation delegates who had long felt their own organisation's lack of profile. As the Northern Division's report put it:

'Concern has been expressed at the apparent growth and strength of the Football Supporters' Association and the fact that they seem able to get publicity in the media that the NFFSC doesn't seem able to obtain.'[85]

The Secretary, Malcolm Gamlen, warned:

The FSA, formed only a few months ago, was said to be the fastest-growing pressure group in the country with branches in most big towns. They are pressing for involvement in both the Football Association and Football League.[86]

Meanwhile, 'Supporters United' had applied for affiliation to the Federation, demonstrating, according to Mr Gamlen, that 'we are a worthwhile body'. (However, the former organisation soon passed into obscurity as quickly as it had risen.) Frank Horrocks of Manchester City was unconcerned about the FSA's interest in dialogue with the football authorities: 'We are recognised by the FA and FL', he reminded delegates. But, along with Jim King at Everton, he was worried about the implied threat to the Federation's status and, particularly, the flow of publicity towards the FSA. To staunch this, he urged the appointment of a Public Relations Officer for the Federation; a call redoubled by Jim King who reminded those present that what the FSA had to offer was *individual membership*. The Federation *had* to respond:

> Our biggest disadvantage is in being fifty-nine years old. Each year the Federation represents fewer and fewer clubs.

That year, current Chairman Tony Kershaw, a Conservative Councillor in Loughborough, was elected by a majority of one single vote. In 1987, Monica Hartland became Deputy Chairman and came to assume the role of Public Relations Officer which Mr Horrocks and others had desired. With the prospect of an increasing number of 'membership schemes' at Football League clubs – and Government talk of identity cards for fans – discussion at the conference in 1988 revealed differing opinions. Some spoke of developing a 'National Federation' membership card (presumably for issue to all members of affiliated Supporters' Clubs); but Frank Horrocks repudiated any form of ID card scheme.[87]

In 1988, the number of Supporters' Clubs represented at the Annual Conference reached an all-time low of forty of which the preponderance (twenty-five) were League Clubs. The small, amateur Supporters' Clubs – once so active, and for so long the bulk of the Federation's membership – were no longer present in large numbers. The agenda reflected the changing times and highlighted the Federation's concern with issues which affected *all* football fans. Amongst the topics for discussion, which included: two-tier pricing; televised matches, all-tickets games, multi-club ownership and international tickets for the HM Forces, only the latter retained the traditional flavour of those, long-ago conferences when the Queen's telegram was received with rapturous enthusiasm.

NOTES

1. See the Federation's *Golden Jubilee* booklet, published in 1977, p. 5.
2. AGM Minutes, 1953, p. 2. See also AGM Minutes, 1987, p. 24–5.
3. The 'Gazette' was a two to three-page section of *Sport Weekly Magazine*, made available to the Federation in return for some help with distribution. For this reference, see 21 August 1948, p. 14.

4. AGM Minutes, 1948, p. 4ff.
5. AGM Minutes, 1948, p. 1.
6. AGM Minutes, 1953, p. 1.
7. AGM Minutes, 1953, p. 6.
8. AGM Minutes, 1948, p. 21.
9. AGM Minutes, 1962, p. 32.
10. AGM Minutes, 1962, pp. 30 and 32.
11. AGM Minutes, 1953, p. 7.
12. AGM Minutes, 1956, pp. 30–1.
13. *Sport Weekly Magazine*, 21 August 1948, p. 14.
14. AGM Minutes, 1948, p. 3 (my emphasis).
15. AGM Minutes, 1956, p. 4.
16. AGM Minutes, 1953, p. 8.
17. AGM Minutes, 1953, p. 27.
18. AGM Minutes, 1954, pp. 9–10.
19. The AGM minutes for 1957 are missing.
20. Personal interview with Tony Pullein, National Federation Secretary at various times between 1960–78. Recorded 28 March 1990.
21. See AGM Minutes, 1964, p. 2.
22. See AGM Minutes, 1965, p. 5.
23. *Sport Weekly Magazine*, 28 August 1948, p. 13.
24. Personal interview with Tony Kershaw, Chairman, NFFSC, recorded 13 February 1990.
25. AGM Minutes, 1960, p. 22.
26. AGM Minutes, 1961, p. 48.
27. AGM Minutes, 1956, p. 10.
28. AGM Minutes, 1956, p. 10.
29. AGM Minutes, 1961, p. 34.
30. See Chapter 8, 'Supporter-club relations.'
31. AGM Minutes, 1965, p. 46.
32. The issue may have arisen before 1962 – the existing records of the 1950s' conference are incomplete.
33. For the text of the debate, see AGM Minutes, 1962, p. 26ff.
34. For a detailed account of these, see Chapter 10, 'Public relations, publications and finances'.
35. AGM Minutes, 1962, p. 26.
36. AGM Minutes, 1962, p. 30.
37. AGM Minutes, 1962, p. 32.
38. AGM Minutes, 1962, p. 33.
39. AGM Minutes, 1963, p. 19.
40. Personal interview with Tony Pullein, National Federation Secretary, 1960–69.
41. Ibid. (EFSA, however, survived to the present day but is currently struggling, with membership in steep decline.)
42. AGM Minutes, 1966, p. 24.
43. For more on this trend, see Chapter 8, 'Supporter-club relations'.
44. For a detailed account, see Chapter 8.
45. AGM minutes, 1966, p. 14.

46. AGM Minutes, 1968, p. 21.
47. AGM Minutes, 1968, p. 21 (my emphasis).
48. Personal communication.
49. AGM Minutes, 1969, p. 30.
50. AGM Minutes, 1969, p. 32.
51. AGM Minutes, 1971, p. 20.
52. AGM Minutes, 1971, p. 30.
53. AGM Minutes, 1971, p. 30.
54. AGM Minutes, 1971, p. 58.
55. AGM Minutes, 1972. p. 28.
56. AGM Minutes, 1972, p. 33ff
57. AGM Minutes, 1973, p. 54.
58. AGM Minutes, 1973, p. 55.
59. *Conference Newsletter*, 1974, pp. 12–14.
60. AGM Minutes, 1974, pp. 44–5.
61. AGM Minutes, 1974, p. 45.
62. AGM Minutes, 1974, p. 47.
63. AGM Minutes, 1974, p. 50.
64. AGM Minutes, 1974, p. 51.
65. AGM Minutes, 1975, page ref. lost.
66. AGM Minutes, 1976, p. 17.
67. AGM Minutes, 1976, p. 28.
68. AGM Minutes, 1976, p. 29.
69. AGM Minutes, 1976, p. 31.
70. AGM Minutes, 1976, p. 36.
71. AGM Minutes, 1978, pp. 10–11.
72. *Nat. Fed. Newsletter*, September 1978, p. 6.
73. AGM Minutes, 1979, p. 22.
74. See AGM Minutes, 1980.
75. See AGM Minutes, 1982, p. 47.
76. For a more detailed account of this episode, see Chapter 6, 'Relations with the football authorities'.
77. *Conference Reflections*, August 1982, p. 26.
78. AGM Minutes for 1983 conference (now dated '1984'), pp. 50–1.
79. See her opening remarks (1983, p. 51) where she castigates one Harold Smith, a visitor to the Conference, who 'thinks that the ladies are an appendage to football and their menfolk' etc.
80. See AGM Minutes for 1983 Conference, p. 51ff.
81. See AGM Minutes for 1983 Conference, pp. 55–6.
82. See AGM Minutes for 1983 Conference, p. 57.
83. See AGM Minutes for 1983 Conference, p. 57.
84. See AGM Minutes for 1985 Conference, p. 43ff.
85. See AGM Minutes for 1986 Conference.
86. See AGM Minutes for 1986 Conference, p. 31.
87. For an account of the Federation debate about ID cards for football supporters, see Chapter 11, 'The hooligan debate'.

6

RELATIONS WITH THE FOOTBALL AUTHORITIES

Spectators are sick of the FA and their unfair administration of unjust laws.
(Players Union Representative, 1909)

Before the war, the Federation had made little headway in gaining 'recognition' from the Football Association. The FA was undoubtedly the appropriate body to approach for a national organisation representing supporters' clubs of many amateur and some professional teams. Federation officers had certainly attended an 'interview' with Secretary of the FA, Sir Frederick Wall, in 1930,[1] but it seems to have been an informal occasion and no record of it survives in FA archives.[2] Precisely what the Federation meant by 'recognition' is not clear, but its officers were preponderantly aldermen and councillors, and one imagines that their idea of 'recognition' would include, at a minimum, *periodic, official meetings with senior FA personnel at which Minutes were taken and circulated*. If we adopt such a definition, 'recognition' seems to have been withheld by the FA for the first fifty years of the Federation's existence.

The question of Cup Final ticket allocations was the single, most important issue to dominate the Federation's relations with the FA. It emerged very early in Federation publications. As we have seen, *The Supporter* of 1935–36 invited discussion of the topic. After the war, the issue re-emerged, but it is clear that what was under discussion was not principally the number of tickets available to the clubs competing in the Final (a chronic complaint amongst supporters), but whether the *Federation itself* could join the long list of FA County Associations and other organisations that received a direct ticket allocation. The FA's traditional practice was to devolve up to three-quarters of the available tickets to recipients other than the competing clubs.

In 1948, Federation Secretary, Leslie Davis, referred to the organisation's (apparently informal) attempts to join the ticket queue at Lancaster Gate:

> Year by year the Federation is getting a little further in its negotiations with the FA as regards a *direct* allocation of Cup Final and International tickets to Supporters' Clubs via the Federation.[3]

The 1948 conference was held in a vibrant mood, reflecting the booming times for football and for membership of the Federation. Chairman Talbot Nanson's opening speech, addressed to 'the biggest meeting that we have ever had', spoke of the 'power' the Federation had become in the football world:

> . . . our relations with the FA are stronger than they have ever been . . .[4]

Stanley Rous, Secretary of the FA since 1935, had become a Vice-President of the Federation, and it was perhaps largely through him that the Federation conducted its 'relations' and 'negotiations' with the FA. There is certainly no official record, in either FA or Federation archives, of the proceedings of any meetings. We must assume that they were, in effect, conversations or private correspondence with Stanley Rous and perhaps other FA officials. (It might have suited both sides to represent these as more significant than in fact they were.) Given the subsequent complaints at numerous conferences throughout the 1960s and 1970s of the FA's failure to recognise the Federation in any meaningful way, there seems a certain irony in Stanley Rous's 'Message' to Federation members in the *Football Supporters Gazette*, of 1948:

> The Football Association is deeply appreciative of the work done by the Federation and is ever mindful of the necessity, not only in the interests of the game, but in the interests of the Community, that such an organisation should have all the encouragement the Football Association can give. May I express the hope that . . . relations with the Football Association will continue to be as harmonious as ever.[5]

The phrase 'all the encouragement the FA can give' is appropriately nebulous.

The Federation certainly needed the kind of encouragement that *official* meetings with the FA at Lancaster Gate would have provided, particularly in terms of the media coverage that might have followed. It also stood in need of any *financial* help it could get – in 1948, the Federation's resources amounted to £108.9.2d[6] and a suggestion emerged that year from the conference floor proposing a particular Saturday, at the end of the season, be designated 'Federation Day' to provide some additional funding to service the Federation's operation. Such an idealistic (though some might argue, quite reasonable) idea was typical of the euphoric atmosphere gripping parts of the Federation at the time, as its nominal membership grew towards the million mark, and in a country where many had recently returned from wartime service, elected the first majority Labour government and perhaps felt 'entitled' to take a fuller part in public affairs than before. Nevertheless, in response to the proposal, President Truett kept his feet firmly on the ground:

> I query very much whether the FA would agree to such a suggestion.[7]

It might have been more appropriate (though perhaps equally futile) to have addressed such a proposition to the Football League, but this body is rarely mentioned in Federation records prior to the 1970s. Whether this was because the amateur representation amongst member clubs was so overwhelming, or because the Federation thought the FA could override the League, is debatable. The Football League management certainly appears *even more distant* than the FA from engaging in serious dialogue with supporters' representatives throughout the 1948–80 period. At least the Federation had, as a Vice-President, the FA Secretary, whereas no Football League official was listed amongst the Federation's patrons.

In the early 1950s, the FA and FL were at loggerheads over the BBC's live broadcasting of Saturday afternoon matches (on radio). The League had banned clubs from allowing such broadcasts on the (somewhat strange) assumption that they would provide an effective alternative to attending a match.[8] (The effect was, in fact, to deprive a lot of people unable for a whole variety of reasons – many including war injuries and hospitalisation – to get to a game.) It was the kind of thinking that did little for football's public image (the 'hospital card' was played constantly) and the FA probably felt some pressure from politicians and the media to sort the problem out, though details are absent.[9] It appears that in 1952, the FA sought from the Federation its approval of radio broadcasts of football, for use perhaps in discussions with League representatives. In the Federation Chairman's resumé of the year prior to the 1953 conference, he mentioned:

> we were able to lend our weight to getting the Ban on broadcasting lifted . . .

(he continued:)

> . . . later we had the honour of a Conference with the FA and put our point of view about Cup Final tickets.[10]

Could such a 'Conference' have been a 'quid pro quo' for the support of the Federation in the FA's attempts to remove the broadcasting ban? Once

again, no FA record of it survives to tell the tale. We should perhaps read
the phrase 'the honour of a Conference with the FA' as an example of the
rather exaggerated and flowery language that often featured at Federation
meetings.[11] It probably referred to yet another 'off the record' conversation or correspondence.

The Federation had sought to draw itself closer to the FA with an offer,
in 1953, of a Vice-Presidency of the Federation to Viscount Alexander,
previously First Lord of the Admiralty, Chancellor of the Duchy of
Lancaster, and now Vice-President of the FA (and of Chelsea FC). He
accepted the honorary position and attended the 1953 conference, though
his constraining presence could hinder rather than help discussions of FA
policy. It is clear from Federation Chairman Ray Sonin's opening remarks
to the Cup Final Ticket debate that year, that the Federation Executive
was now considering *direct affiliation* to the FA in its pursuit of a ticket
allocation:

> We now come to the long and smouldering question of Cup Final Tickets. Every
> year we approach the FA regarding it. Last year we had a conference with them,
> were received charmingly, made a great fuss of and were told what a wonderful
> Federation we are, but we got no Cup Final tickets. Now this year the Executive
> decided to try a somewhat different approach, I personally asked Sir Stanley
> Rous if the Federation were to affiliate to the FA, would it become entitled to a
> quota of Cup Final tickets? Sir Stanley pointed out that the constitution of the
> FA did not permit of the Federation becoming an affiliated body . . .[12]

Ray Sonin went on to describe the action the Executive had taken to
convince the FA that it was a 'bona fide' body through which the tickets
could be allocated for dispersal amongst genuine supporters. The
Federation had discovered an FA Minute to the effect that anyone buying
a ticket at an inflated price should inform the FA so that action could
proceed. The Federation therefore 'instituted certain discreet and tactful
inquiries' and obtained a list of illicit sales which it forwarded to the FA.
Mr Sonin insisted that the Federation was keen to show the FA it wished to
work 'with them; not against them' and that the Federation's request for an
allocation was 'altruistic':

> . . . for the good of football . . . if we can get an allocation . . . we should be
> able to allocate them into channels where people who want to see a Cup Final
> would get a chance of doing so.

At this point, Secretary Leslie Davis sought to head off further discussion as 'indiscreet'. The Federation, he argued, had now presented
concrete evidence to the FA for its consideration and delegates should
await a reply. But some delegates were clearly unhappy with the very

prospect of the Federation seeking its own allocation. As the Aldershot representative pointed out, if they did receive tickets, they would not go far amongst the many members of the Federation: 'My idea is that we should try to get the allocation to the Clubs stepped up so that the Supporters' Club can have more tickets.'[13] Ray Sonin agreed that larger allocations to Finalists were needed as well, and that he had brought that issue up with Sir Stanley Rous who replied that some football clubs could not get rid of all the tickets allocated to them. It was a difficult situation, said the Chairman (perhaps most of all for Federation officers):

> We are awkwardly placed because obviously it would not be right for us to say in front of our patron, Viscount Alexander, that the Football Association is not doing its job. What we do think is that we have a good case for being given a definite allocation of Cup Final tickets.[14]

The delegate representing Spurs supporters – who themselves would take independent action against the FA nearly a decade later[15] – was not convinced that the Federation officers did wish to see the ticket allocation increased to clubs competing in the Final. He reminded the Chairman of his statement the previous year, 'when you suggested that the allocation to Finalists be reduced by some 5000'. The Everton representative concurred, insisting that the Clubs who reached the Final 'are entitled to all the tickets they can get.' Ray Sonin sought to remind delegates of Sir Stanley Rous's remark that some clubs were embarrassed by too many tickets. This made little sense to many supporters present at the conference. They knew Wembley was full to capacity every year, and the annual black market prices for tickets proved that demand always exceeded supply.

It was an unfortunate year to be arguing such a case. The 1953 final, Bolton Wanderers v. Blackpool – the 'Stanley Matthews' Cup Final – had involved two footballing giants and Cup ticket fever had gripped both towns. The Blackpool delegate feared the result of the Federation gaining its own allocation. The Blackpool supporters *had* received some tickets for Wembley from their Club:

> If the Federation had received tickets from the FA then our Parent Club might have said, 'Your Federation has some, go to them.' Would the Federation have been as likely to give us as many as our Parent Club?[16]

At this point, Viscount Alexander interceded in the debate to defend the FA from any charge of its being 'autocratic'; it was, he insisted, a very broadly-based organisation, run 'within the ideas of democracy' and:

> . . . of all the sporting institutions in the world, there is not a single one which could claim to be a better governed body than the Football Association.[17]

In response, Ray Sonin pointed to perhaps the key reason why the Federation felt so strongly that it deserved such an allocation of Cup tickets – the Federation was *very like* the FA. It was broadly based, encompassing amateur and professional teams' supporters alike, and therefore had a similar, overarching concern for the whole of the game at its many levels:

> The Federation, next to the FA, is the most widespread Football organisation in the country . . . we are going along parallel lines to the Football Association.[18]

The Cup Final tickets topic certainly seems to have occupied the attention of Federation conferences throughout the early 1950s. No record of the 1952 conference remains but it is clear from discussions the following year that a resolution had been passed in 1952 calling on all Federation delegates to promote a campaign in the national press and to seek out local MPs for support in changing the FA system. The campaign appears to have been a failure and delegates expressed their annoyance at the apathetic performance of member clubs.[19] A further example of the prevailing level of dialogue with the FA that was available to the Federation is recorded in comments made by the latter's Chairman, in 1954. Once again it is the Cup Final ticket issue that provoked the exchange:

> . . . we sent a memorandum to the FA saying we felt we ought to have an allocation and we followed this up by a personal interview with Sir Stanley Rous who said that there were already too many headaches in the distribution of Cup Final Tickets. Your General Secretary at once offered to take the headaches off Sir Stanley's shoulders, but the offer was not accepted.[20]

The Federation had sent a 'memorandum' presumably because they had no official meetings with the FA at which such issues could be discussed. This had been followed by *a private conversation* with the FA Secretary – 'a personal interview' – at which Sir Stanley offhandedly dismissed the Federation's suggestion that 'we ought to have an allocation' with his complaint that the whole topic was a pain in the head.[21]

A particularly vigorous debate, in 1956, followed another resolution about Cup Final tickets. It read:

> That this Annual Meeting instructs the officials of (the Federation) to press with all publicity the English and Welsh Football Associations for an allocation to be made of tickets for the FA Cup Final and other representative games which come within their jurisdiction, to Football Supporters Clubs who are members of the Federation.[22]

The original resolution – proposed by Guildford and seconded by the Chelsea delegates – had excluded the Welsh FA and had included a reference to the Scottish FA's allocation system, which was thought to be more generous. However, on receiving information from Scots delegates, that reference was deleted.

The Federation's 1956 conference was buoyed up by the first real taste the organisation had experienced of participation in a public campaign which drew media attention. During the previous year a new Lotteries Act has passed through Parliament which had clarified the legal status of small lotteries with limited prizes. Supporters' clubs had, in the past, sometimes fallen foul of local police forces whose interpretation of the old Betting and Gaming law differed from region to region. This meant that, for many football clubs, sometimes no 'fund-raising money' was being donated by their supporters' clubs and the football clubs were consequently feeling the pinch. It was football club directors (and others) who pushed the Federation to campaign for the new legislation. The 1955 Lotteries Act, it turned out, laid the foundation for *football clubs* to develop their own lotteries in future years (to the dismay of the supporters' clubs) but, in 1956, the football clubs were still forbidden by FA regulation to promote such schemes. The Federation, encouraged by club directors, MP's and other lobbyists for the legislation, found itself involved in a real campaign in the press and in Parliament (with a successful outcome). Unwittingly – and with some naivety – the Federation had helped lay the legal foundation for changes which would almost collapse the national network of supporters' clubs a decade later.[23]

Unaware of the subsequent developments which would flow from the legislation, the Federation felt it had done a good job in establishing the grounds for supporter fund-raising and to help the football clubs. It felt it had flexed its muscles on a national stage and achieved success. Consequently, when it came to debating the ticket allocation resolution, Federation speakers hoped for some genuine improvement to result from their efforts. However, it is clear from the Guildford delegate's speech that the Federation saw the ticket issue principally as *a route to the much-sought 'recognition'* from the FA:

The reason my Club has brought this (Resolution) forward is that . . . we are impressed by the great work done in the Headquarters of the Federation in respect of the Lotteries . . . The press has taken the matter up and the Federation has received its due . . . We are now a very strong body . . . the great working machinery of the Federation which is behind you can now go forward with added assurance that will give the Football Associations of England and Wales something to think about . . . *But that august body that runs Football in this country does not recognise you* . . . now is the time when this Federation, in its strength from the past year's work, should take-up the cudgels once more and say that *we are really an important body in the Football World that deserves recognition* . . . the Federation should take off its coat and fight strongly and firmly . . .[24]

Following the seconder's speech, the debate paused to allow a speech from George Wardrope, Assistant Secretary of the Scottish Federation. Mr Wardrope had shown Federation Chairman, Ray Sonin, a collection of press-cuttings illustrating the campaign north of the border to gain tickets both for Scottish Cup Finals and international matches. These cuttings featured headlines like: 'Football Supporters call for Boycott' and 'Fans Declare Ticket War'. As Ray Sonin noted, 'It certainly sounds as if we have some militant gentlemen in our ranks.'[25]

The Scottish delegate weighed into the debate with some surprising revelations. He began with a vehement attack on the Scottish FA, 'the dictators of football' in Scotland. He riled at the operation of ticket touts ('spivs') feeding off the all-night queues outside the SFA offices in Glasgow, where he had seen tickets change hands at up to ten times their face value. Mr Wardrope confirmed that the Scottish Federation had received a 23,000 ticket allocation for the England v. Scotland game at Wembley in 1953 but that, subsequently, SFA Secretary, Sir George Graham, 'made a personal attack on the Supporters Clubs of Scotland', alleging that when it came to ticket allocations, the membership numbers of supporters' clubs were inflated. Mr Wardrope had strongly denied this and the BBC in Scotland had agreed to give him the chance to confront Sir George in public debate. He informed the Federation that when this took place, he would bring home to the SFA Secretary the truth 'that without the loyal support of the rank and file . . . his "gates" are going to drop.'[26]

This kind of talk was quite a novelty in Federation debates (and the possibility of an equivalent, publicly-broadcast encounter on the BBC with the English FA had never been proposed). But George Wardrope had more surprising revelations to make, this time about the existing system of Cup Final ticket allocations in Scotland:

> There is one thing I want to stress quite forcibly . . . you should oppose in England *the allocation of tickets to Nationalised Industries*. We have been faced with that in Scotland in the last ten years . . . My Club won the Scottish Cup after fifty years – a great achievement – and the allocation of tickets . . . gave 29,000 to the participating clubs. Out of that 29,000, the Scottish FA allocated 15,000 to British Railways . . . (and) . . . 10,000 tickets to Scottish Omnibuses and the British Transport Commission. That enabled people to travel to Hampden Park to see the Cup Final but British Railways inflated their ordinary fares by 1/- and Scottish Omnibuses inflated their fares by 1/6d. My own particular Supporters' Club made a direct application for an allocation of tickets and was referred to the Nationalised Industries for tickets . . . (cries of 'shame' from the assembly) . . . I may tell you that my own Club has a Branch composed of engine drivers who drive trains to Hampden. I interviewed the Board of Management and told them distinctly that if the Supporters' Club did not get any tickets, they could take it that there would be no trains for Hampden. When I asked Sir George for a further allocation of tickets he told me . . . 'You and I

are not very good friends – there is another 1,000 tickets to keep your mouth shut.[27]

This amazing tirade (in the context of typical Federation discussions) revealed a system in operation in Scotland which devolved slightly more tickets to competing finalists (less than 25,000 were allocated in England at that time), but which gave an exploitative opportunity to public transport organisations to cash in by raising their ordinary fares. (If supporters had to buy their match tickets along with a travel ticket, they had little choice but to pay the extra.) George Wardrope's parting shot, alluding to the SFA Secretary's offer of '1,000 tickets to keep your mouth shut' was stunning. Federation Chairman, Ray Sonin, seated at the top table alongside Viscount Alexander, thanked the Scottish delegate for some 'very interesting and illuminating remarks.' Conscious of the possible embarrassment such an attack might be causing the Noble Lord, Mr Sonin added:

I think we should hear something from the other side of the fence. Perhaps Lord Alexander would like to say something?

The Vice-President of the FA, however, declined:

I think I had better not speak on this . . . I am an honorary member of the FA Council . . . in order to safeguard my position I should take no part in your discussions here.[28]

The FA Cup ticket issue may actually have been more of an embarrassment to *the Federation officiers* on the top table. Despite the enthusiasm of delegates to see the supporters' organisation 'take off its coat and fight' for the resolution, the senior officers knew from conversations with FA personnel that there was no way the FA could allocate tickets to the Federation. It only allocated tickets to organisations *within* its purview – and the Federation was not attacking *the system itself* but simply asking to be included in it. Asking for a ticket allocation was the Federation's way of seeking a symbolic act of 'recognition' from the FA – a 'gesture' as Ray Sonin describes it below. After so much hard work on the Lotteries Act, the Federation clearly felt it deserved at least something to 'give the troops'. The Chairman described the discussions he and Secretary, Leslie Davis, had attended:

We formed a deputation which attended upon the Football Association . . . We told them exactly our position and that Cup Final tickets had now become a gesture . . . the Federation should be recognised as a body that should get a definite allocation of tickets. At the moment we are denied access to the blue riband of the Football World. The FA were very sympathetic . . . but they said that the Articles of Association of the FA did not permit us to become one of their members to whom only Cup Final tickets were allocated. *We cannot join the FA because of the very structure of our Lottery and other Fund Raising Schemes* . . . The point is this – is it worth while giving up our status and independence for a few Cup Final tickets? . . . *it is public opinion which might cause some differences in the FA* even to the extent perhaps of altering their rules to entitle us to an allocation of tickets.[29]

Again, there is no official record of the discussions with the FA – perhaps the phrase 'a deputation which attended upon the Football Association' means that two or three Federation officers had lengthy, but as always 'off the record', talks with Sir Stanley Rous and others. The situation was deadlocked because, some might argue, in requiring *their own* allocation the Federation was demanding the wrong thing. Ironically, the organisation could not join the FA as an 'associate body' *because of the ways its member-clubs raised money to help keep so many football clubs afloat*. It could not, therefore, gain a ticket allocation. But Ray Sonin's recognition that 'public opinion . . . might cause some difference' was perhaps a more useful approach. However, it seems unlikely that the public would have been greatly aroused by a campaign to get Cup tickets for Federation members – but it might have been for a campaign to devolve many more tickets to *the supporters of football clubs competing in the Cup Final* Somehow the Federation failed to see this.

Ray Sonin did think something had been gained from the Deputation's discussions with the FA. He informed the conference:

. . . as a result . . . a directive went out from the FA to the Directors of all clubs that when Cup Final tickets came along they were to distribute them with special reference to Supporters' Clubs.[30]

But, as the Chairman himself recognised, the FA's action lacked force because it was not based upon any official meetings or minuted decisions. The FA's directive to club directors was, as Ray Sonin's discriminating use of words illustrates, 'a polite directive and not an instruction'. The Cup Final tickets resolution was carried unanimously.

The first record of an approach by the Federation to the Football League management is dated 1958. Some Federation delegates had been arguing the case for reduced admission prices for old-age pensioners. At conference that year, the debate illustrated that some supporters' clubs were already subsidising the cost of pensioners' admission (many amateur clubs offered free admission and a few League Clubs – like QPR – did also). Earlier, the Federation had approached the FL seeking to discuss the question, but the League refused a meeting and replied that reduced admission prices was a 'domestic' matter for the football clubs alone.[31]

That year saw another attempt to raise the Cup tickets issue – but it seemed half-hearted in comparison to the debate two years earlier. Given its aims, there was little progress the Federation could make. The Chairman repeated the remarks made in 1956 that the FA would only allocate to bodies under its umbrella. He reminded delegates that 'it would be fatal for the Federation to sell its liberty of action and place itself under the jurisdiction of the FA . . .'[32]

During the late 1950s and into the 1960s a certain 'anti-FA feeling' developed amongst some Federation members and officers;[33] Leslie Davis, Federation Secretary, seems to have rankled with some FA personnel. A county FA representative told (soon to be Federation Chairman, in 1964), Archie Gooch, that 'the FA would never talk to Leslie Davis – no way'.[34] No progress was made in establishing any official liaison with the football authorities and issues like Cup ticket allocations and reduced prices for pensioners remained unresolved. The Football League's continued insistence on charging supporters' clubs for the right to reproduce the fixture list – and the refusal even to discuss the matter – seemed to add insult to injury for those whose fund-raising activities often kept League Clubs alive.[35]

Cracks began to appear, in 1961, in the Federation's policy of seeking its own allocation of Cup tickets. As the Everton representative pointed out, 'apart from Newcastle supporters', ordinary fans often got but one chance in a lifetime to see their team at Wembley in the Cup Final. The current FA allocation to clubs competing in the Final was such that,

> . . . only one of every two supporters can get a ticket . . . if we as a Federation are going to ask for an allocation, we may be taking some away from the two competing clubs . . . we believe, as a club, that the major allocation should go to the two clubs taking part in the Final (hear hear).[36]

Coventry's Jack Patience thought the current Federation policy a complete waste of time: 'We are knocking our heads against a brick wall with the FA,'; nevertheless the Federation continued in its aim and, warned the Gainsborough Trinity representative, 'we give the football authorities only a further 12 months and then fight them'.[37]

At the conference, twelve months later, the topic was not raised at all. But, in 1962, supporters *did* take action against the FA. Tottenham Hotspurs – winners of the Double in 1961 and back at Wembley the following year – had numerous supporters. Tickets were, as always, in very short supply. At the time, the FA allocated 38,840 tickets (almost 40 per cent of Wembley's capacity) to be shared among the County Associations; around 19,000 tickets were shared between all the Football League Clubs and other tickets were sent to a variety of organisations affiliated with the FA. The finalists themselves had 29,070 tickets between them, and less than 15,000 for Spurs supporters hardly quenchel the thirst for tickets at White Hart Lane. Some Spurs fans formed a 'We Want Wembley' committee and organised a march from Trafalger Square to the FA Headquarters at Lancaster Gate. A few hundred fans took part, demanding an allocation of 80,000 Cup Final tickets to be divided between competing clubs. Apparently, they were 'received' by FA officials and the current allocation system was 'explained' in full.[38]

The organisers of the Spurs fans wrote to the Federation and subsequently met with Tony Pullein, Secretary of the Federation following Leslie Davis's retirement in 1960. According to Mr Pullein,

> . . . there were six of them, good chaps you know, well known, sensible intelligent people'.[39]

But the Spurs' supporters received no support from the Federation in their campaign. The Everton supporters' committee raised the matter with the Federation Executive, seeking some guidance over the 'We Want Wembley' group and expressing the fear that its activities 'will bring disrepute to the Federation as a whole'. The Secretary's reply expressed the Federation's injured pride that the Spurs supporters were 'doing a job that the Federation has been trying to do for many years.' It was suspicious of the bona fides of the organisers and had refused the group's request for a Federation officer to speak at the march to Lancaster Gate:

> We felt, as a Council, that we should have nothing to do with this organisation . . . they were stepping on our toes . . . it was our job which should be done in the proper way and not by marches to FA headquarters.[40]

The Federation's concern in dealing with the FA – its desire not to fall into 'disrepute' by embarrassing Lancaster Gate with any action likely to catch the media's eye – left the organisation unable to pursue vigorously issues of *general* interest to football supporters. The Federation was stuck, as it were, in a 'no fans land' where a march to FA Headquarters to highlight an issue of chronic, popular discontent was not 'the proper way' to proceed. Yet the Federation's Executive thought it 'our job' to take up such issues. But how? The action by Spurs fans probably generated more national publicity over Cup Final tickets than a decade of debating the issue at Federation conferences.

In 1965, with the death of Lord Alexander, Sir Stanley Rous, now the President of FIFA, was elected Patron of the Federation. Archie Gooch (currently President of the Federation and Director of Exeter City FC) had succeeded to the Chairmanship of the Federation in 1964. Mr Gooch was a successful businessman (now retired) and supporter of Ilminster Town FC, and he set about restoring the Federation's standing with the FA which had apparently suffered under the Secretaryship of Leslie Davis. It was proving a difficult time for many Supporters' Clubs. The FA had given sanction to football clubs running their own lotteries and fund-raising schemes, which rocked the Supporters' Club movement to its foundations.[41] There were bitter complaints from Federation member clubs about the organisation's failure to stand up to the football authorities. Leyton Orient's Mr Dunn, called for 'revolutionary action' and decried the 'cap-in-hand' attitude to the FA from supporters who 'are satisfied if they are just tolerated'.[42] The Rochdale delegate bemoaned the absence, after so long, of *any negotiating medium* through which the Federation could raise issues with the FA; it was only with 'recognition', he argued, that 'we can go to the FA and discuss things officially with them'.[43]

Archie Gooch had privately contacted the new FA Secretary, Denis Follows, to arrange a 'lunch' at which he and Tony Pullein would attend. When the Everton representative raised the Cup Final ticket issue, the Executive promised to pursue the matter on the occasion. The proposal from Everton marked a major shift in the Federation's previous policy. It no longer concerned the Federation itself receiving an allocation of tickets but called for the FA to base its distribution to competing clubs 'on the previous season's average gate'. Such a policy would, it was hoped, destroy 'the terrible black market'.[44] Despite the Executive's concern that such a demand might be unrealistic – unlikely to happen before 'Charles is King', according to one – especially if two clubs like Manchester Utd and Everton reached the Final (with an average attendance of 95,000 between them), they agreed the matter would be raised at the forthcoming 'lunch'.

Recalling this – and other – informal occasions when some Federation Officers joined FA Secretary, Denis Follows, for lunch in London, Archie Gooch described the 'off the record' nature of the discussions:

> We talked about what we were trying to do . . . He agreed with us, but said: 'Don't quote me on that!'[45]

Mr Gooch continued to seek to develop a personal relationship with Denis Follows and others in the hope that it might eventually flower into an official liaison-committee. Consequently, when Everton raised the Cup Final tickets issue, following their club's appearance at Wembley in 1966, the Chairman replied:

> . . . this is a question of treading softly, softly. I do not think it is polite to introduce oneself as a responsible officer and then immediately ask for something back. We are hoping that the relationship which we are trying to cement will eventually lead to a certain amount of trust and then maybe a solution will be found.[46]

Demand for action over the Cup ticket allocations continued, nevertheless, on an annual basis. In 1968, the Liverpool SC delegate called for a mass petition to be gathered and presented to the FA, and both Everton and Chelsea representatives presented written questions to the Executive about the issue. The Chelsea contribution recalled the 'heartbreaking scenes' witnessed outside Wembley, when 'thousands of loyal Evertonian fans were locked out', and suggested that each of the Federation's six Areas should be represented on the FA Council 'thus opening channels . . . to an increased allocation.'[47] Secretary Tony Pullein agreed that, without voting power on the FA Council, the Federation could make no progress. He insisted that even when senior FA officers were convinced of the justice of increasing the number of tickets for competing clubs, there was little they could do to make FA County representatives on the Council 'vote away their own tickets'. The only other approach which might have some effect would involve persuading all the First Division clubs to refuse to take part in the FA Cup competition. In conclusion, the Everton delegate called on the Executive:

> . . . to keep fighting . . . we fought very hard for the Gaming Act. Let us fight just as hard for our own rights . . .[48]

The suggestion from Chelsea that regional Federation Areas be represented on the FA Council points up the lingering confusion over what the Federation's policy on Cup Final tickets actually was. In the past, resolutions had been carried calling both for an allocation to the Federation and (more recently) for increased numbers of tickets for competing clubs. In response to another enquiry on the issue, in 1969 from Everton again, Chairman Gooch made it quite clear that the older policy of seeking tickets for the Federation was now superseded:

> . . . I think we need to give up this idea of 'we should have an allocation' . . . It's not on . . . But I think what is on is a bigger allocation for the participating clubs . . . this is the policy . . .[49]

One year later, with the World Cup in Mexico looming, it was still the FA Cup that occupied lengthy debate at conference. It was Chelsea and Leeds Utd (recent finalists), along with Spurs, whose delegates led discussions of 'the unrealistic, antiquated and inhuman allocation of Cup Final tickets.' The Chelsea representative, it seems, had spoken personally to Denis Follows, and had been informed by him that the county associations 'are the first priority'. He rehearsed for the conference the current FA allocation figures ('unjustifiable and perverse') and called upon the smaller and non-League clubs to join the fight for more tickets. With remarkable prescience, Chelsea reminded those present that anything is possible in the football world; that, in some strange and distant future, even the 'Wimbledons of today' might compete at the highest level,

perhaps even at a Cup Final at Wembley.[50] He concluded with a formal
proposition that a subcommittee be formed to 'do all within its power' to
press for changes.

Speeches in support followed, with speakers complaining of the tickets
allocated to all football clubs (nearly 10,000 tickets were shared out
amongst the First Division clubs alone), and railing at the presence in
Wembley of club directors 'and their lady friends', the latter who 'sit there
and do their knitting.' The Leeds Utd delegate, 'representing the golden
failures' as he described himself, inveighed at the annual black market in
tickets and called for an allocation of 30,000 for each participating club.
Another speaker, reflecting on recent news that Government money would
be available to enlarge Wembley, demanded 'the FA use some of its cash
to build a stadium that would hold 200,000 people.' Yet another recalled
the Federation's previous attempts to highlight the black market to the FA
when over-priced tickets were brought and 'taken by Mr Leslie Davis to Sir
Stanley Rous' back in 1957. (Perhaps this had led to Leslie Davis's unpopu-
larity at Lancaster Gate?) Archie Gooch remembered an attempt even
earlier, in 1952, when an eight-page Federation document was presented to
the FA, without result:

> . . . the Football Association are unbending. They are a law unto themselves. I
> think it is time that pressure was brought to bear by the ordinary supporter
> . . .[51]

In the event, the proposition was adopted and a subcommittee established, consisting of some Executive members and representatives from
Everton, Chelsea, Leeds Utd and Manchester City.

> The idea . . . is that we would hope to contact the national Press, radio and
> television and circulate Football League Chairmen in the four divisions and I
> would hope that the delegation would be able to have an interview with the
> Football Association at sometime . . .[52]

The FA flatly refused to meet the 'delegation', but within a year the Cup
Final allocation increased to 20,000 tickets per competing club. The
Federation claimed considerable credit for exerting the pressure which
forced the FA to concede. The Chairman reflected on the achievement:

> . . . we formed a committee and said to the FA by letter that 16,500 tickets was
> ridiculous . . . we did a wonderful job there. The FA would not meet the
> committee. But we are not a militant organisation. The FA knew the committee
> was formed and letters were read to the FA Council and the allocation was
> increased . . . this Federation played a big part. It is an indication that this
> Federation is not a nonentity. It cannot be a nonentity.[53]

Of course the Federation had been exerting such 'pressure' for many years without success. Perhaps the crucial leverage came in reality from *the management of Wembley* who were negotiating with the Government for funds to improve the stadium. Prime Minister Harold Wilson had publicly stated on BBC radio's 'Sport Report' that he hoped to see more tickets available to supporters if public money was to be invested in the stadium.[54]

The issue did not submerge amongst Federation members with the increase in tickets for competing clubs, neither was there any lasting satisfaction in the form of 'liaison' that existed with the FA. Indeed, Archie Gooch found himself, but two years later, bemoaning the fact that, 'as far as the FA is concerned, I suppose we are almost nonentities.'[55] The FA's decision in 1973 not to allow extra time after Cup Finals in future provoked considerable anger amongst delegates and led to Vice-Chairman Southernwood's call for the Federation to 'become a little more abrasive without necessarily becoming militant.'[56] This theme was taken up again by the Hibernian representative who wished to speak about recent developments in Scotland. He reminded the assembly that (as we saw earlier[57]) the SFA used to allocate tickets for the biannual England v. Scotland game at Wembley directly to various Scottish Supporters' Clubs.

Quite foolishly we accepted at one stage that . . . distribution of tickets would be left to the parent clubs which would then pass the tickets on to supporters clubs. This . . . was quite a happy arrangement until the old Scottish Federation collapsed. Then the parent clubs began to assume that the tickets were their private property.[58]

When the Hibs Supporters' Club – a body recognised by their FC – asked for the tickets, its members were told publicly via the local newspaper to 'Get Lost'. The Hibs delegate therefore requested the Federation to take up the matter with the FA and SFA. Unfortunately, as Archie Gooch patiently explained, there was nothing they could do. At the FA, the Federation 'cannot get fair play' and despite a willingness to make approaches to Lancaster Gate, 'I do not see very much hope.' As far as the Chairman was concerned, unless the Federation itself was prepared to get 'a little more abrasive . . . I might even say more militant', nothing would change. With that, the great Cup Final ticket issue disappeared from Federation debates for almost a decade.

In the latter half of the 1970s, the Federation's opportunities for direct liaison with the FA began to increase. As various forms of hooliganism at football continued to proliferate – and its European dimension began to cause acute embarrassment in Government circles – the Federation found itself involved *via Government* with the football authorities.[59] It was Denis Howell MP who probably did more than anyone previously to involve supporters, through the Federation, in the issues of the day. It was he who

had invited the Federation, in 1967, to contribute to the Chester Report,
and (as Minister of State with responsibility for sport) it was he who, in
1975–76, invited the Federation onto his 'Working Party' (Competitions in
European Countries). This Working Party consisted of the Minister, First
Division Chairmen whose clubs were involved in Europe, travel agent
representatives and the Federation, represented by Archie Gooch, now
Federation President.

The inclusion of the Federation in the Working Party was seen as a great
leap forward by the organisation's officers. In 1976, new Chairman, Mr
Southernwood, considered it had:

> . . . done more for the Federation than any other single event in its history . . .
> bringing the Federation to the notice of the Football League and the FA.[60]

At the FA, Ted Croker had succeeded Denis Follows as Secretary in
October 1973. (He remained FA Secretary until February 1989, succeeded
by Graham Kelly under the new title 'Chief Executive'.) Mr Croker's
relations with the Federation at first remained similar to his predecessor's:
he would meet Archie Gooch privately, but still no 'official' meetings took
place. As Archie Gooch remembered it:

> . . . I could always go and see Ted Croker on a personal basis. Mind you, all
> those (FA) officials were always cautious about how far they went with you.[61]

Denis Howell's willingness to involve the Federation in Government
discussions did more than anything the Federation had been able to do in
the past to exert real pressure on the FA to recognise them 'officially'. (The
Minister eventually succeeded Sir Stanley Rous as Patron of the
Federation and became, in Mr Gooch's estimation, 'the most worthwhile
Patron we've ever had.')

There was, however, another pressure on the FA to open up channels to
organised supporters: a desire to *commercialise* its activities. In the year of
the Federation's 'Golden Jubilee', 1977, the FA began to look more
seriously at ways of raising money through the development of sponsorship
and commercial enterprises. Under the headline, 'FA Support – At Last!',
Federation Secretary, Tony Pullein, reported, in March 1978, on a recent
meeting at Lancaster Gate:

> For 50 years the Federation has been battling for some sign of support from the
> Football Association. Now . . . there are real signs of backing from Lancaster
> Gate . . . There is now a far more business-like approach from the FA. *The need
> for cash is uppermost in their minds* and the question of sponsorship is now
> under more serious consideration. The FA will be involving itself in commercial

enterprises . . . and it is hoped that the Federation and its member clubs will be able to participate in some way.[62]

Apparently, this meeting was yet another informal event, but discussions were clearly conducted at a more serious level than ever before. According to Mr Pullein, the meeting was 'intended to reassure the game's leaders of our backing for their plans', and he expected similar meetings would take place with the Football League, PFA, and the Commercial Managers' Association. It is clear that the FA was pressing the Federation at this meeting to include and allow *all kinds of Supporters' Clubs* into membership (thus providing the FA with the maximum possible 'market' of organised supporters). But many 'new' Supporters' Clubs were now run almost entirely by their football clubs as a commercial arm of their 'development associations'. As we have seen, some old member clubs of the Federation objected strongly to the inclusion of such 'supporters clubs' in the Federation, even if the minimum constitutional rules were met.[63] Tony Pullein urged members to accept the inevitable changes and embrace the 'new' Supporters' Clubs, otherwise 'one day we shall become a Federation of unofficial supporters.' He concluded,

> These, and many other interesting matters, were all discussed informally with the men from the FA who have promised the Federation publicity in their quarterly bulletin and who will discuss the Federation and its plans at meetings at all levels of the Football Association.[64]

In May 1978, the Federation attended a meeting of the Sports Council (another door opened by Denis Howell) in company with Alan Hardaker of the League, Cliff Lloyd of the PFA and others. The meeting was a prelude to the launch of 'Football and the Community', a plan pump-primed by Jim Callaghan's Labour Government with cash grants for various regions to develop community sports facilities and social schemes at selected football clubs.[65] Archie Gooch told the meeting that the scheme would greatly benefit from close links to the Football Association (which does not appear to be represented) and the Football League. He urged the formation of junior Supporters' Clubs and recommended the Manchester City example as a model.

In the early 1980s, the Federation's officers were finally admitted through the doors of Lancaster Gate in an 'official' capacity. On 4 February 1981, Federation officers met with FA Chairman Bert Millichip and Ted Croker. Three weeks later, they met with Graham Kelly, then Secretary of the Football League, for a 'useful exchange of views.'[66] The Federation maintained its contact with the Minister of Sport (now Hector Munro) in the new Conservative Government led by Mrs Thatcher and, on 2 March 1981, Federation officers attended the Football Trust Conference.

There was a further meeting with the FA later that year at 3 p.m. on 3 September, at Lancaster Gate. The delicate growth of the Federation's liaison with the FA was under serious threat. The FA was being sued, under the Race Relations Act, by the Scottish Division of the Federation.

It all blew up over the refusal by the FA, in 1981, to allocate any tickets north of the border for the England v. Scotland game at Wembley, following crowd disturbances and a pitch-invasion at the previous match. The decision infuriated Scots supporters in general, and the whole Scottish Division of the Federation in particular unanimously supported the legal action against the FA, though only their Chairman, Charlie Bent, was named in the litigation. They raised the funds to pursue the action which, though eventually brought under the Race Relations Act, they saw as essentially about 'the rights of responsible Federation members to follow their team.'[67] The Federation's Executive, alarmed at developments, decided not to support the Scottish Division (which created deep resentment north of the border), but could not prevent their action against the FA. There were suspicions, however, at Lancaster Gate, which surfaced during the meeting on 3 September.

The FA had drawn up a 'special agenda' for the meeting which was attended by Archie Gooch, Reg Abbott (Chairman), Tony Kershaw (Deputy Chairman) and Malcolm Gamlen (Secretary) for the Federation; Ted Croker and Bert Millichip represented the FA. There was some initial discussion about the effect of the ticket-ban on Scotland's fans and Archie Gooch suggested that 'some good television coverage in Scotland . . . prior to the fixture,' had prevented many Scots from travelling. This TV coverage had apparently included Charlie Bent, for Mr Gooch's remarks provoked an outburst from Ted Croker to the effect that 'Mr Bent was inciting trouble.' At this juncture, Bert Millichip intervened: 'Let's deal with the third item on the agenda'; it read, 'Bent v. Football Association'.[68]

Charlie Bent had attended the previous meeting at Lancaster Gate in February 1981. The FA now had in its possession details of a 'legal conference' which had immediately followed that meeting to discuss the proposed action against the FA.[69] Bert Millichip was concerned to find that Federation Secretary, Malcolm Gamlen, had attended the legal conference despite assurances from the Federation that it did not support the Scottish Division's action. The officers present assured the FA that the latter was indeed the case and Mr Gamlen's presence at the legal conference had been 'as an observer'. They produced the Minutes of the National Council's Extraordinary Meeting which showed the Federation's decision not to support the Scottish Division. With this, the FA officers appeared satisfied. Rather tangentially,

In summarising this topic, Mr Croker thought it may be a good idea for the Scottish ban on alcohol to spread to England for the terraced supporters.[70]

In the event, the Scottish Division took legal proceedings against the FA in the High Court. Judgement was found in favour of the FA on the grounds that steps had to be taken to prevent public disorder.[71] The Scottish Division was left with the costs of the action, which included a debt to the FA of £4,459 (later reduced to £3,211). The Scots had hoped for financial support – they had been encouraged in their legal action by publicity in the *Daily Record* – but none came:

> While eventually the FA waived the last £600, by that time we had paid over £4,000 which had been raised by various fund-raising events. It still grieves me to think what we could have done with such funds but at the time we felt we had to take a stand. It is interesting to note that the average supporter does not now care whether the Wembley fixture ever takes place again, and what was once a significant event in the footballing life of every male Scot has now been consigned to folklore and reminiscence.[72]

In the following year, 1982, the FA refused to sell *English* fans tickets for the Scotland v. England game at Hampden Park which provoked the headline in the *Daily Record* – 'F.A. Ban Their Own Fans'.[73] At the Federation Conference, Chairman Reg Abbott revealed that the whole episode had 'nearly lost the Scottish Division' to the organisation. The Scots had clearly felt let down by the absence of support in the National Council for their action. It was only agreed by the Scots to remain within the Federation on a vote of 6–5.[74] There were worries expressed from the floor, principally through Manchester Utd's delegate, David Smith, that the 'militant' action by the Scots could have done 'irreparable damage to this organisation in its dealings with the hierarchy.'

One effect the legal action did have was to stimulate the FA to meet with the Federation *officially* twice within one year. Subsequently, there appears to have been at least one annual meeting at Lancaster Gate. Items on the agenda of the September 1981 meeting (apart from the Scottish legal action) included:

(a) the Federation's meeting with the Football League;
(b) the Football Trust Conference;
(c) FIFA's allocation of tickets for the 1982 World Cup;
(d) Cup Final ticket allocation's/ticket touts/agencies;
(e) the Federation's financial situation.

This latter item rankled deeply with members north of the border. As David Smith put it:

> . . . the Scottish Division found it distressing that the Federation should will-

ingly supply to the FA details of its financial situation and asks whether a reciprocal report was supplied by the FA.[75]

1982 was the year a resolution was carried at conference which gave the Executive the power to expel any Division of the Federation. It was also the year Charlie Bent called on the Federation to become the 'Paying Customers' Union'.[76] Along with the FA, the League was rapidly seeking to develop additional sponsorship and commercial activity in the face of steadily declining attendances. There was an attempt to launch a 'Football League Supporters' Club' (which was eventually dropped) as part of a 'package' assembled for the League by the advertising agency, J. Walter Thompson. (There was even a jingle written to promote it: 'I was there'.) The League Cup also picked up its first sponsors – the Milk Marketing Board.

The Federation met the FA once again, in December 1982, and discussed the high price of Wembley tickets and the allocation of international match tickets through the Federation. The FA agreed to allocate to Federation members some tickets for the England v. Scotland game (switched to a Wednesday evening), but under certain conditions which included a prohibition on the sale of tickets to Scottish fans.[77] Understandably, the Scottish delegates bridled at these constraints. During 1983, the Federation were invited to contribute to the Football League Chester Report Committee and Sir Norman Chester was asked to address the conference, but declined.

Annual meetings with the FA continued in the years that followed. In 1985, Bert Millichip suggested to Federation representatives that it might be helpful if Supporters' Clubs sought to co-opt football hooligans into their membership – a proposal that was greeted with horror.[78] There was continuing concern about UEFA's methods of ticket distribution for European competitions, but the Federation did not approach UEFA directly, and relied on the FA to represent their views to that body. There was still considerable dissatisfaction in the Federation that the meetings with the football authorities were less than serious:

> (The Federation) has in recent years been granted occasional meetings with the Football Association and the Football League . . . but only ever at its own request, the impression created being that the meeting was agreed to and held as a courtesy rather than with a positive intent to involve the Federation in consultation . . .[79]

The Federation met again with Ted Croker and Bert Millichip at the FA in 1987. But circumstances were already shifting radically, as English football rocked to its foundations under the traumatic impact of the disasters at Bradford and Brussels in 1985. One result – of the Heysel stadium tragedy – had been the formation of the Football Supporters' Association. In addition, the continuing development of a range of 'independent' Supporters' Clubs (unaffiliated to the Federation), and the burgeoning growth of football fanzines, marked a shift in activity amongst supporters away from the traditional Supporters' Clubs that had formed the bulk of the Federation's membership. These new supporters' organisations and publications also appeared to involve, for the first time, substantial numbers of *much younger* fans than those more usually engaged in Federation affairs. Within a year, when meeting with the football authorities, the Federation found itself sitting alongside representatives of the FSA. It had proved a long and hard struggle for the Federation to gain access to official dialogue with the FA and FL, and it was perhaps a little galling for some Federation activists to find themselves joined in discussions by a 'johnny-come lately' organisation like the FSA, which had yet to celebrate its third birthday. For fifty years and more, the Federation had been the only national organisation that could accurately claim to represent Supporters' Clubs and (with less accuracy) supporters in general. Yet during that half century, the only occasions on which the football authorities had deigned to call on the Federation were when they were dragooned by political pressure or commercial desire into starting some dialogue with football supporters. Consequently, it is difficult to characterise the attitude of both the FA and the FL towards the Federation as anything other than cynical. If it had not been for the willingness of Government – and of Denis Howell in particular – at least to attempt to involve supporters in discussions, probably little headway would have been made at all.

NOTES

1. See Chapter 4, 'The Renegades and the Respectables'.
2. I am grateful for the help of David Barber at the FA and for the access to the FA archives.
3. National Federation AGM Minutes, 1948 (my emphasis).
4. Ibid.
5. *Sports Weekly Magazine*, 21 August 1948, p. 15. The *Football Supporters' Gazette* was the official organ of the Federation in post-war years. It comprised a few pages made available by the publishers of *Sports Weekly*. See below, Chapter 10, 'Public Relations, Publications and Finances'.
6. For further discussion of Federation finances, see below, Chapter 10, 'Public Relations, Publications and Finances'.
7. National Federation AGM Minutes, 1948, p. 26.
8. For a brief history of this topic, see S. Wagg, *The Football World*, London, 1984.

9. Unfortunately the Federation AGM Minutes for 1949, 1950 and 1952 have not survived.
10. Nat. Fed. AGM Minutes, 1953, p. 5.
11. For more on the style and language of conference speakers, see the preceding chapter, 'Structure and Membership'.
12. Nat. Fed. AGM Minutes, 1953, p. 18.
13. Ibid., p. 19.
14. Ibid., p. 20.
15. The 'We Want Wembley' Campaign in 1962. See below.
16. Nat. Fed. AGM Minutes, 1953, p. 20.
17. Ibid., p. 21.
18. Ibid.
19. Ibid., p. 5.
20. Nat. Fed. AGM Minutes, 1954, p. 27.
21. A later Secretary of the FA, Ted Croker, expressed very similar feelings in a letter to the FSA in 1987.
22. Nat. Fed. AGM Minutes, 1956, p. 34.
23. See also Chapter 8, 'Supporter-Club Relations'.
24. Nat. Fed. AGM Minutes, 1956, pp. 35–6 (my emphasis).
25. Nat. Fed. AGM Minutes, 1956, p. 36.
26. Nat. Fed. AGM Minutes, 1956, p. 37.
27. Nat. Fed. AGM Minutes, 1956, pp. 37–8 (my emphasis).
28. Ibid., p. 38.
29. Ibid. (my emphasis).
30. Ibid.
31. Nat. Fed. AGM Minutes, 1958, p. 30ff.
32. Ibid., p. 11.
33. According to Archie Gooch, Nat. Fed. President, personal interview, 23 January 1990.
34. Archie Gooch interview, ibid.
35. For discussion of this, see Nat. Fed. AGM Minutes, 1961, p. 31ff.
36. Ibid., p. 33.
37. Ibid., p. 34.
38. 'Cup Final tickets', *F.A. News*, vol. XII, no. 5, December 1962.
39. Personal interview, Tony Pullein, 28 March 1990.
40. Nat. Fed. AGM, 1963, pp. 28–9.
41. For more on this, see below, 'Supporter-Club Relations'.
42. Nat. Fed. AGM Minutes, 1965, p. 46.
43. Ibid., p. 49.
44. Ibid., p. 55.
45. Personal interview, Archie Gooch, op. cit.
46. Nat. Fed. AGM Minutes, 1966, p. 42.
47. Nat. Fed. AGM Minutes, 1968, p. 63.
48. Ibid., p. 64.
49. Nat. Fed. AGM Minutes, 1969, p. 96.
50. Nat. Fed. AGM Minutes, 1970, p. 54.
51. Ibid., p. 57.
52. Ibid., p. 58.

53. Nat. Fed. AGM Minutes, 1971, p. 33.
54. See Nat. Fed. AGM Minutes, 1970, p. 56.
55. See Nat. Fed. AGM Minutes, 1973, p. 34.
56. Ibid., p. 54.
57. See above, AGM Minutes, 1956.
58. Nat. Fed. AGM Minutes, 1973, p. 59.
59. For an account of the Federation's relations with Government, see Chapter 7, 'Relations with Government and Police'.
60. Nat. Fed. AGM Minutes, 1976, p. 17.
61. Personal interview. Archie Gooch, op. cit.
62. Nat. Fed. *Newsletter*, March 1978, p. 4 (my emphasis).
63. The Federation insisted that its member clubs were run by committees with 'a percentage of its members being elected at a general meeting.' Ibid., p. 5. See also above, Chapter 5, 'Structure and Membership'.
64. *Newsletter*, March 1978, p. 5.
65. For more on this, see below, Chapter 7, 'Relations with Government and Police'.
66. Nat. Fed. AGM Minutes, 1981.
67. See *Conference Reflections*, August 1982, p. 25.
68. For an account of these proceedings, see Nat. Fed. *Newsletter*, December 1981, p. 4.
69. These details had been supplied to the FA by Miss Helena Quinn, Secretary of the Scottish Division.
70. Nat. Fed. *Newsletter*, December 1981, p. 5.
71. I am grateful to Martin Rose, current Secretary of the Scottish Federation, for his personal account of the proceedings.
72. Personal communication, Martin Rose.
73. *Daily Record*, 8 February 1982.
74. Nat. Fed. AGM Minutes, 1982, p. 16ff.
75. Ibid., p. 19.
76. See above, Chapter 5, 'Structure and Membership'.
77. Nat. Fed. AGM Minutes, 1983, p. 40.
78. Nat. Fed. AGM Minutes, 1985, p. 6.
79. National Federation Paper for DOE Working Group of Football Spectator Violence, reproduced in *Conference Reflections*, August 1985.

7

RELATIONS WITH GOVERNMENT AND POLICE AUTHORITIES

> Football attendances peaked almost simultaneously with the Labour vote around 1950 . . . The football grounds of England were the Labour Party at Prayer. (Nicholas Fishwick, 1989)

The two most traditional activities of Supporters' Clubs were fund-raising and organising transport for members to 'away' matches. As we have seen, these activities go back to the very beginnings of supporters' organisations, from the 'Brake Clubs' of the 1880s onwards.[1] As the Federation developed during the 1930s, it sought to offer advice to its member clubs about problems they experienced in these mainstream activities. In 1934, the organisation retained its own Hon. Solicitor, G.S. Godfree Esq., 'a member of the Income Tax Payers' Association' to advise on financial matters pertaining to fund-raising.[2]

Many of the legal difficulties encountered by Supporters' Clubs revolved around the interpretation by local police forces of the laws relating to lotteries and to the transport of passengers by coach. There is no evidence, however, of any attempts by the Federation in the 1930s to meet either with Government representatives or police authorities at local or national levels. It does seem, however, that the Federation did take some part in a campaign towards the end of the 1930s to ease restrictions for those organising coach transport for supporters.[3] There is no sign of any criticism of football policing or of police treatment of supporters.

In the immediate post-war period, up to 1955–56, the Federation records show no discussions of issues specifically concerned with Government or policing. In the 'Legal Report' at the 1953 conference, however, Federation solicitor, Mr Griffiths, reported dealing with problems at 'some 60 or more clubs', many of which concerned the old 1930 Road Transport Act which was clearly still presenting problems to organisers of coach parties.[4] Running lotteries was also still an uncertain affair and, in 1954, Mr Griffiths reported on two legal proceedings which police had taken against Gloucester and Torquay Utd's Supporters' Clubs. The Federation had been waiting for a case about lotteries against which it might success-fully make an appeal – and a legal fund had been established to meet costs. A QC (Dingle Foot) was retained to appeal the Torquay case at the Devon Quarter Sessions and, though the case was lost 2–1, one of the judges came out strongly in support of Torquay SC.[5]

The following year, 1955, saw a campaign in Parliament to change the law. The confusion in administering the current regulations concerning lotteries prevented many supporters from attempting such fund-raising schemes. Football clubs (and other sporting associations and charities) were suffering financially as a result, and sympathetic MPs, encouraged by the judge's comments on the Torquay case, were being urged to promote a new Bill to Parliament. Football club directors (some of whom were MPs) were also looking ahead to a time when they might run their own schemes commercially.

The unselfish role of Supporters' Clubs in their efforts to raise money for their football clubs was an effective example for use in the media campaign and in Parliamentary speeches from supporters of the Bill. The Federation 'fronted' the campaign – and was pleased to do so – for the advantages of a clarification in the law seemed clear: Supporters' Clubs could get on with their function of fund-raising and develop their relationships with parent bodies from positions of strength. At first, the Federation approached the Royal Commission on Lotteries and Betting, but as time dragged on, the Federation was urged by football club directors to take further action.

> Clubs asked us what further steps the Federation was going to take because many clubs were bleeding to death for want of funds.[6]

The Federation wrote to the Home Office and subsequently a 'depu-tation' was received by Home Office officials. In 1955, a Private Member's Bill was introduced to Parliament by Sir Eric Errington MP – Director of Aldershot FC and President of the Aldershot Supporters' Club. Sir Eric visited the Federation office in the basement at Pall Mall prior to formulat-ing the Bill, which, whilst receiving support in the Commons, was 'talked out' of time. Another Private Member's Bill followed, introduced by Mr Ernest Davies MP. Meanwhile the Federation called on its member clubs to lobby their local MPs to support the Bill, and speeches in Parliament made frequent reference to the sterling work of Supporters' Clubs. When the Bill successfully proceeded through the various stages to become an Act of Parliament, the Federation officers were euphoric. Understandably (and for Secretarary, Leslie Davis, in particular), it had been invigorating to be engaged so closely in an issue of national significance. What with titled gentlemen popping into the office and:

> Requests by telephone to meet various MPs at the House of Commons were at one time so frequent . . . it seemed that the Federation might have to take temporary offices in the House.[7]

Leslie Davis thought the legislation, perhaps a touch exaggeratedly, as 'one of the finest things that football has known', and he reminded Federation members that, as a result,

> Football Clubs all over the country will be making amorous overtures to Supporters' Clubs before the season is over, because you will once again be able to put them in the money, and how they love your money to be sure.[8]

Four years later, the FA gave its consent to football clubs applying to run their own lotteries.[9]

Throughout the late 1950s and through to 1967, neither Government nor police authorities saw any advantage in meeting with Federation officers. Surprisingly, given the success of the 1955 campaign, the latter did not appear to press for any meetings with Government. In 1967, however, Denis Howell MP invited the Federation to provide written evidence to the commission set up under Norman Chester.[10] The Federation sent questionnaires to 250 member clubs, and eventually received 179 replies. The Secretary, Tony Pullein, compiled a written report to the Chester Commission and later appeared with Archie Gooch to give verbal assistance. There were high hopes amongst Federation personnel that the publication which the Commission would eventually produce (The Chester Report) would 'be of very great importance to this Federation,' underlining its role and bringing it to the attention of the football authorities.[11]

The information presented to the Commission included details of supporters' fund-raising activity over the previous financial year. Of the clubs replying to the questionnaire, their donations to football clubs amounted to £484,023 in 1966–67. With a total membership within the clubs of 453,278, it worked out at just over £1 per member. Nearly half the 179 clubs reported that donations were down on previous years (44 were up), and 30 clubs gave details of disputes with their football clubs in the recent past.[12]

When the Commission's Report was published in 1968, it did include an account of the financial contributions SCs made – and it also recommended that club members and season-ticket holders could be entitled to elect someone to represent their interests on the boards of their football clubs.[13] But great disappointment was expressed in Federation circles that the organisation had been hardly mentioned at all in the Report. It revealed a certain vulnerability about the Federation's situation which was difficult to overcome. When the Federation expected public recognition of its role, it was often the *Supporters' Clubs* within it that received the publicity. Consequently, great expectations of a Federation 'breakthrough' via participation in Government-led discussions were frequently dashed.

The rising incidences of hooliganism associated with football kept pressure on the Government to seek solutions. In 1969, the Sir John Lang Committee was established to look particularly at crowd behaviour and, once again, Denis Howell invited a contribution from the Federation. The resulting document sought to show how difficult a problem hooliganism was for Supporters' Clubs to tackle: 'the culprits in the main are not members of Supporters' Clubs'.[14] The Federation had, for a number of years, sought to arrange 'trouble free' trains for club members and encouraged the latter to report any offenders to the police. It recommended to Sir John Lang 'stiffer sentences' for convicted hooligans and wider publicity to accompany them. In addition, the Federation proposed:

(a) seated areas in 'trouble zones' (cf. behind the goal);
(b) concrete pens for terraced supporters, similar to those at Wembley;
(c) the development of young Supporters' Clubs;
(d) better discipline from players;
(e) more consistent refereeing;
(f) better liaison between SCs and FCs, including joint meetings with local police;
(g) the establishment of a combined liaison committee made up of representatives from Supporters' Clubs, League Clubs, the Referees Association, police and magistrates.[15]

Two years later, the Federation produced recommendations for the consideration of Lord Wheatley's committee on Safety in Football Grounds.[16] The Federation made a particular point of the discrepancy between the tax relief available to football clubs' transfer fees, but not available for capital costs like ground improvements. In this, the Federation was, in effect, representing *the football clubs* which were, of course, keen to persuade the Government to provide wider tax relief. The Federation repeated its previous recommendations for reduced terracing, increased seating, and concrete pens for standing supporters, plus:

(a) grounds should have exits at two levels;
(b) exits should be the same width as approaching stairways or tunnels;
(c) exits should be pro rata to ground capacity;
(d) safety officers appointed for all grounds;
(e) areas set aside for youngsters and adequately stewarded;
(f) grounds should be licensed.[17]

In 1974–75, the Government was still under pressure from the hooliganism issue and the rising tide of media debate. Denis Howell – now Minister of State with responsibility for Sport – set up another 'Working Party' and agreed to quarterly meetings with the Federation. David Smith of the Manchester Utd Supporters' Club produced a detailed document on 'football hooliganism' in relation to his own club which was submitted to the Home Secretary and Denis Howell.[18] In addition, the Federation restated and widened its proposal for an instituted liaison body to be formed, which would include Home Office representatives, probation officers and sports authorities.

At a meeting of the Working Party (Competition in European Countries) on 18 October 1975, discussion in the morning included plans for the distribution of tickets for European matches through supporters' clubs, shareholders and season-ticket holders. The Federation suggested that supporters might be accompanied by 'a person whose voice might appeal . . . over the public address system' should any problems occur. At the afternoon session, attended by Denis Howell, First Division Chairmen, travel agency representatives and Archie Gooch for the Federation, the recent 'Safety in Stadia' report was considered, along with publication of the 'Green Book' (which became the 'Green Guide' for clubs). The discussions agreed that:

> The highest priority would be to control movement on terraces . . . access to pitch, adequate fencing . . . Fencing should not be tight onto spectators . . .[19]

In answer to a question (probably raised by one of the club chairmen present) as to why Supporters' Clubs were involved when they represented but 10 per cent of football's followers, Denis Howell replied that he had been impressed with their report (the David Smith document) and the Minister was 'not concerned with disputes which may have arisen and whether the club supported a Federation or their own brand of Supporters' Club.'

Regular meetings with Denis Howell continued through 1976–79. In addition to Archie Gooch's attendance at the Sports Council launch of 'Football and Community' in 1978,[20] the Federation made input into yet another Working Party (Crowd Behaviour) convened at the Department of the Environment on 17 November 1977. The Federation pressed for some form of control, or licensing, of football coaches, sought co-operation from TV companies not to include obscene chants in their coverage and (along with the FA) pressed the case for corporal punishment.[21]

With the advent of the new Conservative Government in 1979, Hector Munro MP succeeded Denis Howell as Minister for Sport, and he met with Federation representatives on 2 December 1980. At a further meeting on

26 May 1982 (with the World Cup in Spain approaching), the Federation requested the withdrawal of passports from convicted hooligans.[22]

Despite the increased involvement in Government discussions which Denis Howell had encouraged from as early as 1967, the Federation does not appear to have held meetings with senior police officers. The Federation's member clubs were involved in discussions regularly with British Rail authorities concerned with transporting supporters, and there may have also been meetings at local levels with the police. Perhaps surprisingly, there was little *criticism* of various policing methods and tactics which developed during the 1970s and which included the unpopular 'snatch squads' whose role was to spot 'troublemakers' in the crowd and wade in to arrest them.[23] David Smith of the Manchester Utd SC who described the arrest of innocent fans by these squads pointed out in his 1975 report to Denis Howell that:

> . . . in the opinion of many, the police are as much to blame for the current state of affairs as the fans.[24]

Yet David Smith's remarks are the *only* example in Federation documents prior to 1982 of implied criticism of some forms of policing. Perhaps, for most member clubs in the Federation (many of which were associated with smaller or amateur football clubs), the issue was not as significant as it was to First and Second Division supporters. For Manchester Utd fans, however, who (by the mid-1970s) had gained a certain notoriety,

> There have been numerous instances over the past few years when the attitude of the police to any supporter wearing the colours of Manchester Utd has been nothing less than provocative . . .[25]

Following the development of a 'portfolio' system in the Federation in the late 1970s, Ian Todd – a Sunderland supporter based in London – took responsibility for the 'Travel and Crowd Control' portfolio. He was well-placed to take the brief, with experience as a 'Special' constable in the Metropolitan area and, (perhaps more importantly) as a supporter living in London but following Sunderland, he was in a sense an 'away' fan every week. Reporting to the conference in 1982, Mr Todd directed attention at the

> . . . wide difference of attitude by police forces round the country to the way in which football supporters are handled . . . I think this is something we should concern ourselves about . . .[26]

He went on to identify the policing of 'away' fans on Merseyside as a continuing problem for some years and called for the development of 'a file of incidents' by supporters for use as evidence to raise and progress the issue. This was precisely the kind of effective, strategic approach to a topic of real concern to many supporters that, one might argue, had been lacking in much of the Federation's earlier work. It would have been both useful – and of interest to the local and national media – to monitor police tactics in different regions. Such a procedure should also have led to regular meetings with senior police officers. The general problem for the Federation, and for Ian Todd in particular, was *gathering appropriate information from member clubs,* many of whom appeared apathetic to activists within the organisation.

A similar theme regarding differing police tactics re-emerged at the conference in 1983. Following the Chairman's survey of the year, an 'unknown delegate' called for high level meetings:

> . . . different Police forces throughout the country take entirely different attitudes and I think possibly we would need to meet with the Home Secretary . . . In some areas we have proof of Police acting violently, over reacting to the situation and, in fact, making things a lot worse than they should have been . . .[27]

There was no sign of a national initiative from the Federation, but undoubtedly individual initiatives by Supporters' Clubs – often in conjunction with worried parent bodies – did take place. For example, liaison between some clubs involved in European competitions was attempted. The Celtic Supporters' Association, whose members had been amongst Celtic fans attacked by Juventus fans in 1983, had sent representatives to Holland in advance of their match with Ajax in 1984, where they met local police and other officials in Amsterdam. This procedure was also followed prior to Celtic's away leg at Nottingham Forest, but it was expensive to organise and cost the Supporters' Association over £1,000. Though Celtic FC would (it was hoped) meet half this cost, clearly only the richest of supporters' clubs could attempt such imaginative initiatives.

The resources to implement strategies involving pre-match liaison with police, and between rival supporters, were arguably unlikely to be forthcoming from the Conservative Government of the mid-1980s, and neither had such resources been offered by previous Labour administrations. There is no indication either that Federation representatives *asked* for financial support for such initiatives when they met the various Ministers for Sport who held office between 1980–87.

In August 1984, the Working Party considering Football Spectator Violence published its report. Representatives of the Federation met with Department of the Environment officials to consider the report, on 7 December 1984, along with Nigel Bird, Assistant Secretary at the FA and Brian Eames of the Home Office. The agenda that day included:

(a) membership cards;
(b) closed circuit television;
(c) segregation and fencing;
(d) supporters' links with football clubs;
(e) how the Federation appeals to non-members;
(f) travel;
(g) alcohol.

The first item swallowed up half the time allotted for the meeting. The prospect of *compulsory* membership for football supporters (which became known later as the 'ID card' debate) had surfaced in Federation discussions as early as 1974, when the Federation Secretary called for their implementation.[28] On this occasion, the Federation maintained its support for 'the idea of membership cards' and, though Archie Gooch thought that they ought only to be required 'purely for the cheaper turnstiles' (i.e. the terraces), Tony Kershaw agreed with the Home Office that 'the membership card system would need to be comprehensive.'[29] There was talk of a pilot scheme at a selected club and 'any casual supporters would have to enrol as a member of a bona fide Supporters' Club.' It seems that, for at least some of the Federation's officers, the prospect of a compulsory membership system for football fans was viewed as a potentially powerful means to boost the membership and status of Supporters' Clubs.[30]

The Federation expressed its support for segregation, though not for fans to be 'pushed into a cage', and brought attention to the two-tier pricing structure at some clubs which charged more to visiting supporters. Archie Gooch (now both President of the Federation and Chairman of Bristol City FC) outlined some of the tensions which existed between supporters and their football clubs and recommended the 'community' approach. He opposed the idea (previously suggested by Bert Millichip) that Supporters' Clubs should actively seek to recruit 'the hooligan element' to their ranks, and pointed out that organising travel for fans had been taken over by many FCs in recent years. With regard to alcohol on sale within grounds, the Federation (Mr Gooch) drew attention to the considerable revenue that clubs obtained through sales and did not think such contributed to hooligan behaviour.

Not everyone within Federation ranks was happy with the Government's performance, however. In 1985, with Neil McFarlane MP now occupying the position, a motion expressing 'no confidence' in the Minister for Sport – and calling for his resignation – emerged from the floor of the conference.[31]

Earlier that year, the Federation produced a documented response to the Working Party Report on Football Spectator Violence, which had been discussed in the December meeting. In March 1985 Ian Todd wrote a paper outlining Federation policy on the various issues raised. When it came to the membership card proposal,

> The Federation supports the concept of restricting access to football stadia . . . by some form of membership card system . . . only a nationally accepted scheme would eventually be practical. Members of Supporters' Clubs already have renewable cards of some form, in many cases bearing their photograph, and an extension of this administrative arrangement . . . would not be too difficult . . . The Federation would be very willing to be involved.[32]

In conclusion, the Federation welcomed the opportunity to contribute to the Working Party's deliberations and 'to establish its credibility as a responsible organisation.' The document ended with a restatement of the Federation's motto:

'To Help and Not To Hinder'

Within two months of the writing of Ian Todd's paper, English professional football was facing the biggest crisis of its life: the deaths of supporters in the Bradford fire; the loss of a young fan's life at Birmingham City and, at Heysel, following misbehaviour amongst Liverpool's supporters, thirty-nine Juventus fans were mortally crushed. In the aftermath, Justice Popplewell's Commission was established and, in October 1985, the Federation met with Commission officers.[33]

The Government became even keener to progress its idea of compulsory 'membership' for football supporters, as a means of excluding known troublemakers from football matches. The proposal was given encouragement by the implementation, at Luton, of a complete ban on visiting supporters which required a 'members only' scheme, with 'home' fans having to produce membership cards to access the ground through computerised turnstiles.[34] Under the threat of Government action to establish a national membership scheme (which, however, would not – at least initially – involve banning 'away' fans outright), the Football League was required, in autumn 1986, to produce its own proposals (the 'Fifty Percent' membership scheme was the League's response). The comprehensive 'ID Card Scheme' (as its opponents called it) that the Government preferred came under discussion again at the Federation Conference in 1987. Amongst some general support for the proposal (as we have seen), there was also talk of a 'National Federation' card that might come about, but objections to *any* form of compulsory membership card scheme were voiced by Frank Horrock of Manchester City. There still remained a strong feeling amongst many members that, if the Government were determined to introduce compulsory membership, the *Federation* should seek what advantage it could.

Following widespread (if largely unfounded) reports of gross misbehaviour amongst England's fans at the European Championship in Germany in 1988, the Government determined to legislate to enforce compulsory membership for all football supporters. Another Working Party was assembled in the summer to develop proposals, and no supporter representatives were included on it. It was soon clear that the Government's ideas would prove of very little benefit to Supporters' Clubs – in fact, it seemed that the 'national membership scheme' would completely bypass existing Supporters' Clubs. It could also greatly undermine many of them by providing 'parent' football clubs with an extensive database on their existing support. There were already many individuals within the Federation who were utterly opposed to any form of compulsory membership (whether the Federation 'benefited' or not) and, as it was now clear that the Government's proposals could severely damage its membership, the Federation came out in opposition to the 'I.D. Card Scheme'.

The Federation's relations with Government, beginning in the late 1960s through the good offices of Denis Howell MP, had provided the organisation with its first real opportunities to make some contribution on behalf of Supporters' Clubs to serious discussions about football's administration. (though admittedly their scope was largely limited to the hooliganism issue). These opportunities provoked some well-considered papers – like those from Manchester Utd's David Smith and Sunderland's Ian Todd – which Denis Howell clearly found useful. At Government meetings, Federation Officers found themselves alongside officials from the FA and FL, and there can be little doubt that Denis Howell's consideration of the Federation's interest helped lead to the first 'official' meetings between the Federation and the football authorities.

At local levels, some Supporters' Clubs clearly sought to liaise with police – and Celtic's Supporters' Association were proactive in developing liaison across national boundaries – but the Federation itself (at least in the 1970s) had few resources to deploy to meet the costs of such innovative developments. Perhaps private approaches to Government for funds were made by the Federation (using Denis Howell as a sounding-board?) but no official requests for grants appear to have been made by the Federation to any national body before the 1980s. Perhaps the organisations' officers presumed none would be forthcoming.

NOTES

1. See Chapter 1, 'Opening Accounts'.
2. See *The Supporter*, vol. 1, no. 1, October 1934, pp. 1–2.

3. See above, Chapter 4, 'The Renegades and the Respectables'.
4. Nat. Fed. AGM Minutes, 1953, pp. 10–12.
5. Nat. Fed. AGM Minutes, 1954, pp. 18–19.
6. Nat. Fed. AGM Minutes 1956, p. 15.
7. Ibid., p. 17.
8. Nat. Fed. AGM Minutes 1956, p. 17.
9. In 1960, the Federation twice sought meetings with the FA to discuss the lotteries issue but were refused. The FA also refused to supply a list of the clubs applying for consent to run their own schemes. See Nat. Fed. AGM Minutes, 1961.
10. The Chester Report, 1968.
11. See Nat. Fed. AGM Minutes, 1967, p. 67ff.
12. Ibid., pp. 68–9. For more on disputes with clubs, see below 'Supporter-Club Relations'.
13. The Chester Report, pp. 61–2.
14. Nat. Fed. AGM Minutes, 1969, p. 71. See also 'Crowd Behaviour at Football Matches', Report of the Ministry of Housing and Local Government, HM Stationery Office, 1969.
15. Nat. Fed. AGM Minutes, 1969, pp. 72–3.
16. Lord Wheatley Commission, 1971.
17. Nat. Fed. AGM Minutes, 1972.
18. For a detailed account of this, see below, Chapter 11, 'The Hooliganism Debate'.
19. For a summary of the Minutes of the Working Party meeting, see National Federation *Newsletter*, January 1976, pp. 11–12.
20. See above, Chapter 6, 'Relations with the Football Authorities'.
21. See National Federation *Newsletter*, March 1978, p. 6. For more on the Federation's attitude to corporal punishment, see below, 'The Hooliganism Debate'.
22. See Nat. Fed. AGM Minutes, 1982.
23. This writer remembers continuing informal complaints amongst Liverpool fans in the 1970s about this method of policing.
24. See *Conference Report*, May 1975, p. 50.
25. Ibid.
26. Nat. Fed. AGM Minutes, 1982, p. 21.
27. Nat. Fed. AGM Minutes, 1983, p. 44.
28. This topic will be considered in greater detail in Chapter 11, below: 'The Hooliganism Debate'.
29. For an account of this meeting, see National Federation *Newsletter*, March 1985, p. 8ff.
30. There were, however, many people within the Federation opposed to any idea of compulsory membership. When the Government did finally produce legislation to enforce membership (in 1988–89), the Federation, as a body, campaigned against the proposals (see Chapter 11).
31. It was the 'militant' Charlie Bent who proposed the motion; it was defeated. See Nat. Fed. AGM Minutes, 1985, p. 59.
32. See *Conference Reflections*, August 1985, pp. 10–11.

33. See Nat. Fed. AGM Minutes, 1986, p. 24.
34. For an account of the Luton scheme, see *House of Cards*, Sir Norman Chester Centre for Football Research, Leicester University.

8

SUPPORTER-CLUB RELATIONS

The (football) club seemed to think that the money the supporters had raised was their's by right. But it wasn't. It had been raised by a bona fide organisation and it belonged to that organisation. (Archie Gooch, President of the Federation, 1990)

In the years between the world wars, Supporters' Clubs had proliferated widely in relation to football played at both amateur and professional levels. For the vast majority of football clubs, save perhaps for only the richest, the fund-raising activities of their organised supporters were a vital component. The constraint on football clubs (both legal via state and 'moral' via FA regulation) forbidding their participation in 'gambling' schemes like lotteries or prize-draws, liberated the Supporters' Clubs, as voluntary organisations, to occupy a key role as fund-raisers for their 'parent' bodies; a role so significant that, as we have seen, over half of the existing Supporters' Clubs were fathered directly by the football clubs themselves. The organised supporters not only raised money but also provided a whole range of services free of charge, which contributed to the smooth running of match-days.[1]

On the pages of the surviving copies of *The Supporter* in 1934–35, the eye discovers no sign of arguments or disputes between the contributing Supporters' Clubs and their FCs. All seems sweetness and light, as supporters report on beavering away at building stands or dressing-rooms, raising summer wages or transfer fees, purchasing playing kits or goal-posts, producing and selling programmes, distributing cushions in the stands, running tea-bars, etc. But it may have been an *uncomfortable* feeling for many football clubs to rely so heavily on the 'help' provided; indeed, a very few clubs were so embarrassed by their dependent positions, that they offered one member (or more) of the supporters' committee a seat on the Board.[2] The bulk of clubs, however, managed to survive any discomfort without such concessions.

There may have been some football clubs who even *resented* the signifi-cance of the role organised supporters played. (In human affairs, it is not unknown for those 'helped' to despise their 'helpers', especially if the former feel unfairly constrained.) Part of the problem lay in the feeling of many football clubs that their Supporters' Clubs really *belonged* to the 'parent' bodies: that they were, in effect, a fund-raising arm of their private limited companies. This feeling was expressed in the most popular form of liaison – a club director or chairman would also chair or preside over the Supporters' Club.[3] The temptation to 'interfere' with the running of the Supporters' Club was enhanced by this traditional link and it failed to encourage the independent representation of supporters' interests.

In the period immediately following the Second World War, it seems that Supporters' Clubs once again took up the fund-raising and other roles they had been forced to relinquish in 1939 with the outbreak of war. Despite the huge popularity of the game in the late 1940s and the record-breaking attendances, the significance of supporter fund-raising remained high. There were, however, signs of cracks appearing in the traditional relationships which had characterised the pre-war decades. In 1948, the Reading SC representative reported on a breakdown in relations with his club. These sentiments were echoed by Federation Secretary, Leslie Davis:

> I experienced the same treatment some two years back . . . Many of we Secretaries have been in the game far too long to allow any Board of Directors to tell us how to run our Clubs . . . many football clubs are envying us our success and can find no other way to curb our progress than by fault-finding, attempted dictatorship of our policy, and eventual dissociation with our work . . .[4]

Mr Davis's reference to football clubs 'envying us our success' and wishing 'to curb our progress' perhaps signalled something of the resentment some clubs felt towards their organised supporters. Many clubs probably wished to be free of any 'obligation' such a dependent relationship might entail. From the viewpoint of the football clubs, the best thing would be for the legal situation surrounding fund-raising lottery schemes to be clarified and the FA regulations preventing their participation rescinded. This is pre-cisely what the clubs set out to accomplish in the 1950s.

In 1955–56, the Federation threw its entire weight behind a campaign to pass a new Lotteries Act. The Supporters' Clubs were urged and encour-aged by club directors and Federation officers to lobby local MPs in the cause.[5] When the Act was passed, Supporters' Clubs (for a brief period) enjoyed the unfettered right to run lotteries within the new legal para-meters – and therefore to strengthen their positions in relation to their 'parent' bodies. This freedom was short-lived for some. Within a few months of the legislation appearing on the statutes, disputes broke out between supporters and football clubs over the funds generated from lotteries.

In 1956, Bournemouth FC made an attempt to assume direct control of the supporters' funds.[6] Two years later, the Federation conference rang with complaints that 'jealous' football clubs were setting up 'rival' Supporters' Clubs to take over the running of lotteries.[7] One frequent point of dispute concerned the *percentage* of the money raised by supporters which was passed on to the 'parent' body. The attraction of football clubs for setting up their own 'official' Supporters' Club lay in the prospect of being in control of the funds entirely. In 1960, Federation Secretary, Tony Pullein, informed the assembled delegates of news which 'causes all of us considerable concern.' Apparently, it had been discovered that one item on a recent agenda for the Football League had involved discussion of a complete take-over of all lotteries by the League. This prospect, if realised, would mean 'the whole fabric of the Federation and Supporters' Clubs would be at an end'. Tony Pullein continued:

> We must be prepared to offer the strongest possible objection to something which you have made possible, and which has kept football going, being taken out of your hands . . . You are very quiet, and seem stunned by the news.[8]

It is entirely understandable that many Supporters' Club representatives should be 'stunned' by the prospect of football clubs taking over entirely the running of fund-raising schemes. Had they not fought vigorously to see the Lotteries Act through Parliament to clear the way for *Supporters' Clubs* to continue this traditional activity? Had not the emotional weight of so many parliamentary speeches in favour of the Act been centred upon the depiction of *plucky supporters* volunteering their free time to raise money for their beloved club? Had they not been exhorted by football club directors to establish once and for all *the Supporters' Clubs' right* to pursue these activities? Indeed, they had; but now it was becoming clear that, under the rising commercial pressures on football in the 1960s, numerous clubs would have no compunction about taking over the lotteries and depriving many Supporters' Clubs of their raison d'être.

The fundamental problem facing Supporters' Clubs was that they, for so long, had seen themselves almost *entirely within the context that football clubs had provided.* Now that context was changing or being abandoned in the face of new developments, many had little else to fall back on. They had rarely seen their role as one of *representing* the generality of supporters to their Clubs – it was all about raising money, organising travel and developing facilities for their members. If the football club appointed a commercial manager with a brief to establish an 'official' Supporters' Club with precisely those functions, what was left for these traditional groups of organised fans to do?

Twelve months after the League's discussions about taking over lotteries, Tony Pullein broke the news to Federation conference delegates that the FA was now prepared to give consent to football clubs applying to run their own schemes. The Federation twice sought meetings with the FA but the latter refused to discuss the matter or to provide any information about what was happening.[9] The news was received with gloom by many of the Supporters' Club representatives present.

As the new decade wore on, disputes between Supporters' Clubs and their 'parent' bodies multiplied. The Federation's Legal Advice system began to collapse under the strain. The Federation normally retained a solicitor to provide member clubs with assistance – and during the 1950s he was usually on hand at conferences to report on the year's activities and answer queries. In the early 1960s, however, he rarely appeared, and instead sent communications which indicated his increasing difficulty dealing with the number of requests for help. He suggested 'a younger man' might be found for the role and resigned in 1963.[10]

The Federation felt a considerable threat to its structure as the traditional foundations of Supporters' Clubs began to tremble. The Secretary described 1963 as 'one of the most critical years in the entire history of Supporters' Clubs' – a sentiment repeated in one form or another with annual regularity for the next ten years.[11] By 1964, disputes between SCs and their FCs were so numerous that Federation members called for the setting up of a permanent 'liaison committee' to intercede between the warring parties.[12] There was considerable bitterness emerging, particularly amongst long-standing supporters' committee members, who found themselves not only 'brushed aside as unwanted anachronisms' but also *deprived of access* to facilities and amenities which they themselves had built years before. So many of the traditional relationships between SCs and FCs had been based on 'goodwill' alone. They were rarely *institutionalised* relationships involving properly formed agreements. When supporters raised money to build club-rooms, refreshment bars – even 'wash and brush-up' facilities (as at Luton Town) – *inside* the football ground, to whom did these amenities actually belong? Without any written agreements, when the 'goodwill' dissolved (i.e. when the club no longer required a voluntary body as a fund-raising arm) possession became the full nine-tenths of the law, and supporters found themselves barred from the very facilities they had paid to construct.

At Coventry City in 1964–65, the Supporters' Club financed the construction of extensive premises for their members, located in the Sky Blue Stand, to a cost of £27,587 (more than a quarter of a million pounds in modern terms). The organised fans also took responsibilities for a much bigger sum: the £41,000 overdraft on the Sky Blue Stand itself. As news began to circulate amongst Coventry fans about the difficulties some Supporters' Clubs were encountering – and realising that 'we never owned a brick of it' – the Coventry SC began to worry about the strength of the 'gentlemen's' agreement' which gave them access to their own premises.

> We asked for some security of tenure . . . we were learning from the problems other clubs had . . . Jimmy Hill refused to give us security of tenure . . . we'd built every brick . . . its *our* ground . . . we were the workhorses, the Club had taken all our money . . . it was the straw that broke the camel's back . . . So we struck out on our own . . . eventually built our own club outside the ground in 1978 . . . (The Football Club) . . . set up the Sky Blue Club with a puppet committee – not elected like us – it was a 'social committee' there to do what it was told . . . In the early 1980s, we approached the Club because we were struggling financially. We hoped in the light of the huge financial contributions we'd made in the past, they would help us . . . We were *begging*. We got nothing . . . we don't hate the *team* – we're supporters, you know – but the Club hierarchy, well their attitude never changes does it?[13]

As the Supporters' Club network shuddered under the impact of new commercial developments at football clubs, Federation officers sought to stabilise the structure by outlining possible future roles for supporters clubs. They had some difficulty, however, in seeing *beyond* the traditional fund-raising role the SCs had occupied for so long. In 1965, Federation Secretary, Tony Pullein, sought first to emphasise the unavoidable new reality that members must face:

> At one time it was our proud boast that football couldn't survive without the aid of Supporters' Clubs. That statement is no longer entirely true. True, only *supporters* keep the game alive but it is not necessarily the *Supporters' Clubs* that are the backbone of the game today.[14]

In the face of this reality, Mr Pullein argued, the Federation should seek to negotiate at first with the Football League, and later the FA, a businesslike arrangement which would standardise the relationship between supporters' clubs and their 'parent' bodies – a 'code of conduct' to be observed by both sides. In short, Supporters' Clubs would guarantee to raise a given sum of money per annum and receive in return access to the facilities they needed or had developed. (In other words, the supporters should pay a rent for premises which they had provided the capital to build in the first place.) As far as Mr Pullein could see, raising *more* money for the football clubs was the only way to ameliorate the situation:

> . . . the only possible way we can retain our strength and build is to take the lead in the fundraising world. In football, as in any other industry, money counts.[15]

There were clearly a number of problems with this argument. In the first place, many SCs had been raising money for fifty years or more, without succeeding in establishing any proper, institutionalised relationship with their clubs. (As Tony Pullein admitted in his speech, 'Some have been striving for years to obtain official recognition from parent bodies'.) Secondly, many SCs – like Coventry – could hardly swallow the bitter pill of raising money now to pay some sort of 'rent' for (what they saw as) their *own* premises. Finally, the kind of negotiations with the League and FA that were envisaged as a basis for an agreed 'code of conduct' could not take place anyway, as *no official relationship existed between the Federation and these football authorities*. In fact, Tony Pullein got the cart firmly before the horse when he suggested at the end of his speech that if the Federation *could* possibly 'bring about a proper understanding' between FCs and SCs, the organisation would

> be held in much higher esteem generally and it would give us some standing for negotiating . . . whereas at the moment our efforts are recognised only unofficially.[16]

Perhaps fifteen (or even thirty) years previously, the Federation might have been in a better position to negotiate from strength. As one delegate from Leyton Orient put it, in the opening of the debate on the 'Future of Supporters' Clubs' that afternoon in 1965:

> The question of the future . . . is one which should concern all of us deeply . . . But I'm not putting all the blame on to the parent clubs. I feel that much of the blame lies with us. We have been, in the past, too apathetic . . . too much going cap-in-hand to parent clubs . . .[17]

The new developments at football clubs could create a terrible confusion for some delegates. The representative of Workington Town SC described the strange identity crisis which had overtaken his life:

> I have to stand here . . . because I do not know where I am. Three or four years ago the Workington directors sacked the Supporters' Club of which I had been a member for 20 years . . . But the committee asked if I would become President because they felt it could be saved. Just a few weeks ago, after having led the rebels, and the directors themselves having brought into being their own supporters' club . . . they asked me to become chairman. I am still President of the rebels. But I am now also Chairman of the Club's own club . . .[18]

For the Gainsborough Trinity supporter, it was incomprehensible that SCs should find themselves in such difficult straits with their clubs. For their part at Gainsborough, they had contributed over £60,000 to their club in recent years and they enjoyed 'excellent relations' with the 'parent' body. Surely it was just a case of needing 'to get round the table a little more and thrash out your difficulties?' (At this point the Coventry representative interceded to say that his FC thought 'good relations' amounted to: 'Keep your ruddy nose out of our business and we'll run yours for you'.[19]) The Everton member sought to remind delegates that his club 'has never needed our money' but had 'recognised' the supporters' club none the less as an organisation 'that will uphold our parent body's reputation'. Corby Town pointed out that most of the clubs represented in the Federation were 'non-League or small clubs' – and it was at this level that innovations could be attempted. The delegate from St Neots Town agreed and described the recent developments at his club, following a decade of 'constantly fighting the football club'. A joint 'finance committee' had been formed, consisting of six members of the FC and four of the SC. All the accounts went through this committee, whether it concerned expenditure by either body, and it proved so successful that a similarly constituted 'management committee' was subsequently established. Such a structure was, suggested the St Neots man, 'the solution to this problem'.[20]

Unfortunately for many of the Supporters' Clubs present, such a solution was already beyond the bounds of reality. A substantial number were currently engaged in bitter wrangles about usurpatory 'official' SCs formed by football clubs to take over fund-raising. The Federation itself was facing difficult decisions. Its own rules required that membership be open 'to all properly constituted Supporters' Clubs' who apply. 'Properly constituted' appeared to mean that (at least) some of the SC committee must be elected at a public meeting, but it seems that football clubs could get round this provision in a variety of ways, and the Federation found itself facing applications for membership from some of the new 'official' clubs that were directly rivalling the traditional ones still in membership of the Federation. A case in point, in 1965, was that of QPR FC and its Supporters' Club – a case worth considering in detail as it was typical of many, and the QPR supporters were one of the first groups in later years to form an 'independent' organisation themselves.[21]

The QPR delegate at the 1965 conference read a lengthy statement to the assembly. It had been prepared in response to the Federation's Executive Council decision to accept into membership the 'Queens Park Rangers Sportsmen's Association' (QPRSA). The delegate began by reminding those present that his club – originally the QPRSC but now known as the Rangers SC – had joined the Federation in 1938 and had continued in membership ever since. In 1962–63, a disagreement had broken out between the SC and FC centring (as did so many disputes) upon the latter's demand to assume control of the 'pools scheme' run by the supporters. The FC promptly 'threw out' the SC and immediately set up its own 'official' version: the QPRSA. Early in 1965, the Secretary of the Football Club, Mr Smith, contacted the still functioning Rangers SC to offer a deal that would allow the new 'official' club to become a member of the Federation. What the proposal actually amounted to was a merger or amalgamation of QPRSA and the Rangers SC. It was an offer of some interest to the original organisers until they learnt of the details of the proposal. The supporters suggested to Mr Smith that *both* committees should resign; a public meeting should be held to form the new body, and a new committee be elected by those present. This suggestion turned out to be unacceptable to Mr Smith who insisted on a guarantee that all existing committee members of the QPRSA would pass unopposed on to the new committee. This in turn was refused as 'unconstitutional' and when the original organisers asked if a 'veto' over supporters' committee decisions would be operated, Mr Smith affirmed that the board of directors would retain a right to veto. Clearly, for the Rangers SC supporters, Mr Smith's proposal was beyond the pale.

But why should Mr Smith and QPRFC *want* their 'official' club affiliated to the Federation in the first place? (There were few obvious advantages to the club.) As the plot thickened, it turned out that the 'official' club was desperately short of active members and had sought to recruit some 30 or 40 members of the Rangers SC who played in supporters' football teams. (This ruse may have been part of a wider strategy to give the 'official' club more of a semblance of a 'real' Supporters' Club – and therefore make it more attractive to QPR supporters.) To tempt these supporter players, generous 'expenses' were offered (and accepted) – but Rangers SC had known nothing of this until the news appeared as a 'fait accompli' in the club programme. The problem for Mr Smith and the FC was that the supporter players they had subvened were in teams which played in the *Federation's* Sunday Football League. They had been promised that this could continue, hence the necessity to arrange some form of 'affiliation' with the Federation!

Subsequently, the QPRSA 'secretary' (a club director) made a formal application via Tony Pullein for membership of the Federation; Mr Pullein informed the Rangers SC and asked if they had any objection. Despite their lodging, as one might imagine, a vigorous protest at such a proposal, the Rangers SC heard shortly afterwards that the new 'official' supporters' club had been accepted into the Federation. They were livid. As the QPR supporters' statement argued, this was not a serious matter just for themselves, but represented a real threat to the independence of the Federation itself:

> . . . it is well known these days that football clubs are increasingly anxious to take full control over their Supporters' Clubs. If this is ever achieved and those controlled Supporters' Clubs are allowed into the Federation, it could . . . materialise that the Federation itself was controlled by the football clubs.[22]

Following this statement, the Cardiff City delegate briefly outlined his own club's position – one not dissimilar from QPR's – where the new 'official' SC had its Chairman, Treasurer and Secretary appointed from the Board, and the Spurs representative (rather prophetically) reminded the assembly that these circumstances could develop anywhere. It was clear that, at least from the floor of the conference, many Federation members thought it simply wrong to allow *another* Supporters' Club into membership when the 'old' one was still around (regardless of whether the former was 'properly constituted' or not). The Executive, however, felt differently. Its concern, as expressed by Tony Pullein, was that, as an increasing number of club-sponsored, 'official' SCs appeared, if the Federation refused them representation, it would become itself more and more an 'unofficial' organisation. What was more, there were no rules forbidding 'double representation' providing the applicants fulfilled the basic requirement of being 'properly constituted'. Finally – and possibly most significantly – the Federation had *always* been a body which included 'official' Supporters' Clubs. As Mr Pullein reminded the conference, half the current membership of the Federation consisted of Supporters' Clubs that 'were formed at the suggestion of the football club'.[23]

It was clearly a ticklish problem. Supporters' Clubs were rapidly dividing up into two types: one which raised money via lottery schemes, etc. (and which was now, more often than not, run directly by the football club); and another which performed the 'social' functions of a club, offering a meeting-place, perhaps organising 'away' travel and football teams for member supporters. In 1966, Tony Pullein was still grappling with the issues involved and seeking to offer the Federation a way to deal with them. The previous years' debate about the two clubs at QPR had forced the Executive to re-examine its admission of the 'official' version (QPRSA) into Federation membership. It turned out that, on enquiry, the new club had *not* been 'properly constituted' (there had been no properly advertised inaugural meeting) and consequently the QPRSA was expelled.

A draft plan for the future was put to the 1966 conference in an effort to sort out the general issues. Mr Pullein suggested that 'the only ultimate solution' would involve the creation of 'two types of membership of the Federation – one for the officially recognised Supporters' Club; one for the club concentrating on social activities.' He outlined three typical circumstances which were occurring with increasing frequency:

(a) The FC's appetite for money grows beyond the point where it can be satisfied by the Supporters' Club's fund-raising efforts. The FC therefore forms another, subsidiary organisation (which may work in harmony with the SC).

(b) A dispute breaks out between FC and SC. The latter refuse to make *any* 'donations' and the FC creates its own club to raise money. If and when the dispute is resolved, the FC is already committed to support its own official club.

(c) The original SC 'through lack of new blood' gradually deteriorates to the point where it no longer performs 'the accepted tasks' and the FC therefore launches its own SC.

Tony Pullein then suggested the appropriate response from the Federation to each of those possible circumstances:

> If (a) then the Federation should *accept* the new SC (providing it was 'properly constituted'). Loyalty to the old SC should not turn into extended sympathy. 'There is no place for sympathy in a virile organisation.'
>
> If (b) the Federation should *still* admit the new SC (if 'properly constituted') according to the 'law of logic'. There was a Federation rule (Rule Six) which gave the Executive power to expel any member club which acted against the best interests of the Federation or against '*the Parent club to which it is attached*'. Mr Pullein argued that, if a Supporters' Club was *refusing to donate money*, it was 'indeed acting in a manner detrimental to the parent club whatever its motives for withholding payment'.
>
> If (c) the Federation must look very closely at the SC in question to decide whether it still functioned properly.[24]

The General Secretary recommended these suggestions for consideration by delegates in the sure knowledge that these issues would re-emerge at subsequent conferences. Though Tony Pullein's 'draft plan' expressed the feeling of the Executive, clearly many Federation members were unhappy with much of it. From the Federation's traditional position, there was a certain logic to Tony Pullein's plan. Supporters' clubs run (to all intents and purposes) by their football clubs were the very stuff of which the Federation had been made. As Tony Pullein argued, 'many supporters' clubs have the same officials as the football clubs they support'. ('Parent club' was no misnomer.) Consequently these Supporters' Clubs had hardly been constituted to represent the interests of the supporters (if necessary) *against* their football club. By the same token, the Federation was not there to act similarly for Supporters' Clubs *against* the football authorities. It was there 'To Help and Not To Hinder'; indeed, as Rule Six stated, if a member club acted against the interests (however defined) *of its football club*, it could be expelled from the Federation. In other words, the Federation was not geared up to fight on the very issue which most concerned its members. It could (and did) use the 'good offices' of its senior officials to intercede in disputes. (Archie Gooch, Federation Chairman at the time – and later to become Chairman of Bristol City FC – was a successful businessman with some contacts amongst football club directors.) But *the logic of the Federation's history demanded that it accept the new 'official' clubs into membership*, even if the latter were elbowing

out old members of long standing from Federation ranks. The organisation's rules offered no resistance to the new 'official' clubs, providing they
fulfilled the basic requirements of proper constitution. Nevertheless, it
rankled with many of the representatives of Supporters' Clubs within the
Federation. These developments triggered the steep decline in membership which ran through the following decade and more. For many member
clubs simply dropped away, seeing little point in remaining in the
Federation – whilst the majority of new official clubs sponsored by the
football clubs saw little point in joining it.

There were exceptions to the general air of dissatisfaction which prevailed
amongst Federation members. Not all football clubs negotiated the fund-
raising transitions without sympathy for the traditional supporters' clubs,
and some of the latter were just so *efficient* at running schemes that their
football clubs knew they could do no better. At Aldershot Town, for
example, the SC raised £124,000 in the fifteen years prior to 1976, and it was
currently stumping up £20,000 a year. The SC Chairman had been recently
elected (1967) to the Board of Directors, an elevation of which he felt 'very
proud'.[25] Similarly at Wrexham FC, both the past and the current Chairman
of the SC had been elected on to the Board. At Fulham too, the club had
negotiated with some skill the change-over of responsibility for running the
lotteries, and the Supporters' Club was happy to take a part and enjoy
certain rights and privileges.[26] These examples serve to show that it *was*
eminently possible to manage skilfully what were often inevitable changes,
forced by the commercial revolution which the 1960s heralded. The provision (at Aldershot, Wrexham and a few other clubs) of *board representation*
for the old SC was a sensible and sensitive way of recognising and paying
tribute to the heroic efforts which many Supporters' Club members had put
in. If those perennial fund-raising contributions from individual SCs were
added together, they would, in all probability, amount to more than the
money contributed by many serving directors. In a sense, the supporters had
bought the right of board representation without even considering the
myriad other ways in which organised supporters had helped their football
clubs. The outstanding fact is the *rarity* of some form of proper recognition
of the role supporters had played. It seems that football was so poorly
managed and administered that, during the 1960s, at a time when crowd
disturbances and misbehaviour were rising to crisis proportions, it managed
to alienate and abuse the very organisations from which relationships with
supporters could be developed and improved.

A more typical example of the way old-style Supporters' Clubs were
dealt with by their football clubs was provided, in 1967, in a vivid account
from the Ipswich Town representative:

> Some of us have served the game in supporters' associations for over 30 years
> . . . I was on the amateur committee before professionalism was introduced at

Ipswich and negotiated with the professional body. We also have three members who have each served over 30 years on this committee . . . Two years ago we gave the football club £42,000 in twelve months. That was the year they started their own competition (i.e. lottery). We have done everything they have asked of us . . . We have paid for everything on the football ground: the stands, the offices and the dressing rooms . . . We have never tried to dictate their policy . . . but . . . tried to look after our own business. That is perhaps where we have gone wrong. Two years ago . . . their policy suddenly changed . . . They told us to cut off our social club and to stop running our bingo because it clashed with theirs, which we did. When we started a new competition, they told us in writing that we must not start any further competitions unless they tell us . . . Without warning, a notice appeared in the press saying that they no longer recognised our Supporters' Club and a new one had been formed . . . This came as a complete surprise. We went to the Boardroom and were given our notice – the secretary and myself after 31 years and 35 years service. We were not thanked . . . we did not ask for thanks and we certainly did not get them . . .[27]

This was hardly even basic 'public relations' from the football club towards a group of Ipswich Town supporters of whom Archie Gooch himself insisted, 'there is not a better organised or more business-like group of people anywhere'.[28]

Within the next few years, many similar stories were recounted by Supporters' Club officials. Federation Chairman, Gooch, spoke of 'evidence of many clubs which have been disowned by their parent body'.[29] At the 1969 conference, the Bedford Town delegate told his tale of woe:

. . . we have experienced this very bad thing of being thrown off the football ground. I think this is due to the FA . . . they gave the board of directors the chance to run their own fund-raising schemes. So what did the board of directors do? They looked around and said, 'Supporters' Clubs, fund-raising machines. Right, we'll take them over' . . . From 1950, to 1965 when we were kicked off the ground, we have given our football club in cash and kind over £175,000 . . . Every single building on Bedford Town football ground was built by Bedford Town Supporters' Club with their money that they raised . . .[30]

Some SCs – notably Northampton Town and Norwich City – could alternatively claim that they had been well treated by their parent bodies. But, as the delegate from Bath City was keen to point out, so much depended on the *personalities* involved on the club's board. Harmonious relations (of which Bath City had a long history) could collapse with changes of personnel:

It's all right to say that you are getting on well with your directors, but the point is these directors could very well change within the course of twelve months . . . As regards Bath City, we have put thousands and thousands into our parent body even though we are only a small club. In the last five years, we have paid off our floodlights which cost us £12,000; we built a clubhouse which cost just over £4,000 . . . and in the meantime we are also making donations to the club. Only last season we actually sold our houses in order to keep the club afloat yet we were given ten weeks notice to close our own clubhouse because the parent body wanted to build theirs . . . We put our new plans to the directors that we would build this (new) clubhouse; we would form a joint committee to run it; we would want a lease; they agreed on all these things; and within two weeks there were headlines in the paper that the Club were going to do this and we were ruled out of it completely . . . the only participation we have now is just to go in and help run the bingo . . . How can you trust people who treat you in the way we have been treated at Bath?[31]

The absence of proper, written agreements between SCs and FCs meant that little could be done in law to defend the supporters' organisations whose 'property' was confiscated on the grounds that it was *inside* the football ground. None the less, the Federation launched a 'Legal Fund' (with around £600 in it in 1969) with the intention of picking a case to fight. The easy-going, hopeful – and essentially *trusting* – relationships which characterised the supporters' leaders and their FCs in the past had left the 'parent' bodies unconstrained. The legions of councillors, aldermen and justices of the peace who set the tone of those relationships were either too easily manipulated or simply too unquestioning to look ahead and protect their members' interests. As Archie Gooch recognised:

We are, to a great extent, to blame for the situation we are in. We have been an affable – a lot of affable societies – handing money out ad lib . . .[32]

In reality, there was now little the Federation could do to prevent so many Supporters' Clubs 'being toppled like ninepins' as the commercial managers moved in to run 'development associations' and 'official' clubs.[33] In 1970, with the impending establishment of the Association of Football League Commercial Managers, it was clear that soon most fund-raising activity would be under the umbrella of another organisation, though Federation officers still urged further fund-raising efforts from Supporters' Clubs. There was legal action taken in at least one case (but not funded by the Federation). It was at Corby Town, when in 1973, the Football Club went bankrupt and was only rescued after the Supporters' Club raised £12,500 to pull it round. The British Steel Corporation (BSC) held a majority of shares in Corby Town FC and also (more significantly) owned the ground on which the team played. Following the supporters' rescue of the club, BSC demanded a sudden and massive increase in the 'rent' of the premises the SC had themselves built earlier inside the ground. BSC wanted £10,000 a year plus 75 per cent of the net profits on the bar in the premises.[34] The supporters refused and instigated legal proceedings, eventually winning their case.[35]

In the Federation, moves to include a 'wider cross-section' of supporters' organisations continued in the early 1970s. In 1971, a suggestion emerged to add the words 'and Associations' on to the end of the Federation's full title. The suggestion was not accepted.[36]

Disputes at football clubs continued to break out but in general, only those Supporters' Clubs with written agreements survived with their club premises intact. Football clubs could be quite unscrupulous in their efforts to outmanoeuvre even those SC's with contracts in writing. As Archie Gooch recalled (in 1990) at Bristol City where he himself had been the Board's Chairman earlier, a dispute developed over the 'rent' of SC premises inside the ground. The supporters had built the facilities themselves at a cost of £40,000 and paid a nominal £1 a year rent. They subsequently spent a further £25,000 on improvements, but eventually the Board wanted the supporters out and demanded £15,000 a year rent. By then, Mr Gooch was no longer involved with the Board but was a trustee of the Supporters' Club. Consequently, he was invited to intervene. He argued from the Landlord and Tenants Act that it was simply unjust to seek to raise a rent by 15,000 times, but:

> . . . the Club were very devious – they got all the ground staff and the directors to join the Supporters' Club . . . to overthrow the committee . . . but they failed and in the end it all worked out alright.[37]

One of Mr Gooch's attempted interventions almost led to a libel action against him. In 'the early 1970s' Yeovil Town FC were broke. They did not even have the money to pay for the team's travel to its next match. The Supporters' Club, however, had a few thousand pounds in the bank and the FC desperately wanted it. Mr Gooch was invited to attend a crucial meeting between the Supporters' Committee and half a dozen directors. The supporters complained that, though the FC wanted their money now, it had never listened to their requests nor took sufficient concern for them in the past. In a private meeting with the supporters, Archie Gooch persuaded them to hand over the £2,000 to the club in return for a promise of much greater co-operation in future.

> This was on Friday. On Monday, they threw the Supporters' Club out. I was contacted by the local press (and) I called it a confidence trick . . . and promptly received a letter from their solicitors threatening libel . . . You see, the Club seemed to think that the money the supporters had raised was theirs by right. But it wasn't. It had been raised by a bona fida organisation and it belonged to that organisation.[38]

The piecemeal dismemberment of the old network of Supporters' Clubs continued throughout the 1970s, in tandem with a steep decline in membership of the Federation. Without their traditional raison d'être, many Supporters' Clubs just disintegrated or became wholly incorporated into the commercial development of their football clubs. Even down at the Isthmian and Southern League levels, the football clubs themselves increasingly took over the lotteries and organised travel to 'away' matches on a commercial basis.[39] If fund-raising had been one of the great foundations upon which Supporters' Clubs were built, the organisation of 'away' travel had been the other. The simultaneous removal of both these fundamental functions often proved a mortal blow.

The commercialisation of organising 'away' travel was deeply resented. In 1978, Ian Todd contrasted the different attitudes of the old Supporters' Clubs and the new development and travel associations, co-ordinated by commercial managers:

> . . . the aim of the Supporters' Club run by supporters was to get as many as possible to see their team play; the Supporters' Clubs run by commercial managers aim to make the maximum amount of money out of supporters.[40]

In many instances, the organising of 'away' travel by football clubs was less efficient and more likely to include known 'trouble-makers' than when organised by supporters themselves. Archie Gooch noted at Bristol City FC that, following the Club's take-over of the Travel Club,

> . . . the Parent Club allowed anybody on payment of a small fee and took passengers whom the Supporters' Club would never have allowed near coaches.[41]

Previously, the supporter-run Travel Club had been trouble free.

Some football clubs ended up with no Supporters' Club at all; others spawned new style 'Independent' associations.[42] For those traditional SCs that survived the upheavals of the 1970s, some managed to develop reasonably amicable relations with their, commercially-expanded football clubs, while for others hardly any contact existed at all. Very often, it seems, harmonious relationships could be disrupted by changes amongst the club's directors. This might also work in reverse: at Aldershot FC, where the SC had been excommunicated in the 1970s (despite its previous representation on the Board!), a new Board of Directors took over in the early 1980s and re-instated the old supporters' committee.[43]

In 1986, the Federation Secretary, Malcolm Gamlen, described the membership as consisting of '150 affiliated clubs, over a third of whom support Football League teams'.[44] Just over thirty League Clubs were represented at conference that year, and it seems that some of those that did not attend no longer felt very enthusiastic about their membership:

Today, we only pay lip-service to it. We don't send any representatives anymore . . . The Federation is struggling for lack of support, really.[45]

Those that did attend conference heard an enlightened (if occasionally confused) account from Wallace Mercer, Chairman of Hearts FC, about his 'new deal' for supporters at Tynecastle. Mercer had taken over the struggling Hearts Club in the early 1980s – at a cost of around half a million pounds in cash – and had been immediately struck by the poor links between the club and its fans. He quickly appointed 'a director responsible for fan relationship' with a view to encouraging contacts with the 'customers':

We have tried to turn Heart of Midlothian into the people's club . . . no one can actually own a football club . . . I tried to approach (it) as a community project . . . In reality you're only acting as a custodian of the social interest . . . I'm quite ruthless . . . People may say it's autocratic, but sometimes one needs a degree of democratic autocracy . . .[46]

Under Mercer, the club sought to encourage the formation of a network of Supporters' Clubs and 'developed very aggressively' a Juniors Club with a current membership of over 1,500 youngsters. The Hearts Chairman thought football clubs should 'actively encourage fan responsibility . . . (and) . . . re-invest money in developing Supporters' Clubs.' The supporters are 'the most valuable tool that the club has' and, as far as Board representation went, 'they must make their own decision', though he was not sure of the benefits. Finally, Wallace Mercer restated his perception that 'ownership' of a football club gave a position with local obligations: 'I felt that you have got a social obligation to use that platform.'[47]

Five years on, the network of Supporters' Clubs associated with Hearts FC has evolved an effective institutionalised relationship with the club. In an account of that relationship provided in 1991,[48] it appears that there are currently forty-five member clubs of 'The Federation of Hearts Supporters Clubs'. These forty-five elect a committee of eight members – four Executive officers and four others – with no more than one committee member allowed to come from any particular member club. There are regular, monthly meetings at which two delegates from each member club meet with the committee. The latter maintains 'direct access, two way' to the Board 'by phone, by letter, any time'. The shareholders' association is one of the member clubs. There is a once a season meeting of the ninety delegates with the Chairman and his Board, and an annual meeting between the executive committee and the Board. The director specifically appointed to deal with 'supporter-relations' usually attends the monthly meetings.

The Hearts Federation meets annually with the local police, sits on the post-Taylor Report 'Advisory Group' for Tynecastle; produces its own fanzine and uses a page in the match-day programme. Members receive a ticket allocation (after shareholders and season-ticket holders) for 'big' games. Yet the Hearts Federation remains entirely independent of its football club – just as each member club is also independent of the Federation, according to its constitutional rules.

From the outside – and in contrast to much that prevails elsewhere – the Supporters' Club relationship at Hearts FC seems admirable (though Wallace Mercer may not be so popular with Hibs supporters [49]). It certainly illustrates how these relationships *can* be managed with respect and imagination on both sides. Unfortunately for the history of relations between Supporters' Clubs and their 'parent' bodies in England – especially during the difficult transitional period in the 1960s and 1970s – very few attempts were made to accomplish the changes with skill and sympathy. At the time, the National Federation was ill-equipped, impotent and too confused about its role to negotiate these changes effectively. Though efforts were made by individual officers, without some genuine care and concern from the football clubs, little progress was achieved. As a result, the Supporters' Club movement almost collapsed.

In retrospect, by the mid-1960s, the time had long gone for the kind of negotiations from strength that Federation members called for. It might have been possible, either in pre-war times when Supporters' Clubs were contributing such huge sums of money, or even in the late 1940s and 1950s when, at first, the Federation contained hundreds of member clubs with up to one million football fans inside them. If then, the Federation officers could have pulled the membership together to demand some proper relationship with their clubs and appropriate representation to the FA and League – or else no more 'donations' would be forthcoming – they might have pulled it off. If they had been prepared to 'hinder' a little, in between so much 'helping', perhaps some real purchase could have been gained on the football authorities. The difficulty was always that the supporters often valued – even loved – their own particular clubs too highly for their own best interests. They saw it as their first duty to 'support' and hoped thereby to gain their 'parent's' esteem. They trusted and hoped their clubs would treat them decently. In response – and especially when the commercial 'crunch' came – most football clubs quite simply traded on their affections. The supporters were sold down the river which flowed from their own overpowering loyalty.

NOTES

1. See Chapter 3, 'The Fund-raisers and their Football Clubs'.
2. See Chapter 3, ibid.

3. See Chapter 3, ibid.
4. Nat. Fed. AGM Minutes, 1948.
5. For more on the campaign, see chapter 7, 'Relations with Government and Police'.
6. Nat. Fed. AGM Minutes, 1956.
7. Ibid., 1958, p. 12ff.
8. Ibid., 1960, p. 26.
9. Ibid., 1961.
10. Ibid., 1962.
11. Ibid., 1963, p. 17.
12. Ibid., 1964, p. 15.
13. Personal interview, Jim Hamill, current President, Coventry SC. Recorded 27 February 1990.
14. Nat. Fed. AGM Minutes, 1965, p. 12.
15. Ibid., 1965, p. 12.
16. Ibid., 1965, p. 14.
17. Ibid., 1965, pp. 45–6.
18. Ibid., 1965, p. 47.
19. Ibid., 1965, pp. 47–8.
20. Ibid., 1965, p. 50.
21. The Queens Park Rangers Loyal Supporters' Association (QPRLSA).
22. Nat. Fcd. AGM Minutes, 1965, p. 59.
23. Ibid., 1965, p. 61.
24. For the full account of Tony Pullein's 'draft plan' see Nat. Fed. AGM Minutes, 1966, pp. 13–14. (My emphasis).
25. Ibid., 1967, p. 69.
26. Ibid., 1967, p. 71.
27. Ibid., 1967, pp. 69–70.
28. Ibid., 1967, p. 71.
29. Ibid., 1969, p. 80.
30. Ibid., 1969, p. 81.
31. Ibid., 1969, p. 83. It is difficult to know precisely what the Bath City delegate means when he states, 'we actually sold our houses in order to keep the club afloat'. It might refer to property bought from supporters' club funds and used to house players.
32. Nat. Fed. AGM Minutes, 1969, p. 81.
33. Ibid., 1970, p. 28.
34. Ibid., 1978, p. 13.
35. Ibid., 1979, pp. 25–6.
36. Ibid., 1973, p. 30ff.
37. Personal interview, Archie Gooch. Recorded 23 January 1990.
38. Ibid.
39. See 'Federation must open its doors', by Tony Pullein in National Federation *Newsletter*, September 1978, pp. 5–6.
40. Nat. Fed. AGM Minutes, 1978, p. 19.
41. National Federation *Newsletter*, March 1985, p. 7.
42. These became part of the 'Alternative Football Network'.
43. National Federation *Newsletter*, March 1985, p. 6.

44. Nat. Fed. AGM Minutes, 1985, p. 13.
45. Personal interview, Jim Hamill, 1990.
46. Nat. Fed. AGM Minutes, 1985, pp. 71–2.
47. Ibid., 1985, p. 74.
48. Personal communication. I am grateful to Hearts Federation Secretary, Alex Jones, for his account of the relations to his club.
49. Mr Mercer recently led an unsuccesful attempt to merge Hearts and Hibs.

9

ATTEMPTS AT INTERNATIONAL RELATIONS

Today everyone knows what a power – a friendly power – the Federation has become in the football world . . . we should now go forward and promote an International Federation of Football Supporters' Clubs. (Talbot Nanson, Mayor of Brighton and Federation Chairman, 1948)

From the formation of the Federation in 1927, to the outbreak of war in 1939, there is little evidence in the organisation's surviving documents of any real interest in making contacts with football fans of other nations. Perhaps in this the supporters within the Federation reflected accurately the insularity of British football at the time; its isolation from FIFA and World Cup competitions. International affairs are mentioned but twice in the available editions of *The Supporter*, between 1934–35. In one column, subheaded: 'A peep into the future', the prospect of air-travel for football teams – sparked by the recent arrival by plane in London of the German national side – is discussed. Apparently one or two English clubs which regularly faced long journeys to League matches (like Plymouth Argyle) had sought to organise air-travel but the FA 'had placed its taboo on the plan'. Interestingly, remarks by Major Frank Buckley of Wolverhampton Wanderers (one of the first English clubs to seek entry into European competitions some twenty years later) indicate discussions of an 'International League', consisting presumably of *national* sides playing mid-week fixtures, with air-travel a necessary component of the organisation.[1]

In another article, in 1935, the topic of 'substitutes' was aired under the headline, 'Continental Idea Which Would Not Work'. It betrays a somewhat chauvinistic attitude towards what are seen as 'suspect' tactics deployed by European sides using substitutes. The writer – 'A Student of the Game' – fears the difficulties administrators might face distinguishing between players genuinely injured and those merely 'tired', and concludes that the practice of substitutions should not be allowed in English League football. There is, after all, the writer insists: 'Little wrong with the Game' as it is (in Britain).[2]

The Second World War and the subsequent international developments which led to the formation of the United Nations had a significant impact on Federation attitudes. In 1948 – a time of great optimism in the football world as the game's popularity reached new heights – the Federation conference was a buoyant affair. Members were not only celebrating the organisation's 21st Anniversary but also revelling in the record attendance of delegates at the conference and the (seemingly) ever-expanding number of Supporters' Clubs coming under the Federation's umbrella. Chairman Talbot Nanson – Lord Mayor of Brighton and founder-Chairman of the organisation – was exuberant. The horizons for developing supporter organisations internationally seemed to stretch forward limitlessly.[3]

Unfortunately, the records of Federation meetings between 1948–52 are incomplete but we may assume that discussion of the 'internationalising' of Federation affairs continued. Little, however, appears to have been done to make any European connections, though some Irish Supporters' Clubs had been contacted (and an Irish Federation was formed in 1954). The 'international' issue reappeared in 1953, introduced by Chairman Nanson as 'a matter which is very near to my heart'. The Lord Mayor of Brighton had discussed the prospects with Federation Patron Viscount Alexander:

> As Viscount Alexander said to me last night, this is a platform not only between people of one race but between people of all races, and might quite possibly be a means of going far towards world peace, which means so much to all of us.[4]

These high hopes for the power of football as a common link across national divides were frequently expressed in Federation circles in the 1950s. The practical difficulties, however, of actually linking up with (or even discovering the nature of) supporters' organisations in Europe and elsewhere, were substantial, as the Federation was already discovering. Mr Mountford of Romford Supporters' Association reported to the conference in 1953:

> I want you to realise that the setting up of an International Federation . . . is not going to be an easy matter to accomplish, as there are no bodies or Federations of Supporters' Clubs in places abroad with whom we can co-operate.[5]

Mr Mountford regularly travelled 'on the continent' (probably in a business capacity), at a time when such travel was comparatively rare. He had been commissioned by the Federation Executive to sound out the prospects of developing links abroad. He had recently visited Holland and made contact with several secretaries of Supporters' Clubs there. He discovered that some were constituted in a very different fashion to their English counterparts – often being loose organisations of season-ticket holders. Mr Mountford had succeeded in arranging a meeting with the Dutch FA (the Royal Netherlands Football Union) at The Hague and had been greatly assisted by its Secretary, Mr Brunt. (It seems the Dutch FA were easier to approach than the equivalent English body.) The Secretary of the Dutch Trainer's Union had also helpfully provided a list of supporters' clubs and their secretaries. There was no sign of any *national* organisation, like the Federation, with which direct relations could be established though Mr Mountford felt 'very optimistic' about future developments. Subsequent discussion revealed that Arsenal supporters already had some contact with clubs in Malta and Holland, and the Spurs delegate referred to contacts with fans in Denmark, Sweden and Belgium.[6] Whether these 'clubs' and 'contacts' involved European supporters of *English* clubs (like Arsenal and Spurs) is difficult to gather. Certainly, support for English football had long existed in Malta and in the Benelux and Scandinavian countries. In conclusion, the progress of an International Federation was left 'safely in the hands of the Executive Committee'.

The following year offered a great opportunity to develop international relations between supporters' organisations. With the 1954 World Cup staged in Switzerland (and England now involved, having entered the competition in 1950, only to be defeated 1–0 by the USA), the distance to travel was, at least for some, not too great. But little advantage of the international competition was taken by the Federation officers, though the Secretary does mention that some of 'the very large numbers of supporters from England that went out to the World Cup matches' were Federation members who took special badges with them to distribute amongst other nation's fans.[7]

Federation Secretary, Leslie Davis, spoke none the less of the 'considerable progress' that had been made on this 'question very dear to the hearts of all of us'. There seemed, however, little to show for it, bar the presence at conference of a representative of the Dublin club, Shelbourne's, supporters. Mr Davis produced an impressive list of countries where 'much progress' had been made, including Sweden, Austria, Belgium, New Zealand and Malta. Discussion was brought to a close with the promise, from Chairman Nanson, that 'This International Union is going to be a great organisation and one which could cover the world.'[8]

Throughout the remaining six years of the decade, no real progress was made to establish contacts in Europe or further afield. In 1956, speakers were still warning Federation members that Supporters' Clubs abroad 'were not quite the same as our own. They are more or less big Social Clubs . . .'[9] This probably indicates that, in Europe, fans did not play the significant fund-raising roles that their English counterparts did. In Europe, few clubs were private limited companies on the English model, and many of them were closely tied to their local authorities. The *community's* money was usually channelled into its football club via these local councils (who might, for example, own and administer the football stadium). Consequently, European Supporters' Clubs had found little reason to develop national bodies, like the Federation, to serve in an advisory capacity for member clubs dealing with substantial amounts of cash. If the Federation was trying to 'sell' the idea of an umbrella organisation like itself to European supporters, it was clearly proving difficult. Hopes were expressed that *Germany* might be the most fertile ground for future developments.

It seems that, in the event, little did develop. The topic did not resurface in Federation affairs until 1961 when the recently recruited (and comparatively young) General Secretary, Tony Pullein, picked up the thread. The prospect of a World Cup staging in England in five years' time was an additional stimulus, leading Mr Pullein to write to some twenty football associations – 'all the important ones, plus Canada and Australia'. His most enthusiastic reply came from Australia where the antipodean FA was urgently seeking to popularise the game. Tony Pullein's letter had been reproduced in the AFA *Bulletin* which sparked a number of replies from Supporters' Clubs; one, the Box Hill Supporters' Club, claiming a membership of eighty.[10] Such organisations were astounded to discover that English SCs (of professional clubs alone) raised nearly half a million pounds annually in support of their 'parents'. They were urged to get fundraising and establish their Australian Federation of Supporters' Clubs.

Replies from non-English speaking nations were sparse. Mr Pullein had received letters from Brazil and France most recently, but could not comment on them as 'I am afraid I cannot read them'. The reply from Spain, however, had been translated and it informed of the strange situation prevailing there where each Supporters' Club *was* the football club. The fans became *members* of their particular football club by paying a fee of £2–£3 at the start of a season. Social and sporting activities were available at the club's stadium or elsewhere and, before Franco came to power, 'members' used to *elect* the President of their FC.[11]

Contact had been made (via the Chelmsford SC representative) with supporters of clubs in the South Africa National Football League. (Their 'parent' clubs were no doubt keen to promote the kind of supporter fundraising bodies that operated in England.) The Chelmsford delegate, while recognising that South Africa was 'undergoing a bad time', felt that politics do not enter into football 'and hoped for deepening relations with South African supporters'. Only one Federation member raised any objection to such a prospect, the Coventry City delegate:

One of the speakers said that politics do not enter into football. I would say we

. . . do not care what a man's creed or colour is as far as football supporters are concerned.[12]

The momentum continued through 1962, with Secretary Pullein announcing that a proposed Constitution for an International Federation was to be circulated for discussion. The prospective founder-member nations were to include England, Scotland, France and (despite the Coventry delegate) South Africa. But, once again, progress proved difficult and, in 1963, the topic was hardly raised at all. In 1964 it did not feature on the conference agenda at all.

The truth was that the Federation was too busy dealing with its own internal problems to worry too much about international possibilities. Supporters' clubs were struggling to survive in many places, as football clubs increasingly incorporated their traditional functions under a 'commercial' wing.[13] Someone did raise the 'international' matter from the floor of the 1964 conference, but clearly not much was happening for the Executive to report on. One of the Federation's Dutch contacts had developed a friendship with Tony Pullein (to the point of honeymooning in Mr Pullein's house, it seems) and, interestingly, the Secretary reports that his guest was starting up a Federation in Holland with a grant of £2,500 from the Dutch FA.[14] The South Africans were reportedly still 'very keen' but nothing had been heard from them of late. One wonders just *how* the Federation hoped to include, in any meaningful way, representations from supporters based some 10,000 miles away, in a country where government regulation banned black and white players or supporters from being together in the same stadium.

In any event, the discussions of the great expansion of the Federation into an international body of supporters' organisations disappeared from the agenda for almost fifteen years after 1964. It was the most difficult period – both financially and in terms of morale – for supporters engaged in running clubs or the Federation. Membership and, most significantly *active* members, were in steep decline, as the Federation struggled to establish a new identity for itself and its member clubs, in the post-commercialisation phase. In the early 1970s, there was even talk of changing the Federation's name to omit the word 'football' in an attempt to include all kinds of sporting clubs under the organisation's wing. In one speech (in 1974) by the Ipswich Town representative (who was pleading for individual membership to be available for any football fan), the vision was expounded of the Federation embracing 'any sports club' and pursuing vigorously 'the inauguration of an international set-up for supporters of football all over the world'.[15]

In 1978, the topic resurfaced with a splash as 'The Birth of a European Federation' was proclaimed in headlines of the March *Newsletter*. Under the subheading, 'Result of nations meeting in Dusseldorf', Archie Gooch (now President of the Federation) reproduced the press-release which marked the occasion:

> Delegates from six Europeans countries have agreed to form a European Federation of Football Supporters' Associations (EFFSA). The six countries represented at a meeting in Dusseldorf, West Germany were, BELGIUM, ENGLAND, HOLLAND, SCOTLAND, WALES AND WEST GERMANY. HUNGARY AND SWITZERLAND were unable to attend for domestic reasons and EAST GERMANY were apparently prevented for political reasons.
>
> The decision to form EFFSA, emanating from a formal proposal, was unanimously agreed. The National Federation of Football Supporters' Clubs (Great Britain) was by far the most experienced Federation having been in existence for 50 years, the others having been formed during the last decade.
>
> It was agreed that EFFSA should transcend all political barriers and be built upon friendship and good sportsmanship: to give every support to EFFSA members in particular; to combat all forms of hooliganism and to arrange for orderly visits of supporters and to assist in the organisation of such visits.
>
> Mr Augule de Smet (Belgium) a delegate lawyer, undertook to study the legal requirements of such a European Organisation.
>
> Mr Carlo Sperrle (West Germany) was elected Secretary and Co-ordinator and other delegates accepted the following briefs:
>
> (a)   Developing contacts and membership in Eastern European countries.
> (b)   Extending membership to such footballing nations as ITALY, FRANCE, SPAIN, PORTUGAL, etc., and if where necessary to assist in the formations of Associations.
> (c)   To organise a European Championship for Supporters' Clubs Football Teams in 1979.
> (d)   To draw up a directory of all Supporters' Clubs throughout Europe.[16]

The document went on to outline the delegates' discussions about hooliganism and travel abroad, and their hope that a system of ticket distribution (for Euro-matches) via Supporters' Clubs might cut off the supply to misbehaving fans. A two-year target was set for the establishment of the new organisation 'on a sound legal footing'. This beginning was the 'culmination of 20 years work in Britain and abroad' and would, hopefully, soon spread to all European countries East and West.

At conference a few months later, Mr Gooch sketched out some of the developments. The Dusseldorf meeting had been attended by himself and Secretary, Tony Pullein – representing England, Scotland, Wales and N. Ireland – along with West Germany, Belgium and Holland. Language barriers had proved a difficulty but, fortunately, it had been decided that English should be the language of discourse in the International Federation. The new organisation 'would be built on friendship, sportsmanship and give every support to Football Associations'; it would also 'keep in

contact with UEFA' as regards ticket allocations. True to its own traditions, the (English) Federation saw the principal aims of its international
counterpart, not in terms of *representing* its members to the appropriate
authorities, but in giving 'every support to Football Associations' and
(rather hopefully) keeping 'in contact' with the European governing body.

At first, it seemed that support for the establishment of an International
Federation might even be forthcoming *from* the FA in England. It was
planned that meetings of delegates would take place 'in each country from
time to time' and Archie Gooch informed those present that the FA's
enthusiasm was short-lived. Reflecting on the events in 1978 and the
subsequent collapse of the venture, Mr Gooch recalled some twelve years
later

> Tony Pullein and I had the makings of a considerable international Federation
> . . . with Prince Rainier of Monaco as our Patron. We had about seven or eight
> groups (i.e. founder-members). Our meetings were televised over there . . . It
> fell because the German guy was made Secretary of the Steering Committee,
> there were no Officers; 'you organise the meetings', we said to him. But the
> question of how to finance travel to these meetings arose – we were paying our
> own fares, I think. But anyway, the German began to appoint a Chairman and
> Secretary. We said, 'Enough' . . . and it collapsed. The FA, anyway, were
> opposed to it . . . I think Ted Croker said it wasn't a good idea.[17]

The International Federation did not collapse immediately. In summer
1979, Archie Gooch reported on the appointment of Carlo Sperrle ('the
German guy' referred to above) to do the groundwork of developing the
new body. There had been a recent meeting in Amsterdam and, clearly,
things were already not proceeding smoothly:

> These meetings did not go as we would have liked; they had not stuck to the
> rules but had just carried on without prior discussion. We protested about this
> and told them so . . . They got a fright and . . . were very anxious to try and
> please us and suggested that the next meeting would be in London.[18]

Only the West Germans, Belgians and Dutch 'had anything like a federation' so one of Carlo Sperrle's primary tasks was to encourage into life
other federations of Supporters' Clubs in other countries. Despite the early
difficulties, Mr Gooch remained confident that the 'Euro-Federation'
would be successfully established within a few years.

Within a year, the Euro-Federation initiative was lost. Sadly, Archie
Gooch informed the conference in 1980 that the 'problems of trying form
an organisation of federated bodies' in Europe had proved insuperable,
and the Secretary chosen to co-ordinate the network (presumably Carlo
Sperrle) 'had disappeared'.[19] The project sank without trace, though hopes
still remain amongst current Federation officers that, given the social and

political developments in the European Community, eventually some kind of 'Euro-Federation' will emerge.[20]

Clearly, the financial problems involved in co-ordinating a network of supporters' organisations in Europe were considerable. The costs of travelling, especially from and to Britain, were prohibitive for organisations that often had difficulties financing activities within their own borders. However, in the early 1980s, the Federation was richer than it had ever been. Involvement with a pool/lottery company in Bath had profited the Federation enormously, netting over £10,000 in 1980. In 1982, the Federation's assets included £36,000 on deposit.[21] Yet none of this capital was apparently expended on developing the Euro-Federation – or indeed on any major campaigns to promote supporters' interests inside or outside the national boundaries. With prudence most in mind (and conditioned by decades of hand-to-mouth financing), the Executive felt that the Federation's future was best secured by retaining the capital and, in effect, living on the interest it produced.

Yet lack of money or a reluctance to spend it was not the real reason for failure. In reality, there was neither the appetite nor the common organisation ground between European supporters' organisations to allow for the growth of a healthy body. As it was, the English Federation had its own very real difficulties seeking to preside over its widely various membership. Its original (and abiding) raison d'être was to service Supporters' Clubs who were fund-raising and organising travel for supporters' and, in many European countries, supporters' relationships with football clubs were widely different from the English models. In short, the Federation was a *very loose* conglomerate of, often very busy, Supporters' Clubs with little energy to spare for Federation affairs or initiatives. If this, already loose, Federation had loosely federated with the few other (and in most cases) equally vague federations of European Supporters' Clubs, what would have been gained?

The real 'international' work was going on at local level and particularly in *Scotland* with some combined efforts by football clubs and their fans. In 1984, the Celtic Supporters Association urged the Federation Executive 'to implement the idea of liaison between member clubs when engaged in European ties'. The Celtic spokesman, Mr N. Gallagher, gave an account of how liaison had developed between themselves and other clubs, following the problems their fans had experienced at the Juventus match in 1981, when five Celtic fans had been stabbed in Turin. The following season Celtic were to meet Ajax in Amsterdam:

> We sent people on ahead 2 or 3 days prior to the arrival of our team – we met local police, stadium officials etc. to ensure exactly where our fans would be placed. We discussed and agreed as to where our buses would arrive . . . and insisted on police protection for the buses whilst the game was in progress . . .

Similar organisation has taken place with other teams from abroad. Last season when we played Nottingham Forest, four of our people went down and met the police and the Notts Forest Supporters' Club a week in advance of the game. It was heartening on the day to see how amiable both sets of fans were, no animosity but plenty of good humour. However, this is a very costly exercise – it cost Celtic Supporters over £1,000 since its implementation and Celtic themselves (i.e. the FC) are, hopefully, going to contribute 50% of the cost.[22]

This account by the Celtic representative gives a good picture of what could be done but it also indicates how expensive the advance liaison abroad might prove. Even with the help of their football clubs, most Supporters' Clubs could not meet these kinds of costs. There was certainly no guarantee either that trouble would not break out amongst fans despite serious attempts to make early contact and organise transport properly. UEFA had consistently refused, for the past decade, to stop the sale of tickets on the day of a match, which encouraged 'unofficial' travel by supporters for whom little could be planned in advance. Mrs Black of the Liverpool Supporters' Club gave, in response to the Celtic account, a chilling picture of the events that greeted the Liverpool fans in the summer of 1984. Liverpool FC were to play Roma FC in the European Cup Final and, by some peculiar circumstance of UEFA's making, the English club had to play the Final at the home ground of their opponents. Realising that it would, inevitably, be a 'difficult' fixture, Liverpool FC, its supporters' club and the City Council had made major efforts to smooth out any foreseeable problems in Rome. According to Mrs Black:

> Our Secretary along with supporters from our club, plus 15 people from Liverpool City Council . . . were sent on a mission to Rome a week in advance. We were well received and had every co-operation. Peter Robinson (then Secretary Liverpool FC) went over three times . . . all coming under the jurisdiction of Liverpool FC, we were told where we would be positioned in the ground and how to behave . . . However, it had to be seen to be believed – it was a near bloodbath . . . The attitude of the Roma supporters . . . was one of provocation . . . Rockets and bottles were thrown at us . . . When we came out of the ground after Roma lost, it was terrible – they burnt their flags and we took a barrage of abuse . . . bricks were flying in all direction and children were screaming . . . The Roma supporters were hiding in bushes, running in gangs with knives and we saw a man stabbed . . . Eventually we got back to our coaches and were advised by the police to stay indoors. So, on the night we won the European Cup for the fourth time, we had to go into our hotel, sit there and wait for our flights back next day.[23]

Later that year, Liverpool played Juventus in Turin in a one-off match between the European Champions and the winners of the European Cup Winners competition. More violence took place that night. It was, in retrospect, the penultimate stage on the terrible road to the Heysel tragedy the following year, when Liverpool met Juventus once again, in the European Cup Final of 1985. The crushing to death of thirty-eight Italian fans that day occurred after fighting Liverpool fans caused panic in the stadium and a wall collapsed at the Italian rear. With it collapsed any immediate prospects of 'international relations' between English supporters and their European counterparts.

NOTES

1. See *The Supporter*, Official Organ of the National Federation, vol. 3, no. 4, December 1935.
2. *The Supporter*, vol. 2, no. 1, September 1935.
3. Nat. Fed. AGM Minutes, 1948, p. 3.
4. Ibid., 1953, p. 27.
5. Ibid., 1953, p. 28.
6. Ibid., 1953, pp. 28–9.
7. Ibid., 1954, p. 23.
8. Ibid., 1954, p. 23.
9. Ibid., 1956, p. 43.
10. Ibid., 1961, p. 42.
11. Franco disenfranchised Spanish supporters who were 'members' ('socio') of their football clubs in order to gain control of the clubs in 1939. With Franco's demise, in 1975, the Spanish clubs reverted to the traditional system and, currently, Spanish fans who are 'members' (and over 18 years old) elect the club President once every four years. Legal changes in Spain are presently forcing all clubs to become Plc's. It remains to be seen how this will restructure the element of democracy unique to Spanish football.
12. Nat. Fed. AGM Minutes, 1961, p. 43.
13. See Chapter 8, 'Supporter-Club Relations'.
14. See Nat. Fed. AGM Minutes, 1964, p. 42. This substantial sum of money (about £30,000 or more in modern terms) indicates a keenness on the part of the Dutch FA to *assist* in the development of supporters' organisations, something which has been markedly absent from the English FA or FL. Today, the Dutch Government employ a Supporters' Liaison Officer who works *within* the Dutch FA (KNVB) but is funded independently from it. The English FA's *Blueprint for Football* (1991) has included proposals to provide money for the development of supporter representation, though it is, as yet, unclear precisely what the FA is proposing.
15. Nat. Fed. AGM Minutes, 1974, p. 45. For a detailed account of the debate over individual membership of the Federation, see Chapter 5, 'Structure and Membership'.
16. Nat. Fed. AGM Minutes, 1978, p. 17.

17. Personal interview, Archie Gooch, President of Federation, January 1990.
18. Nat. Fed. AGM Minutes, 1979, p. 20.
19. Nat. Fed. AGM Minutes, 1980, p. 21.
20. Personal interview, Tony Kershaw, Chairman of Federation, 1990.
21. For more on this see Chapter 10, 'Public Relations, Publications and Finances'.
22. Nat. Fed. AGM Minutes, 1984, pp. 45–6.
23. Nat. Fed. AGM Minutes, 1984, pp. 46–7.

10

PUBLIC RELATIONS, PUBLICATIONS AND FINANCES

A lot of work has been done. I have travelled tens of thousands of miles. I have sought publicity wherever I could find it . . . We have never for the last twenty five years, had the publicity we deserve. (Archie Gooch, Federation Chairman, 1974)

Throughout its long history spanning sixty-five years, the Federation's relations with the media, its ability to produce its own publications and the organisation's level of funding have all proved tenuous. Yet ironically, within the membership of the Federation, there were always many supporters' clubs operating effectively with their (local) press, producing regular supporters' magazines or match programmes, and raising substantial amounts of money by various means.

From its earliest days, the Federation failed to capture or stimulate the kind of national publicity it thought appropriate. In 1935, one Federation member lamented the almost complete absence of any recognition afforded to the Federation by the national and sporting press.

When we come to the world beyond the confines of the football ground, what is the status of the Supporters' Movement there? Frankly it hasn't one. Who has seen any interest taken . . . in one of our national journals? Has anyone ever seen there a reference to the Movement, its objects and its importance? To all sports editors, it is non-existent.[1]

This acute feeling of being ignored by the pundits of the day became a chronic complaint as decades passed. In the most recent Federation meetings, voices are still heard lamenting the organisation's failure to make a proper impact in the national media.[2]

Member clubs joining the Federation in the 1930s paid a fee: one guinea for those supporters of Football League clubs and half a guinea for others. With a membership growing from just over twenty clubs at the end of its first year (1927) to 'something like sixty clubs' in 1934[3] – and recognising that the majority of these member clubs were non-League (i.e. half-guineas) – the Federation had to operate, in these early years, on a sum between 15 and 35 guineas a year (roughly equivalent to £1,000 to £2,250 p.a. today). The Federation's affairs were run on a voluntary basis, almost entirely, though a 'retaining fee' was presumably paid to the organisation's Hon. Solicitor, G.S. Godfree Esquire. Member clubs received for their fee, advice on legal matters (and about the income tax due on the funds they raised) and, 'the most valuable asset of all – the interchange of ideas and views'.[4] The balance of the Federation's funds were probably spent on correspondence, printing and travel.

From 1934–36, member clubs also gained the benefit of *The Supporter* – a monthly broadsheet which operated as the 'Official Organ' of the Federation, priced at 3d (i.e. £1.50p) per copy. It too was a voluntary effort, edited by Jack Williams of the Wrexham Supporters' Club, but it failed to attract regular contributions (in the form of articles) from Federation members nor did it sell in sufficient numbers. Recalling those days some twenty years later, Jack Williams reflected:

> I produced an eight page printed newspaper for three years. Unhappily, it was not supported as it should have been, even though it was distributed throughout Europe. It was owing to the increase in printing costs . . . that we had to close down.[5]

Following the war and the recommencement of the Football League in 1946–47, the Federation's membership swelled to over 200 supporters' clubs.[6] No attempt was made to restart *The Supporter* – or any equivalent – but by 1948, the Federation had at its disposal (usually) two pages of an existing publication, *Sport Weekly Magazine*. These pages were open to the Federation to fill with news of Supporters' Clubs activities and publicity about the existence of the Federation. Under the heading, *Football Supporters' Gazette*, the first edition offered a 'A Personal Word to all Real Supporters of Football', penned by Federation Secretary, Leslie Davis. On the opposite page 'A Message from Stanley Rous Esq. CBE', Secretary of the FA, wished the *Football Gazette* every success. Presumably, the publishers of *Sport Weekly Magazine* hoped that by including the Federation's pages as a 'Supplement', it would sell more magazines amongst the enormous nominal membership of the Supporters' Clubs affiliated to the Federation. Member Clubs of the Federation were expected to sell copies of *Sport Weekly Magazine* to their members and other supporters. An arrangement had been made (though no details of it survive) that the

Federation itself should benefit financially, depending on the number of copies sold through its members.

Southend Utd Supporters' Club were the mainstay – and probably the prime movers – of the Federation's partnership with the publishers. They sold the magazine vigorously, 'twelve hundred copies in twelve weeks', and the Federation benefited by some £10–£15. Unfortunately, only twelve other Supporters' Clubs were making any effort to imitate Southend's success selling the magazine. These twelve were a coterie of Southern and South Coast Supporters' Clubs; an awkward regionalism for a national organisation which was reflected in contributions under the section in the *Gazette*, entitled: 'Touring the Clubs'. They were exclusively from Barking, Brighton, Chelsea, Horsham, Maidstone, Colchester, QPR, Torquay, Hitchin, Littlehampton, Bromley, Byfleet, Gool Town, Watford and Wimbledon.[7] With only a dozen or so Supporters' Clubs showing any enthusiasm for either selling or contributing to the *Gazette*, the Federation could make little money from it and the partnership with the publishers soon petered out. Yet, in 1948, Federation Treasurer, Mr Manley, informed the conference that 155 clubs were 'paid-up' members and the cash balance at the bank stood at £108.9. 2d.[8] It was felt necessary that the membership fee be doubled to 2 guineas and 1 guinea (for non-League SCs) and a suggestion was made that the football authorities be approached for help in staging a 'Federation Day' one Saturday towards the end of the season to raise money.[9]

By 1952, the Federation had organised an 'agency' in the office basement at Pall Mall which acted as the organisation's HQ. It offered tickets to members for a variety of entertainments, including 'Theatre, Circus, Amateur Cup and miscellaneous match tickets'.[10] The growing profitability of the ticket agency was, at first, insufficient to defray other expenses and, in 1952 and 1953, deficits of £392 and £128 respectively were recorded. In 1954, the Federation had a scheme running which, in one form or another, continued up to the present day. It was an insurance scheme, offering member clubs the chance to insure their individual members 'against accident whilst travelling to away matches'.[11]

Complaints continued from Federation members about the low public profile of the organisation. During 1954, in an attempt to generate some publicity, it was suggested that the Federation organise a beauty competition amongst the female members of Supporters' Clubs. There would be regional heats and a grand final at the end of the football season. Chairman Ray Sonin presented the idea to conference:

> . . . much of the work of the Federation must, as it were, be 'back room stuff' . . . There is little or no outside propaganda or showmanship . . . the Federation needed a little boost – or to put it more bluntly – 'showmanship' . . . and one of the ideas put forward was the running of a National Football Queen

Competition. Some of you may think that such a competition is something strange for the Federation to stage . . .[12]

In fact, some Supporters' Clubs had been staging similar competitions for years. In *Sport Weekly Magazine*, in 1948, Maidstone SC are congratulated on the election of a Supporters' Club 'Beauty Queen'.

None the less, some members did find the prospect of a national Football Queen competition rather strange. The originators of the competition (in 1954) were members of Doncaster SC. The regional heats were designed to raise local publicity for clubs (and the grand final, it was hoped, would work similarly on a national level). The whole competition was run in conjunction with *The People* newspaper – but the sponsor soon got fed up with the lack of enthusiasm and threatened to desert the competition if more clubs did not get involved. Delegates at the 1954 conference complained that it was proving difficult to get their local papers interested in the heats (as it would, inevitably, with a single newspaper as sponsor), but the most interesting and significant complaint came from the (male) Spurs representative:

> We put the suggestion to our lady members but they would have nothing to do with it . . . They thought that, if anything, there should be a competition for the most beautiful man (loud laughter). That was the attitude of the ladies.[13]

This gem was so rich that Chairman Ray Sonin felt he had to repeat it for those at the back of the hall: 'It is the *men* that should be judged – not the ladies', he added to make absolutely plain the full revolutionary force of the Spurs females' suggestion.

In response to the complaints about lack of publicity, Mr Sonin informed his audience:

> Speaking personally, you might like to know that a couple of months ago I had the honour of being invited by the Midland BBC (radio) . . . where I was able to say a piece about the Federation. Everybody seemed to think that this little snip of propaganda for the Federation was good . . .[14]

It is clear from comments like this (and continued complaints from members) that the 'honour' of appearing on regional radio was a rare one, even for the Federation's Chairman, who assured the conference in 1956 that 'your Federation is going all-out in its endeavours to get greater publicity'.

A deficit in the Federation's finances was recorded for the third year running in 1955, but it only amounted to £60. In the meantime, the Federation's assets had been growing – perhaps from the profits of the ticket agency – to £702 in 1953, reaching £1,003.1.1d in the following year – a quite considerable sum. By 1956, the Secretary, Leslie Davis, had become the first salaried officer of the Federation – at £688.10.6d per annum – presumably drawn from the assets.[15] By now the ticket-business was probably so busy that voluntary aid was not enough to ensure the running of it.

In addition to any profits from the ticket agency, the Federation did receive irregular donations from its richer supporter club members. These monies were often drawn from funds raised by their lotteries. In 1957, the Federation showed a profit of £406, but a sudden drop in 'donations' the following year forced the Federation back to a deficit of £37. By 1958, some football clubs were taking advantages of the Small Lotteries Act, for which the Federation had lobbied so hard two years earlier.[16] Consequently, some Supporters' Clubs were themselves feeling the pinch and donations to the Federation slumped as a result. Membership fees for member clubs now stood at 4 guineas and 2 guineas, but the loss of donations forced a proposal to increase them to 5 guineas and 3 guineas. Though little enough for large Supporters' Clubs raising hundreds of pounds a year, these fees were beginning to hurt the smaller clubs within the Federation. The Dorchester SC representative reminded members that some clubs were attached to teams watched by 'about fifty people'. The Treasurer, too, confirmed,

> . . . the main bulk of the Federation consists of smaller clubs of the 400 clubs (sic), a great proportion are non-league clubs . . .[17]

In the end, a proposition of 5 guineas and 2 guineas was approved, with the Executive empowered to waive the 2 guinea fee for some of the smallest clubs. It failed to prevent a financial 'crisis' in 1959, when member clubs were asked to stump up for a deficit of £89.

Throughout most of the 1960s, the Federation's finances undulated between surpluses and deficits of around £400–£500 per year. The worst was 1968, with a deficit of £1,143. Assets, however, continued to grow, reaching a peak of £11,779 that year. Part of the Pall Mall basement office had been sublet in the late 1950s, greatly cramping the voluntary and paid staff who ran the ticket agency (and various lotteries) from there.

After the demise of the *Football Supporters' Gazette* in the *Sport Weekly Magazine*, the next publication to include the Official Organ of the Federation within its pages was the *Sporting Record* after 1958. Mr Clifford Webb of the *Record* wrote to all the Federation's member clubs with a proposal for a monthly magazine for Supporters' Clubs. It was, he explained, the brainchild of Charles Buchan whose *Football Monthly* sold widely. Mr Webb included 'a little slip at the end of the letter about how many copies you would want to sell'. He assured Federation members that 'with a magazine of your own you could make up for all the deficiencies in the National Press.'[18]

Mr Webb spoke at the 1960 conference (as it happened, Charles Buchan died on holiday during the same weekend), where he further outlined the proposal for a supporters' monthly magazine. He was asked what minimum number of sales via the Federation would be required. His answer revealed how little he knew about the way the Federation worked:

> . . . we shall want a circulation of almost 100,000. Frankly I do not think that is a lot bearing in mind that you have 400,000 members in all your clubs . . .[19]

The representative of Wrexham SC – the club that launched the Federation's first publication in 1934 – was enthusiastic and hoped the Area Secretaries would contribute regular articles. Ilminster's delegate (probably Archie Gooch) reflected on the Federation's failure to gain national publicity, even when initiating projects of wide interest, like the much-discussed international Federation. Another delegate, from Truro, revealed that efforts to attract television interest in the Football Queen Competition had been futile, but the *Sporting Record* had covered the event (*The People* newspaper had dropped out four years previously) and increased their sales as a result. With that in mind, he felt that the publishers of the proposed monthly magazine should pay a 'remuneration' to the Federation, providing an additional incentive for member clubs to sell more copies.

This suggestion provoked a sharp response from Clifford Webb. It had been extremely difficult sometimes, he explained, to get any information at all out of the Federation with which to fill the available space in the *Sporting Record*:

> Meetings are held (by the Federation) but nobody, apparently, is responsible for telling the Press. Even though . . . we are now the Official Organ of the Federation, we get complete silence . . . a magazine of this sort (the proposed monthly) would cost a considerable amount of money . . . As for the idea that we should contribute to the National Federation, I'm afraid that is rather laughable . . . that we should pay for the privilege of putting your work before the public is completely out of the question.[20]

The Football Queen Competition, described by its supporters as 'one of the highlights in the world of football', continued despite the earlier objections of female fans of Spurs.[21] The Southern Area was principally responsible for its organisation, co-ordinating the five regional heats before the final which was held on the Saturday evening following the Federation conferences. Retiring Secretary in 1960, Leslie Davis, urged more clubs to get involved and more husbands to put forward their wives for selection:

> . . . If you are the proud possessor of a wife who will ultimately become the

Football Queen, you will be on velvet from that day until you die. If she is your
wife or sweetheart, bring her to the preliminary bouts, put her in, and encourage
her to carry off the club area and grand final . . .'[22]

The competition also caught on in South Africa and, in 1962, the
Federation received an official visit from Meryl Lemarque, the reigning
South African Football Queen.[23]

When the chance of some real, national press coverage did come along,
the Federation's inability to deliver responses from its members often
wasted the opportunity. In 1961, for example, the *Daily Mail* wanted to
research an article about supporter opinion. It circulated (via the
Executive) a questionnaire to 75 member clubs of the Federation. When
only 29 of them replied, the newspaper dropped the article.[24]

The Federation lost money for three of the four years 1961–65. In an
attempt to raise funds, the Federation sought to run a national lottery/pool
(amongst its member clubs) in 1962. At first, it was to be based on a one-off
horse race, but the very idea of *another* fund-raising scheme for the officers
who voluntarily ran their own schemes for Supporters' Clubs was a burden.
Inevitably, any regular Federation lottery or pool would interfere with the
existing, local schemes. In that same year, the Federation sought a 3d levy
on all individual members of their affiliated clubs, but the motion was
defeated.[25] Consequently, a further rise in the membership fee was proposed and the debate that followed revealed some of the stresses and
strains in an organisation seeking to cater for such a widely divergent
membership.

The debate was opened by the proposer, Coventry City, who laid bare
the irony that supporters within the Federation raised large sums of money
for their football clubs, while, every year, the Federation's Executive was
required to 'pass the bucket' to keep the organisation afloat:

> You represent organisations which are raising hundreds of thousands of pounds
> for football clubs. You do not, by and large, have any say in the management of
> those clubs. But you are allowing an organisation which you own to run into the
> red every year . . .[26]

He urged a doubling of the membership fee to ten guineas, and four
guineas for non-League clubs.

There was some support from the floor for the proposal, but soon a
troop of small Supporters' Clubs representatives lined up to present their
objections. Wisbech, Dorchester and Yeovil Town's delegates spoke of
their inability to meet these increases. Wealdstone – a club with under a
thousand members who paid the full five-guinea fee – actually spent
around £60 a year on Federation activity, taking into account the travel and
other expenses incurred. Cheltenham asked: 'What do we get back for our

subscriptions?' and Romford concurred. Northerners (of Guernsey) thought the fee should be left entirely to the discretion of the Executive. Meanwhile, Grimsby Town – a large and thriving Supporters' Club – suggested a sliding scale of fees dependent on membership numbers. The Grimsby delegate promptly wrote out a cheque for twenty-five guineas which he handed over to loud applause. In reply, the Coventry representative returned to his original theme.

> By the time you have given money to your parent bodies, you are broke. I am suggesting that instead of giving all your money to your parent bodies, give a bit to the Federation.[27]

In the event a 50 per cent increase was carried, with discretion for the Executive to deal kindly with the smaller, poorer clubs. The proposal was, however, reversed at conference the following year. In 1962, the Federation's association with the *Sporting Record* ended, to be replaced by a column in the *Soccer Star* magazine. Secretary, Tony Pullein, complained at the failure of many clubs to send material for use in the Federation's official organ. It seems, he said, that 'most Supporters' Clubs just do not want the publicity'.[28] The Federation began to make some money taking part in a national, weekly competition called the 'Players' Pool' which was run by the British Sport Guild originally as a scheme to raise money for the PFA. In 1963, the Federation made a £600 profit on this competition alone and it urged more member clubs to take part, if necessary at the expense of ditching their current lotteries. (At the time, both the FA and FL were keen to run similar national pools schemes, following the Betting and Gaming Act of 1960.) The Federation and its member clubs stood to gain considerably if the competition became popular with supporters. For every ticket sold, 6d accrued to the Supporters' Clubs plus 15 per cent 'distribution allowance' which enabled agents to be paid something for selling the tickets. If agents worked voluntarily, it meant that, for every £100 put into the competition, £65 was returned to the local Supporters' Club.[29]

The following year the Federation recouped £1,100 from the 'Players' Pool' – though still recorded a deficit overall of £668. Secretary, Tony Pullein, however, felt optimistic for the future. The Football League's attempt to run a national sweep had failed and the FA's project had never left the starting-post. The Federation more than doubled its profit from the 'Players' Pool' in 1965 (£2,612) and was able to declare an overall surplus of £500.[30]

The decade of the 1960s saw the first modern wave of commercialism sweep over football. With the players' maximum wage limitation gone and increasing coverage by television, the costs and opportunities to make money multiplied. As the first 'commercial managers' took up their posts at football clubs, other businesses – those who ran lotteries and gambling schemes in particular – looked around for suitable vehicles to penetrate the football market. To some of these businesses, the Federation, with its large, nominal membership, seemed a likely prospect; a ready-made network of hundreds of local organisations associated with football, run by volunteers. As the Federation did not have its own publication, one firm – *Dance News Ltd* – offered to produce for the Federation a regular, weekly newspaper to be sold to members, price 6d (of which 2d would be returned as profits to the Supporters' Club). The publication was to be tied up with a national bingo scheme.[31]

In the event, the weekly Federation newspaper failed to appear. But two years later, in 1967, yet another magazine emerged which offered space for Federation news. It was a monthly, called *The Football Supporter*, which featured articles of general interest to supporters and a regular column for Federation affairs. To supplement this, the Federation decided also to produce its own *Newsletter* for circulation principally to the officers of the organisation and the committee members of Supporters' Clubs in affiliation. Federation stalwart, Jack Williams, who had edited *The Supporter* some thirty years previously, took on the task of ensuring its production.[32]

With a deficit in 1967 of £1,143, the Federation sought to raise money via a variety of schemes and funds. There was an Auxiliary Association, a Development Society and an Improvements Fund, along with bingo tickets with one-armed bandit prizes, lucky numbers and a 'Goldmine Scoop' in operation. In addition, there were regular appeals for loans or gifts to the Building Fund. The Federation was seeking to purchase a house on the outskirts of London (one was eventually bought in Luton) as the small basement HQ in Pall Mall was increasingly swamped, not only by the secretarial staff required but also 'a hell of a lot of work now going on in pools.'[33] Meanwhile, the 'Players' Pool' had collapsed from lack of enthusiasm and participation, and with it went the much-needed cash it had produced.

Another deficit the following year of £1,115 plunged the Federation deeper into financial crisis. With membership falling steeply as well, Archie Gooch described the years 1967–68 as 'the most difficult . . . that any Chairman of any organisation could ever have had'.[34] On top of these difficulties, the resignation of Secretary, Tony Pullein, to pursue a career in free-lance journalism, exacerbated the organisation's problems. Each new scheme – the 'Goldmine Scoop' being the latest – soon foundered on the rocks of apathy (and probably exhaustion) which were constant features of the Supporters' Clubs' committees required to promote the schemes. Remembering these years some two decades later, Tony Pullein reflected:

> The problem was that most of the member clubs were so apathetic . . . all those schemes we tried to run that only half a dozen clubs would bother with . . . the huge fusses at Conference about raising the fee from £5 to £7.50 – when these

clubs were raising up to £50,000 a year for their parent clubs! Really, the clubs were very small-minded, only concerned with their own areas.[35]

The new monthly magazine. *The Football Supporter* was also struggling after seven issues. The Federation's member clubs had greeted it without enthusiasm – and the price, at 2/6d, proved prohibitive. The magazine in fact included very little about Supporters' Clubs or the Federation, as it was aimed at a mass market of (mostly young) football fans who often cared little for the former and knew nothing of the latter. The proposition that the Federation should be involved in *The Football Supporter* had come from Frank Adams – the same Frank Adams who was subsequently jailed for five years after England supporters' money for travel to the Mexico World Cup disappeared.[36] Mr Adams initially invited the Federation to invest in the magazine but the organisation baulked at the prospect, deciding only to lend its good name to the publication. Some members thought the Federation's name alone was worth some form of financial remuneration but no deal existed. In return for the Federation's 'approval', Frank Adams offered the magazine as a vehicle for any major campaigns or issues of general interest that the Federation wished to pursue. He was, however, not interested in publishing the internal difficulties and minutiae of Supporters' Clubs affairs.

On his resignation, Tony Pullein became editor of *The Football Supporter* and a Director of Frank Adams' publications firm, Focal Advance Development (FAD). Fears were expressed at the 1969 conference that the name and the 'approval' of the Federation were being used in other ventures, without the expressed sanction of the Executive. Frank Adams had obtained the franchise to organise travel for supporters to Mexico and was also involved with the England Football Supporters' Association (EFSA), of which Tony Pullein was a founder member. One Federation member, Mr Hooker of Aldershot SC, was particularly concerned when he saw (on a visit to Wembley) publicity about a company called 'Shaw's International Sports Travel Ltd' which advertised itself as 'official agents for EFSA and the Federation of Football Supporters' Clubs'. Mr Hooker feared that the Federation was being openly exploited: 'We are a lucrative market for all speculators. Mr Frank Adams and his associates are running us for their own ends.'[37]

By 1970, the Federation's financial crisis had receded, though it is difficult to account for the improvement. It was a record year in the Federation's history, with a surplus of £4,000 declared and assets standing at £8,166. From 1970–74, the Federation recorded consistent surpluses with assets rising to £12,296 in 1973.

Tony Pullein temporarily rejoined the Federation Executive as Public Relations Officer in 1970. With Supporters' Clubs 'being toppled like ninepins', however, the organisation still faced major difficulties.[38]

Publicity and media relations remained a regular source of complaint from members, as they insisted that, beyond the confines of its conferences and Executive meetings, the Federation 'is unknown'. In response, Chairman Archie Gooch insisted that the Federation *did* receive publicity, and letters to himself from Jim Callaghan (then Minister of the Crown) and Ted Heath (soon to be Prime Minister) proved that the organisation was well known.[39] What particularly annoyed some members was any publicity that was gained by supporters *outside* the Federation's ranks. When, in 1970, the Manchester Utd SC leader, David Smith (not yet a Federation member), appeared in the press calling for Cup Final tickets to be allocated in accordance with the average attendances of the two finalists, the Everton delegate (who had himself made a similar proposal five years earlier) fumed at 'the Federation for allowing him to gain the publicity that rightly belongs to the Federation of Supporters' Clubs.'[40]

The following year complaints were renewed about the Federation's failure to publicise its existence effectively. Chairman Gooch was forced to concede that,

> The Federation since 1927 has lacked very considerably in public relations. There is no doubt in my mind that if you talk to a football follower in the street . . . he does not know what the Federation stands for.[41]

It could have been added that most football fans did not even know of the Federation's existence at all, and even those who were members of supporters' clubs affiliated to the Federation often knew little, if anything, about the organisation.[42]

As membership dwindled throughout the 1970s – and the media's concern about football hooliganism grew – the Federation found itself increasingly sidelined from the burning issues of the day. In 1974, both the Midlands and Northern Divisions were expressing considerable concern about the organisation's 'slide into obscurity', with poor public relations, slow reactions to emerging issues, chronic apathy and falling membership.[43] The great swell of Supporters' Club delegates which once attended the Federation conferences of twenty-five years earlier was reduced to a rump of middle-aged and older representatives. As the Wrexham delegates put it, there were too many empty seats in the conference hall: '. . . you would think it was a Mother's Union meeting, not a National Federation meeting . . .'[44]

The age and appearance of the Federation's leading spokespeople and activists were probably not attractive to a media dominated by concerns about hooliganism amongst young football fans. Even to 'insiders' – football supporters who were members of clubs affiliated to the Federation – the organisation could appear too gerontocratic and introverted to be in touch with the real issues and experiences that affected football fans on

Saturday afternoons. One such couple – Elaine and Geoff Walker, both Chelsea supporters – visited a Federation conference in 1973 as 'observers' and wrote a revealing account of the weekend. The 1973 conference was held at Warners Village Holiday Camp, near Harwich, and the camp's Entertainment Manager had specially commissioned a trophy and medals for the winners of the Federation 'Football Competition', staged on Sunday, on the assumption that the competition would be a *football match*. But, as the Walkers explained,

> It was in fact a quiz . . . and it seemed rather odd that with such a gathering of football supporters, and with a pitch available, no organised football had been arranged. Possibly one of the reasons for this was that a quiz more physically suited the majority of the delegates, for it was quite apparent that most of them, and nearly all the Executive Committee, were past their playing days . . . They all seem to want to disassociate themselves from the real hard core of supporters . . . we were continually brainwashed into believing that age was a great asset by the persistent mutual admiration among the Executive Committee and a few of the delegates who felt that twenty years service was twice as commendable as ten. One of the overriding impressions that we came away with was that so much of the business of the conference was far divorced from what we had imagined football supporting was all about.[45]

With conferences like that described above, the various media correspondents who might have covered the discussions as representative of the views of football's fans clearly shied away. Some Federation members were well aware of the discrepancy between the age of many delegates and that of the majority of football fans. That very year in Warners Holiday Camp, the new (and, at under fifty, comparatively young) Vice-Chairman, Mr Southernwood, called for the Federation 'to promote conferences with younger delegates if possible . . . and make (them) generally more interesting'.[46]

To date, the Federation still struggles to attract young supporters into active roles in the organisation. The only way young people can reach the Federation's organisational levels is through the individual Supporters' Clubs affiliated, and these are often either still dominated by older fans or simply unattractive to young potential members. As current Federation Chairman, Tony Kershaw, put it:

> . . . its very hard to persuade the younger members to take any responsibilities . . . it's disappointing that Supporters' Clubs should mirror the football club boards, dominated by older people, but young people don't want to make the commitment to committee work.[47]

By the mid 1970s, the Federation's annual surpluses of the first years of the decade turned into regular deficits. The various lotteries and bingo schemes run from the Federation's HQ in Luton still raised some money, but less and less came from participation in these schemes by member clubs of the Federation. In 1973, out of 129 clubs selling the Federation's fund-raising tickets, only 11 were members of the organisation. The remaining clubs consisted largely of cricket and other social clubs, unconcerned with football.[48]

The Federation continued to lose money throughout the period 1974–79 and was only maintained by drawing upon the assets the organisation had built up earlier. These latter might eventually have been drained altogether were it not for 'a stroke of luck' in 1979, as current President Archie Gooch described it:

> . . . a firm in Bath ran big lotteries on behalf of a fisherman's organisation. They needed a football organisation to run an equivalent one . . . So this firm came in with us – and our member clubs didn't support it! – but (the firm) had so many people selling tickets that we were picking up £15–20,000 a year . . .[49]

This continued for three years until the firm – the 'Sports Club Pool' in Bath – were no longer prepared to subsidise the Federation's involvement. As one Federation officer put it:

> The money we were getting was immoral . . . It was money that wasn't paid out to winners of unsold tickets . . .[50]

The Federation's HQ, which had moved to Saville Row, Bath, after 1979, was subsequently closed down and Secretary, Malcolm Gamlen, the only salaried officer, returned to voluntary status. But the money accrued over those three years set the Federation on its first firm financial footing since its inception over half a century earlier. By 1983, the Federation's assets stood at £33,746, and the interest from the sums on deposit (plus profits from the insurance scheme for member clubs) has enabled the organisation to live reasonably comfortably, despite annual deficits in four of the last eight years, until the present day. The current debate in Federation circles centres around whether the present assets (£27,368 in 1989) should now be used partly to salary a full-time official to run the organisation. At the moment, the Chairman, Tony Kershaw, has been employed by the Federation for one year, in the hope that salaries for subsequent years can be raised by various sponsorship deals.

In 1980, the Federation was offered a page in the FA's publication *Football Today*, to serve as an 'official organ', but the paper ceased publication in 1983. The Federation's *Newletter* – for internal distribution only – continued on, edited by the seemingly indefatigable Jack Williams of Wrexham. Currently, the Federation officers are served by a quarterly Newsletter, retitled *End to End*.

Despite the potentially heightened public profile offered by Denis Howell's concern to involve the Federation in high level meetings through-out the 1970s,[51] complaints still emerged about the organisation's failure to gain sufficient media access. In 1978, Archie Gooch rued the absence of any national coverage of the Federation's attempts to launch an inter-national supporters' body (in contrast to his experience in Europe).[52] Four years later, there was some discontent that the Federation had lost the opportunity to publicise itself during the year of the World Cup in Spain.

The 'personality' competitions – like the 'Football Queen' competition – designed to raise both money and publicity for the organisation, often failed to attract the interest of member clubs. The 'Supporter of the Year' competition was poorly supported and complaints about the very nature of the 'Football Queen' event (now renamed 'Miss Football Supporter') were rising. In 1984, the 'Miss Football Supporter' competition was sponsored by Pontin's, but objections from both male and female members threa-tened its future. One member called it 'outdated' and another – Maureen Robinson of Preston North End – reckoned: 'There's something wrong with the whole concept.'[53]

The problem was: was it a beauty competition? If so, many members thought it anachronistic. Though its defenders and organisers (principally Tony Kershaw, at the time) insisted it was not a beauty competition, the Barnet delegate countered: '. . . the prettiest girl wins . . .'·As it did raise some funds for the Federation, the competition continued.

Worries about the Federation's poor public relation's reached a peak with the advent in 1985 of a new, national supporters' organisation, the FSA. This body almost immediately became the subject of considerable media attention, emerging from Liverpool in the wake of the Heysel Stadium tragedy. The FSA kept up a series of high profile, public cam-paigns which kept it in the media spotlight and, inevitably, drew a stark contrast with the Federation's historic failure to grab the media's attention. For some Supporters' Club representatives, like Frank Horrocks of Manchester City, who had worked long, hard and effectively at local level, it was more than disconcerting to watch the rise of the FSA to national prominence. When Chairman Tony Kershaw explained his personal preference for 'unsensational publicity', Mr Horrocks feared: '. . . that it wasn't getting us anywhere, whereas the Football Supporters' Association was getting maximum coverage.'[54]

In reality the rise of the FSA appears to have *benefited* the Federation, in making it easier for supporters generally to put their views forward. The strategies employed by the FSA led the national media – probably for the first time – into the habit of consulting supporters' representatives, over a period of great public and Governmental concern about the future of football and its fans. In the end, the FSA's efforts raised the public awareness of supporters (as opposed to 'hooligans') to a level that also raised the Federation's profile. Those leading the Federation were not unaware of it, as Tony Kershaw readily admits:

> The additional weight of the FSA has helped to break a few doors down . . . the Federation has traditionally suffered because the media has little interest in 'good news'. I think the FSA's success with the media has washed back, particularly at the *national* level. It's now a great deal easier to gain access to a national audience.[55]

NOTES

1. *The Supporter*, Official Organ of the National Federation, vol. 2, no. 3, November 1935, p. 5.
2. See below.
3. *The Supporter*, vol. 1, no. 1, September 1934, p. 5.
4. *The Supporter*, vol. 1, no. 1, September 1934, p. 1.
5. Nat. Fed. AGM Minutes, 1967, p. 67. What level of distribution of *The Supporter* was achieved in Europe is difficult to estimate. Jack Williams died in 1990, after a lifetime of activity in Federation circles. With him, departed a substantial portion of the Federation's history. He was the longest serving member and his oral account of the Federation's history would have been invaluable.
6. See Chapter 5, 'Structure and Membership'.
7. See *Sports Weekly Magazine*, 21 and 28 August editions, 1948.
8. Nat. Fed. AGM Minutes, 1948, p. 4.
9. Nat. Fed. AGM Minutes, 1948, p. 26. Needless to say, this 'Federation Day' failed to materialise (see also, Chapter 6, 'Relations with the Football Authorities').
10. Nat. Fed. AGM Minutes, 1953, p. 8.
11. Nat. Fed. AGM Minutes, 1954, pp. 2 and 7. One of those supporters who died at Hillsborough in 1989 was an insured member of Liverpool SC.
12. Nat. Fed. AGM Minutes, 1954, p. 9.
13. Ibid., p. 27.
14. Ibid., p. 10.
15. Ibid., 1956, p. 9.
16. See Chapter 7, 'Relations with Government and Police'.
17. Nat. Fed. AGM Minutes, 1958, p. 8.
18. Ibid., 1960, p. 27.
19. Ibid.
20. Ibid., p. 29.
21. Ibid., p. 8.
22. Ibid., p. 30.
23. Ibid., 1961, p. 46.
24. Ibid., p. 48.
25. See Chapter 5, 'Structure and Membership'.

26. Nat. Fed. AGM Minutes, 1962, p. 38.
27. Ibid., p. 43.
28. Ibid., p. 10.
29. Ibid., 1963, pp. 53–5.
30. Ibid., 1965, p. 7.
31. Ibid., p. 11.
32. Ibid., 1967.
33. Ibid., p. 53.
34. Ibid., 1968, p. 21.
35. Personal interview, Tony Pullein, March 1990.
36. See Chapter 5, 'Structure and Membership'.
37. Nat. Fed. AGM Minutes, 1969, p. 89.
38. Ibid., 1970, p. 28.
39. Ibid., pp. 29–30.
40. Ibid., p. 55.
41. Ibid., 1971, p. 30.
42. For example, see *Chelsea Blue*, The Official Journal of the Chelsea Supporters' Club, October 1971, vol. 4, no. 1, pp. 4–5.
43. See *Conference Newsletter*, 1974, pp. 12–14.
44. Nat. Fed. AGM Minutes, 1974, p. 44.
45. *Chelsea Blue*, August 1973, vol. 5, no. 6.
46. Nat. Fed. AGM Minutes, 1973, p. 55.
47. Personal interview, Tony Kershaw, 13 February 1990.
48. See *Chelsea Blue*, August 1973, vol. 5, no. 6.
49. Personal interview, Archie Gooch, 23 January 1990.
50. Nat. Fed. AGM Minutes, 1982, p. 29.
51. See Chapters 6 and 7 above.
52. See *Conference Report*, 1978, p. 17.
53. Nat. Fed. AGM Minutes, 1984, p. 40.
54. Ibid., 1988, p. 19.
55. Personal interview, Tony Kershaw, 13 February 1990.

11

THE HOOLIGANISM DEBATE

Suppose we were to build stocks on either side of the goal in which trouble-makers might instantly be imprisoned? (Kenneth Wheeler, *F.A. News*, 1971)

Football has been associated with a variety of crowd disturbances and misbehaviour since at least the beginnings of the professional game in the 1880s. More generally, riotous behaviour had sometimes accompanied the 'folk' forms of football throughout the centuries it was played in Britain. The period up to 1914, for the professional game, was marked by regular outbreaks of 'hooliganism' which could involve physical attacks on players, referees and (less frequently) fights between opposing fans. Pitch 'invasions' – most usually triggered by gross overcrowding – were also not uncommon and the football authorities employed a variety of sanctions to punish offending clubs.[1]

In the period between the two world wars, 1919–39, there is some indication that, along with a growing national acceptance of the game, crowd trouble was less acute than in earlier times, though by no means unknown. When the Federation was first developing in the late 1920s, it was at a time when, with crowds regularly increasing, football was keen to present its most 'respectable' face and to distance itself increasingly from the 'vulgar' associations of a previous period. The eminently respectable leaders of those Supporters' Clubs who joined the Federation in its first decade clearly wished to play their part in representing football's 'fanatics' as mature and worthy folk, with a proper sense of their place. They were there 'To Help and Not To Hinder', a motto used almost as if to identify themselves as utterly different from *some other kinds of supporters* that the game attracted. In the first edition of the Federation's newspaper, in 1934, *The Supporter*, each member club is extolled,

. . . in honour bound to do all in its power to put down any unsportsmanlike behaviour and by this means stop unfortunate happenings that mar football.[2]

Just as the game of football wished to become more acceptable and establish its place in the heart of English cultural values, so some of its supporters wished *to be accepted* by their, fondly-styled, 'parent' clubs:

> . . . our aim is to assist them by helping to carry out our part as supporters, in a clean and proper sportsmanlike manner, and to be of assistance to them in various ways . . .[3]

If this included voluntarily stewarding crowds, producing magazines 'to provide helpful propaganda' for their football clubs,[4] counteracting barracking of players and the use of bad language, then these Supporters' Clubs were prepared to play their part. Their general desire was to raise the 'tone' of football supporting and play a helpful role in the economy of their football clubs.

When the Federation reconstituted itself following the Second World War, it rapidly grew into a substantial body which included within it hundreds of thousands of individual members. The great flowering of football's popularity in the late 1940s appears unsullied by any substantial fears about crowd violence, though crowd safety was another matter. Dozens of supporters *did* lose their lives at Burnden Park, Bolton, in 1946, when failure to control the entry of crowds at a Cup match led to a terrible crush on the terraces.

It was not until the mid 1950s that the topic of supporter misbehaviour surfaced in Federation discussions. The train-wrecking exploits of Liverpool and Everton fans in the 1955–56 season,[5] following FA Cup matches in Manchester particularly, provoked comment from the Liverpool delegate at the 1956 conference. Referring to the 'vandalism' involved, the delegate was most concerned that these exploits would reflect badly on organised supporters like themselves: 'The Teddy boy type of football follower is dragging the Supporters' Clubs' name down.'[6]

Perhaps surprisingly, the subject of hooliganism did not resurface in Federation national circles for another eight years, though problems associated with unruly football fans had grown considerably in the meantime.[7] In 1964, only the briefest of references to 'so-called fans who . . . make a damned nuisance of themselves' occurs, in the address by Federation Chairman (and Vice-President of QPR) John Hancock. The following year, however, the first detailed discussion about 'football hooliganism' (the latter phrase by now the accepted term) took place amongst delegates, after the topic had been raised by Secretary, Tony Pullein.

The Federation's chief concern seems to have been clearly to demark the transport of Supporters' Club members from the 'unofficial' modes which (the organisation felt) included troublesome fans. Tony Pullein felt it was 'inevitable that . . . there will be irresponsible actions by a small proportion of fools on the terraces' and called on Supporters' Club members to 'give evidence against offenders taken to court'. On the Federation Executive's behalf, he had sent letters to all member clubs suggesting that each Supporters' Club 'be given sole agencies for all football excursions,' but only ten clubs had bothered to reply to his suggestion. The Executive, none the less, planned to meet with transport officials (i.e. British Rail personnel),

> to take what steps we feel necessary to safeguard the reputation of Supporters' Clubs and to ensure that their travel facilities are not suspended for the actions of the irresponsible few.[8]

In the debate that followed, the anger that some delegates felt about the besmirching of the 'good name' of supporters in general often confused the issues discussed. It was, of course, entirely understandable that these representatives of 'supporter-respectability' should boil with frustration, contemplating the rapidly lowering opinion of football fans in the public mind. They were torn between the desire to separate themselves off unmistakably from the 'irresponsible few' and the urge to take matters into their own hands by physically confronting the hooligans. Chairman Gooch (Justice of the Peace) kicked off the debate with a statement that accurately mirrored feelings expressed in many football boardrooms:

> . . . hooliganism is . . . not just only connected with football or Supporters' Clubs. Hooliganism is occurring all over the country and when one sits in magistrates' courts one realises that this is a problem probably of the present day.[9]

The representative from Leyton Orient SC confirmed that it was 'a national problem' but did not think it one 'confined to the young. Some of the older people . . . also indulge in it'. He was most concerned about the way football hooliganism would taint an organisation like the Federation, and recommended:

> I do not think we can do any better or any more than to issue public statements disassociating ourselves with persons who cannot act as decent citizens . . . The Clubs have the law upon which to call to rectify any misdemeanour . . . I feel sure we can clear our name, as it has always been in the football world, an honourable one.[10]

But Archie Gooch, in response, felt this was simply not enough. If Supporters' Clubs organised transport, they had to take responsibility for those transported, not as 'vigilantes' necessarily but as people willing to report (and give evidence against) offenders. In a rather confusing final sentence, he maintained:

We just cannot go along saying this is nothing to do with us; these people are not our people; we can say this.[11]

The Everton SC delegate continued the 'debate' with a diatribe about misrepresentation of his club by the newspapers ('The Press thrives on this'). The coverage of hooliganism associated with Everton supporters had deeply angered his members:

So action is necessary and I would say strong arm action wherever necessary. We have taken this action . . . to put down any signs of hooliganism . . . They (the hooligans) only know the iron fist and we have incorporated that wherever necessary, and we have got results.[12]

This view was warmly supported by the representative of Ilford SC, himself a train driver: 'There is only one way to stop it; the iron fist on football specials.'[13]

At this point Chairman Archie Gooch obviously felt the discussion was itself getting slightly out of control and, deploring the suggestion of the use of the 'iron fist' (somewhat difficult to imagine amongst the late middle-aged majority of Federation delegates), he brought the organisation's first hooliganism debate to a close.

The topic only briefly surfaced in 1966 when Federation President, John Hancock, proclaimed that,

Members of the (Federation) can and will stamp out these undesirables.

Yet he added rather confusingly:

They are not and never will be members of a Supporters' Club because no Supporters' Club would have them . . .[14]

The following year the Midlands Area report urged delegates to recognise that their *own* supporters were sometimes involved in hooliganism. The speaker knew this to be true from painful personal experience. He was

. . . on the receiving end of a violent attack, necessitating hospital treatment . . . Needless to say the culprits were so-called supporters of my own club.[15]

That year the conference was addressed by Mr Trainer, the (perhaps appropriately named) Divisional Passenger Manager for the Merseyside Region of British Rail. In his introduction to Mr Trainer, Archie Gooch reflected on the Federation's debate in 1965 and recalled the threatened cancellations of special trains for West Brom supporters attending the

League Cup Final. Following Mr Gooch's personal intervention, trains were apparently put on but the 'scourge' remained unsolved.

Mr Trainer opened by congratulating the hard work Everton and Liverpool Supporters' Clubs had put in to counter the 'image' of Merseyside's fans in recent years. He added:

> I have seen Rangers and Celtic on New Year's Day and some of the things I have seen in England are nursery stuff by comparison.[16]

Mr Trainer went on to illustrate the kind of damage inflicted on carriages (slashed seats, wrecked toilets, broken windows, etc.) and the frequent pulling of 'communication cords' which disrupted rail traffic over a wide area. He insisted that his job was to make *a profit* on the special trains he ran ('. . . and I am not ashamed of that') and described some of the counter-measures adopted on Merseyside. These included:

(a) using only open or corridor stock where travelling fans were able to be surveyed by other passengers or 'the vigilantes on the job';
(b) not allowing any agents or suburban stations to make bookings, thus guaranteeing everyone gets a seat;
(c) including two plain clothes policemen on every train dressed in club colours;
(d) not stopping the trains at any suburban station and ensuring that they arrived on time. ('There was a school of thought creeping in that these people were hooligans and it did not matter whether they got there on time or not; in other words we were making a rod for our own back . . .'.);
(e) prompt departure times to prevent after-match drinking;
(f) no alcohol on sale on the trains;
(g) no half-fares ('. . . this age group are very prone to do the damage so if they are coming with me they pay full fare').

Mr Trainer recommended the development of 'charter agreements' in which Supporters' Clubs indemnified a sum against possible damage to (or delay of) the train by supporters. He could not understand why it was *football* supporters who caused such damage ('I have never had a penny-worth of damage done by Rugby League Supporters') and he concluded:

> This is big money for us, Mr Chairman, In my division alone in 1965–66 I had £80,000 revenue. I know we had a bumper year. Everton came to the Cup Final . . . It is good business: we want to hang on to it . . . Profitability must always be with me because that is my job.[17]

Amongst all the Federation delegates, it was only Jack Patience, the

Coventry representative – often the sole 'radical' voice in Conference debates – who took exception to the profit-oriented considerations of the British Rail Manager. At Coventry, he insisted, the 'Sky Blue Train' (chartered by the SC) offered three different rates (adults, youngsters and juniors with parents) without problems. It was British Rail's keenness to make money – and meanness in providing too few policemen on football trains – that created difficulties where none need exist. With a hyperbolic flourish, he maintained:

> . . . the people who are mainly responsible for damage to trains are British Railways themselves.[18]

The discussion concluded with a Spurs supporter who thought that the 'mods and rockers' who wrecked seaside towns in the early 1960s had transferred their activities to football. There was only one just solution: '. . . give them the birch; they will not boast afterwards.'[19]

In 1969, the Federation was invited by Denis Howell to submit evidence to Sir John Lang's Committee investigating crowd football behaviour.[20] At the Federation's conference that year another British Rail representative produced vivid accounts of the damage done to trains. He claimed the mere prospect of Saturday misbehaviour was now driving increasing numbers of ordinary passengers on to other forms of transport.[21] One member from the conference floor stood up to insist that the 'hobnailed boot brigade' were not 'supporters'; they were properly termed 'followers':

> . . . there's a supporter and a follower. I'm proud to say we're all supporters here and we'll deal with our own supporters in our own way. If they misbehave, their card goes and they're no longer a supporter as far as I am concerned.[22]

This position was supported and elaborated by Wrexham's delegate:[23]

> Firstly with us; we have got to live with it . . . These people are carrying club colours . . . How many times . . . do we see things thrown from the crowd and the police go in to try to arrest somebody? Straightaway, the crowd – who are not youngsters, but men – stand shoulder to shoulder to stop police from getting somebody.[24]

The Romford supporter described how he himself had disarmed a fan with a piece of scaffolding in his hands and taken him to the club Chairman who called the police.

> There is only one way to do it: act ourselves and rid ourselves once and for all of them.[25]

Though the Newcastle SC representatives vocally quailed at the prospect of

individual supporters seeking to stand in the way of the Gallowgate End
fans rising en masse to march towards the opposition when a second goal
went in against them, once again Everton's delegate – Mr Bailey – insisted
that supporters must 'become involved'. He blamed poor refereeing,
overly aggressive players and 'a lack of Christian faith in the community'
for the rise of hooliganism. It was Sunday School and Bible classes that had
helped him and many others of his generation to keep themselves in check
in years gone by:

> . . . the ruthless savagery that exists today was unthinkable then, and if the
> powers that be and the religious teachers would put more zeal and willpower
> into their efforts to expound the Christian faith, it would at least help to curb the
> abnormal amount of hooliganism that exists . . .[26]

Mr Bailey's speech was greeted with wide applause and congratulations
from the floor of the 1969 conference. It was followed by calls for 'stiffer
sentences' for convicted hooligans from the President and the General
Secretary.

The Federation's 'policy' towards hooliganism at football matches – as it
developed throughout the 1960s – was hardly a cohesive one. It did, in fact,
reflect quite accurately much of the prevailing opinion emanating from
boardrooms and football authorities at the time:

(a) It was not football's fault.
(b) Hooligans were not 'real' supporters.
(c) It was a 'law and order' issue.
(d) Birching (and/or compulsory national service) was required amongst
     other 'stiffer penalties'.

Individual Supporters' Clubs, however, sometimes worked hard and effectively where they could to minimise some forms of misbehaviour and to
present an alternative 'image' of football's fans. Clubs like Everton and
Coventry stewarded their trains to good effect; Wrexham Supporters' Club
operated a 6d a year membership club for 'youngsters' which was manda-
tory for entrance to the ground and it cured the problem of pitch invasions
quickly. Many Supporters' Clubs worked with police and parent FCs to, at
the least, provide a relatively trouble-free channel for away match travel-
lers. The Federation Executive, too, was occasionally able to liaise with
transport authorities and keep 'specials' going when threatened by withdrawal. Yet perhaps the most remarkable thing about the Federation
hooligan-debates in the 1960s is not what was said, but what was *not* said.
Despite the occasional 'radical' outburst from Coventry's Jack Patience, no
one raised the simple questions:

(a) What does football deserve after the long history of a failed relationship with its (always active) audience?
(b) What does the game expect of its supporters, when they have been chronically, badly (and unsafely) accommodated; poorly provided for; ignored or patronised in varying proportions, depending upon their ability to raise and donate money?

What makes the absence of such questions even more remarkable is that many of those gathered at Federation conferences knew only too well how cavalier football clubs could be with their organised and dedicated – usually older and more 'respectable' – supporters, never mind the rest. In the debate that immediately followed the hooligan discussion in 1969, some delegates complained bitterly of the new commercialism of their football clubs and the brutal process of their summarily 'divorcing' the old Supporters' Clubs and establishing new, 'official' clubs run by commercial managers.[27]

Federation conferences had been riven with such complaints (and the harrowing accounts that accompanied them) for the previous decade.[28] Yet no one as yet made any connection between the *attitude* of football's clubs and authorities (the latter who still refused even to meet officially with supporters' representatives) which was betrayed by such disregard. In other words, no one even attempted to answer the question posed by Mr Trainer, the British Rail Manager: *Why football?*

It was 1974 when the first circumstantial link between supporters' behaviour and their general treatment was suggested in Federation debate. It came following Chairman Gooch's 'Review of the Year' – a depressing account of falling membership and income for the Federation, coupled with reflections on the growing 'export' of English hooliganism to Europe, in particular the violence in Rotterdam earlier that year involving Spurs fans.

In response to the Chairman's 'Review', Federation Secretary, J. Harris, representing the whole Executive, suggested a solution which, a decade and half later, found great favour with Mrs Thatcher. He suggested that all football fans should carry identity cards:

> . . . we think the time has come when the National Federation could put forward the suggestion that every person entering a football ground must be issued with an identity card. We hope that the National Federation, in conjunction with the Football League and football clubs in the FA will work out the administrative side, with a slight charge at the first match of the season to the members going in. He (i.e. 'the supporter') would produce his photograph and if a person misbehaves on a football ground the card could be taken away from him and he would not be allowed to enter a football ground anywhere in the country or even abroad.[29]

It was this proposal which drew a riposte from some representatives that linked police and football clubs' treatment of fans with their behaviour, for the first (and last) time in Federation discussions. First the Millwall supporter:

> . . . a lot of clubs could provide better facilities for fans. If they treat people as animals – and I am thinking of toilet facilities etc. on grounds – they will not get a different reaction from fans. . .[30]

Millwall fans had suffered acutely from some of the worst ground facilities in the Football League. The club which, in 1991, is currently in the vanguard of developing community and supporter relations in partnership with its local authority,[31] had a long history of bad provision for and poor relations with its followers. (It also had a reputation for crowd disorder and hooliganism.) Even in the 1930s, rather than encouraging the development of a Millwall Supporters' Club, the directors set up a rival, commercially-based enterprise, 'The Millwall Lions Subscribers' Club'.[32] Those who managed the club – 'an oligarchy of directors and officials who were jealously protective of their positions of influence'[33] – had continually frustrated any attempts by supporters to organise and involve themselves with the club. Yet, despite everything, Millwall's fans often rallied round in times of financial difficulties, offering money and interest-free loans to their Football Club. It won them little in the way of consideration and, almost incredibly, there were no women's toilets at all at the Den until the early 1960s.[34]

Encouraged by the Millwall supporters' interjections, the representative of Hearts SC, Mr Hunter, suggested that *some* of the responsibility for misbehaviour by fans should be laid at the feet of 'the major official European bodies' (i.e. UEFA) who organise football matches.[35] He was followed by Coventry's Jack Patience who, in a strange mixture of 'civil rights', 'trade union activism' and 'law and order' emotions, addressed the assembly:

> I do not think the people in this country would stand for (identity cards). We shall be getting in the State Police next to examine identity cards because the gateman would just not have a cat in hell's chance of doing it . . . (On hooliganism) . . . There is going to be a tragedy that we cannot imagine now but it has got to happen . . . I would like to see solid steel cages put up away from the ground . . . Let them (the hooligans) stay put in there as long as the police are busy doing other things . . . the *other* hooligans in football – I am talking about certain directors of football clubs – have seen fit to kick Supporters' Clubs in the teeth . . . no one has got the guts to get up and say we will do something and I think here a lead should come from the top. I would applaud Archie Gooch . . . if I saw him leading a crowd of pickets round the ground which had been closed to Supporters' Clubs . . .[36]

Jack Patience's speech triggered a further interjection from a Scottish supporter – and one most rare in Federation discussions – a complaint about the quality of policing at football matches. Mr Cranston of Hibernian insisted:

> . . . there is one question we have not covered . . . when someone is arrested at a match and eventually found to be innocent. I think we have to have due regard for these people. I quote a particular case of a member of our club . . . the police made a complete mess of the case.[37]

The unusual trend of this discussion towards criticism of the football clubs, authorities and police in relation to crowd behaviour clearly disturbed many Federation members. These speeches were quickly followed by various restatements of the traditional position the Federation assumed – one reflecting the pent-up fury and frustration of middle-aged, and older 'respectable' supporters forced to witness the damaging unruliness of youngsters. The Basingstoke representative was first to react:

> Mr Chairman I am an old man you might say. I am 70 . . . It is not the place of 'Supporters' Clubs to control the people who are hooligans. They are not supporters. They do not belong to the Supporters' Clubs . . . what is a Supporters' Club for? To better facilities for supporters. It is nothing whatever to do with a Supporters' Club to control supporters.[38]

But members of Supporters' Clubs did misbehave according to another speaker:

> I reported an incident I saw at Wembley when approximately fifty members of Liverpool Supporters' Club broke into Wembley . . . The answer to this (hooligan) problem Mr Chairman and fellow delegates, I am afraid, goes back to the cessation of military service and the abolishing of the birch. The sooner this is brought back, the better. Until we get a different Minister of Sport who has the guts to stand up and thrash this out . . . etc.[39]

Finally, Jack Lambert, the representative of Dorchester and one of the oldest Federation members concurred:

> What we need is a deterrent. I am sick and damned tired of these do-gooders with dented haloes who go around telling me not to use any discipline on some of the scum who come on our football grounds . . . There was a cane in my family. I am a great grandfather and I am proud of the discipline in my family, because I had a cane . . .[40]

As was often the case, the best work on behalf of the Federation was produced by individual Supporters' Clubs. In 1975, the Federation produced a report for Denis Howell MP about football hooliganism. It was written by David Smith, Chairman of the Manchester Utd SC, and concerned particularly the problems amongst fans of his own club.[41] The report recognised that, regardless of the wider issues of 'society in general' in relation to football hooliganism, the latter had become a 'recreational activity' on Saturday afternoons. Manchester Utd – with its huge number of supporters, especially at 'away' games – experienced little trouble at Old Trafford, but undoubted problems when visiting other grounds. The most serious incidents took place before and (particularly) after the match, outside the football ground, and these incidents often occurred when the 'home' attendances were smaller than the visiting 'Red Army'. (Manchester Utd were in the Second Division at the time.) In addition, influential factors included:

> . . . 'pre match publicity' . . . given concerning the reputation of United Supporters; (and) where an additional admission charge had been effected for United Supporters only.[42]

These circumstances, in combination with poor or inexperienced policing, were very likely to provide opportunities for outbursts of hooliganism and disruptive behaviour.

The report outlined in greater detail the responsibilities of the press and other media sources in 'promoting' images of violence in association with football. It recognised the pressure on reporters to provide whatever their editors thought appropriate and cited an example in which the *News of the World* had published a photograph of United's 'hooligans' on the pitch 'brandishing their spoils of victory', when in fact it was a picture of United supporters helping to remove debris from the pitch, with the full permission of the police.[43] These and other examples of self-serving reportage led David Smith to conclude that, while the actions of misbehaving fans were at the root of United's 'reputation', none the less:

> . . . biased and irresponsible publicity has played an important part in promoting such activities.[44]

The police, too, bore some responsibility according to the report: '. . . in the opinion of many (supporters) the police are as much to blame for the current state of affairs as the fans . . .' The newly-formed, so-called 'snatch squads' of policemen brought forth the heaviest condemnation:

> In the event of what the police call 'ungentlemanly behaviour', constables jump into the massed spectators in an attempt to quell the so-called trouble and, as a result of the tightly packed crowd and therefore the inability to reach the designated location, (the police) proceed to evict many innocent supporters . . .

There is no doubt in the minds of a great many supporters that the majority of arrests made within the confines of a football ground involve innocent supporters and this fact together with the overall attitude of the police, which in many instances is one of 'over-reaction', has brought about the current attitude of even the genuine football supporter, towards a policy of non-co-operation.[45]

The report concluded with a series of recommendations specific to the problems facing Manchester Utd.[46]

David Smith's report probably reflected much more accurately the concerns of many (especially younger) football fans; nevertheless, the public attitude of the Federation remained one of a 'law and order' stance towards hooliganism. In 1977, the 'Golden Jubilee' year for the Federation, a special, celebratory publication included an outline of current 'policy' for the future. The piece is littered with the same vocabulary utilised by the very elements of the press that David Smith's report condemned. The words 'louts', 'hoodlums', 'wreckers', 'rowdies' and 'plague' are liberally used throughout, as the Federation calls for 'more seats', a ticket allocation system that would allow 'spectators on the terrace a place among respectable people' or 'the right sort of people', and 'better arrangements for police to dispose of the hoodlums'.[47] In this the Federation mirrored quite accurately the FA's own position which, at its wider reaches, included a return of the birch and the implementation of stocks at football grounds:

> Suppose we were to build stocks on either side of the goal in which trouble-makers might instantly be imprisoned?[48]

The Federation and the FA both called for the return of corporal punishment at the 'Working Party into Crowd Behaviour' meeting at the Department of the Environment in November 1977:

> The question of corporal punishment was raised. The FA seemed to be much in favour but the Minister discouraged discussion on this subject.[49]

Undeterred, a year later Monica Hartland again called, on the Federation's behalf, for a return of the birch, though it is unclear upon whom it should be used, as Monica provocatively proclaimed that 'the main reason for hooliganism is sociologists'.[50]

The Federation's call for compulsory membership ('identity cards') for football supporters – though opposed on practical grounds (pace Jack Patience) by some Federation delegates – continued into the 1980s. Tony Kershaw (then Vice-Chairman of the Federation) was one of those originally against the idea but converted, in 1982, to recommending identity cards with photographs for all 'away' fans 'to keep out the undesirables'.[51]

Two years later at a meeting involving the FA, the Home Office and the Department of the Environment in December 1984, Mr Kershaw expressed the Federation's support 'for the idea of Membership Cards' if a solution to the problem of delays at turnstiles could be found.[52]

Archie Gooch, President of the Federation,

> . . . felt that the introduction of a laser system for membership cards would be a good idea, although such cards should be purely for the cheaper turnstiles, thereby excluding season ticket holders.[53]

But both Mr Kershaw and Mr Eames (of the Home Office) argued that 'the membership card system would need to be comprehensive' (i.e. compulsory for all supporters). It was felt that a pilot-scheme might need to be introduced at a particular club and the meeting agreed that 'any casual supporter would have to enrol as a member of a bona fide Supporters' Club, in order to gain entrance to a ground'. It was perhaps this latter prospect, *of compulsory membership of Supporters' Clubs*, that lay at the root of some Federation officers' enthusiasm for the prospect of identity or membership cards. During a debate on membership/identity schemes at the Federation conference in 1987, the prospect of a 'National Federation Card' was talked of, though opposed by others (particularly Frank Horrocks of Manchester City SC). But the Executive's position was most accurately encapsulated by Monica Hartland's insistence:

> . . . if the membership scheme was inevitable then *we* should do it . . . (we) should be prepared to accept change . . .[54]

However, when it came to the actuality of Government legislation in 1988–89 to enforce 'identity cards', there were no offers of any advantages either to individual Supporters' Clubs (many of whom vigorously opposed the very idea) or to the Federation as a whole. Conservative Councillor (and now Chairman) Tony Kershaw found himself leading the Federation's opposition to the 'Football Spectators Bill' proposed by his own political party. Opposition to the Bill was widespread, but a determined Prime Minister through her Minister for Sport, Colin Moynihan, ensured the passage of the legislation despite vigorous protest across the whole spectrum of football. In the event, it was the deaths of ninety-five Liverpool fans at Hillsborough in April 1989, and the bold condemnation of the legislation in Lord Justice Taylor's consequent Final Report, that proved decisive in preventing the implementation of compulsory identity cards for all football supporters.

The Federation was poorly equipped to make an effective contribution to the hooligan debate, as it grew throughout the 1960s and 1970s. Its opinions reflected accurately the general age of its active membership, and the role they perceived for organised supporters wore the indelible stamp of the Federation's pre-war origins. Despite the bitter experiences of many Supporters' Clubs as they were swamped by the wave of commercialism that swept over football, few Federation spokespeople emphasised the *context* in which hooliganism had re-emerged; one of a chronically failed relationship between the game and its supporters. Highlighting that failed relationship was, perhaps, the real contribution the Federation could have made, on behalf of all football fans. Instead, and again despite the good work of many individual clubs within its membership (and the production of documents like David Smith's report), the Federation did not provide an *additional* voice to the debate on hooliganism. It was not so much 'the voice of the supporter' as the echo of the football establishment in its willingness to see the problem, simply, as a 'law and order' issue. The best efforts of some Supporters' Clubs *empowered* football fans, actively liaising with the police and providing roles as organisers and stewards, while the worst efforts both of the FA's and the Federation's people called for the birch and national service. For the Federation, in fact, the emergence of the hooligan issue into full national debate in the 1970s was a great *opportunity* to put itself on the map – especially in terms of its public profile – but that required it to represent a *particular* voice; one unique to football fans, not one which both washed its hands of the matter whilst simultaneously calling for 'iron fists' in the form of stiffer penalties and ID cards.

NOTES

1. For a detailed history of this, and subsequent, periods, see *The Roots of Football Hooliganism*, ed. Dunning *et al*. London, 1988.
2. *The Supporter*, vol. 1, no. 1, October 1934, p. 2.
3. *The Supporter*, vol. 1, no. 1, October 1934, p. 2.
4. *Sport Weekly Magazine*, 28 August 1948, p. 14.
5. For more on this, see *The Roots of Football Hooliganism*, op. cit., p. 142ff.
6. Nat. Fed. AGM Minutes, 1956, p. 45.
7. Individual Supporters' Clubs, however, did get involved in iniatives to control hooliganism. The Supporters' Clubs on Merseyside in particular met with the press, local police and railway officials in 1959, according to Everton's delegate. See Nat. Fed. AGM Minutes, 1965, p. 54.
8. Ibid., p. 14.
9. Ibid., p. 53.
10. Ibid.
11. Ibid., p. 54.
12. Ibid.
13. Ibid., p. 55.

14. Ibid., 1966, p. 1.
15. Ibid., 1967, p. 22.
16. Ibid., p. 57.
17. Ibid., pp. 57–60.
18. Ibid., p. 61.
19. Ibid., p. 63.
20. See Chapter 7, 'Relations with Government and Police Authorities'.
21. National Federation Conference Report, May 1969, p. 66ff.
22. Ibid., p. 71.
23. Probably Jack Williams.
24. Ibid., p. 75.
25. Ibid.,
26. Ibid., p. 78.
27. See, for example, the speech by the Bath City rep. (p. 83).
28. See Chapter 8, 'Supporter-Club Relations'.
29. National Federation Conference Report, June 1974, p. 35.
30. Ibid.
31. Millwall FC won the Football Trust's 'Football and the Community' Awards in 1989 and 1991.
32. For more on this, see Chris Downham's illuminating MA dissertation: *Dockers, Lions and Bushwackers*, University of Warwick, 1987.
33. Downham, ibid., pp. 48–9.
34. Downham, ibid., p. 81.
35. National Federation Conference Report, June 1974, p. 36.
36. Ibid., pp. 38–9.
37. Ibid., p. 40.
38. Ibid., pp. 42–3.
39. Ibid., p. 43.
40. Ibid.
41. Conference Report, May 1975, p. 48ff.
42. Ibid., p. 49.
43. Ibid.
44. Ibid., p. 50.
45. Ibid., p. 51.
46. Ibid., pp. 56–7.
47. National Federation *Golden Jubilee* Booklet, 1977, p. 15.
48. 'Now Kick the Hooligans Off the Terraces!' Editorial in the *F.A. News*, by Kenneth Wheeler, November 1971. There were other outlandish ideas circulating in the 1970s. Labour MP Arthur Lewis suggested spraying hooligans with indelible dye in 1977, and the call for use of the stocks was repeated by Lady Emmet of Amberley in the House of Lords in October 1976. See Ian Taylor, 'Class, Violence and Sport', a talk presented to the International Symposium on Sport, Culture and the Modern State, Queens University, Kingston, Ontario, 27 October 1979.
49. From Federation Minutes, reproduced in the *Newsletter*, March 1978, pp. 5–6.
50. See National Federation *Newsletter*, September 1978, p. 23.

51. National Federation Conference Report, 1982, p. 59.
52. See *Newsletter*, March 1985, p. 8.
53. See *Newsletter*, March 1985, p. 9.
54. National Federation Conference Report, 1987, p. 27ff.

EXTRA TIME

12

FOOTBALL AND ITS FANS: THE FIRST HUNDRED YEARS

Clearly we have entered an age when every football club needs to establish a new partnership with its supporters. Who will lead the way . . . in the months ahead? (Albert Sewell, 1964[1])

In the tumultuous folk-game of football that hurtled through medieval city streets or rural fields, 'supporting' and 'playing' the game were probably hard to discriminate from one another. Spectating at football seems rarely to have been an entirely passive experience. This tradition was revivified in the dawning of the modern game as it expanded and professionalised in the last quarter of the nineteenth century. Once the rules of 'association' football were established, it was the combined enthusiasm of a wide spectrum of players and watchers that promoted the mushrooming of a myriad of football clubs. Most of these emerging football clubs offered membership to those keen to join in, and they were run largely by committees elected by the members.

Groups of 'supporters' – at a time when that word was only used pejoratively – were quick to organise themselves either on an ad hoc basis (to raise funds by running one-off events) or more systematically to co-ordinate and make available transport to both 'home' and 'away' matches. The close ties between many football clubs and their immediate communities which intensified especially in some urban and industrial areas during the first decades of the professional game, formed the backdrop against which football clubs could appeal for additional money, and supporters could organise to provide it. The community's support for its football club was often channelled through the opportunities provided by its organised supporters. In addition to all the individual 'patrons' for whom the provision of funds might provide a position of authority and power within the football club, without the active engagement and generosity of local people and local supporters' groups, the professional game could never have spread so widely nor rooted so deeply.

Ironically, the intense desire on the part of spectators to participate in supporting a *winning* team produced some of the pressures which led to most professional clubs assuming the status of private limited companies. The requirements to take full part in a national League, to purchase better players, produce a better team and to provide a stadium in which to stage their matches, forced many clubs – perhaps the majority – into a cycle of almost continuous insolvency which only an equally continuous stream of public and private 'donations' could assuage. The issue of shares and the status of a private limited company, with its Board of Directors, often effectively divorced the football club from its supporters. When individual benefactors provided funds for a club, they usually bought their way into the private company and on to its Board of Directors; when the community and its supporters provided funds, they usually *gave* the money to their football club with few strings, if any, attached. In general, football supporters have been (and apparently still are) unattracted by the idea of share-ownership in a football club; their 'investment' is of a different order.

Faced with a developing rift between themselves and those who 'owned' the football clubs, the supporters around the turn of the century could react in a number of ways. If they wished to organise, they could either seek to establish themselves independently and press for involvement in the club's affairs, or organise in a manner and form explicitly approved of by the football club, as a 'child' of the 'parent' body, largely for the purpose of continuous fund-raising. Of the Supporters' Clubs that emerged and survived, clearly the latter proved in the majority. Supporters who sought to organise independently of their football clubs (while also fund-raising) – and particularly if they sought to *represent* the views of their members – were singularly discouraged and refused recognition. Those who administered the game wanted to have their cake and eat it. They were embarrassed by football's popularity (and explosive potential) amongst the rougher sections of the crowd and wished to distance themselves and the once-aristocratic game from it all. Yet, when it suited, they were equally keen to trade on the very same intense local identification with their club that was involved in such strong emotions. When money was required to be raised from local people, the football club was usually presented as an intrinsic part of the community it represented; when local supporters wished to organise independently and take a wider role in their club's affairs, it was seen as 'interference' in a *private* business.

Football clubs much preferred to stimulate the emergence of a supporters' club themselves and to select the personalities to lead it. The kinds of people who came to dominate the committees of these 'approved' Supporters' Clubs were very often men who were already involved in local government and public affairs. Aldermen, councillors, Justices of the Peace, local MPs and churchmen were particularly to the fore. There were obvious advantages to local politicians and other 'personalities' in being closely related to (but not directly responsible for the playing form of) their football clubs. Local publicity about their activities, the impression that they shared the popular life and enthusiasms of the 'common man', and the opportunity occasionally to hob-nob with the club's directors (often also men of considerable local influence) were probably reward enough. They rarely appear driven by the desire to represent the views even of the members of their Supporters' Club, never mind the mass of the football crowd. They were largely 'respectable', middle-aged men; an aspiring, mirror-image of many a club's Board of Directors. With one of the latter usually installed as Chairman or President of the Supporters' Club, these organisations often worked more to represent the interests of the football club to its supporters than vice versa. The rank and file members of most Supporters' Clubs seem to have been content to work voluntarily in weekly fund-raising schemes or other activities as a way of providing additional 'support' for their team, and to trust that those 'in charge' would administrate the club in their best interests. Above all, perhaps, they hoped to earn the respect of their football club and feel more closely involved in its destiny.

Football supporters in general were in a position where they needed to gain the 'respect' of wider society. The occasionally ferocious condemnations of the very idea of *watching* football – the despised 'spectatorism' – set against the backdrop of the aristocratic origins of the modern game and the great amateur versus professional divide – left football's supporters in a no-fan's-land. They were neither straight 'consumers' of a leisure product, nor were they legitimate participants in the game. The poor provisions for supporters attending matches; the generally primitive and inhospitable state of many football grounds; the almost complete absence on the part of the FA or the newly formed Football League to take the interests of spectators and their safety into serious account; these features of the game's landscape were rooted in the social and historical circumstances surrounding the game's birth as a modern sport.[2] They grew to become permanent features on that landscape.

The process of commercialising, and then professionalising, football was quite haphazard. The powerful local links between the inhabitants of particular towns, and districts within cities, and their football clubs were able to root deeply over the years, in part precisely because, as Eric Dunning has argued, the absence of purely profit-motivated commercialism to a degree forced 'a limited form of accommodation to spectators' interests.'[3] Among other factors, the FA's limit of 7½ per cent profit on dividends meant that the football clubs did not become easily manipulable tools of commercial interest – as many equivalent sports clubs did in the

USA – and, they were, consequently, forced to rely on the 'psychological profit' they could provide for local, wealthy gentlemen, as well as the dedicated enthusiasm of local supporters.[4] These conditions *immobilised* the football clubs at their places of birth and made time for intense local identities and traditions to develop. They also helped leave the game badly managed and under-funded.

Supporters and local communities were involved in raising money for their football clubs from the earliest days of the professional game. Periodically, between 1900–60, it is apparent that very substantial sums of money were raised by Supporters' Clubs for their 'parent' bodies. It seems almost as if (excepting some of the larger, rich clubs only) facilities like roofing the 'popular' terraces and the provision of toilets, refreshments, bars, programmes and stewards were left entirely to the supporters' efforts to accomplish. Despite some spectacular feats of fund-raising, like those at Luton Town in the mid-1930s, these were tall orders even for well-organised groups of supporters to fill. That there remain so many professional football clubs in England still operating is surely a tribute to their efforts none the less; given the poor and dilapidated state of many of those football grounds today, what would they have looked like *without* the decades of supporter fund-raising that kept them going? Would they exist at all?

Some football clubs were prepared (at certain times) to operate in close liaison with the representatives of organised supporters; most were not. Many appear completely cynical in their dealings with supporters, readily benefiting from the deeply rooted affection that their football clubs enjoyed locally, while remaining, it seems, unnecessarily secretive and exclusive about details that, one might argue, were of legitimate concern to active fans, like the size of attendances and transfer fees. Some clubs (like Leicester City[5]) even refused representations from organised supporters about half-time entertainments, toilet facilities and stewarding practices.

At a national level, the Football Association and the Football League could see no advantage in developing any real dialogue with the game's supporters. Though members of both administrative bodies must have been aware of the sterling works of fund-raising and organising by supporters that kept so many amateur and professional clubs afloat, they did not offer any 'recognition' that would involve official encounters and debate with supporters. Even after the emergence of the National Federation of Football Supporters' Clubs in 1927, which at the least provided a forum for some supporters to meet with football administrators, no meetings took place until the last decade of one hundred years of the professional game. It was, in fact, the Government (in the form of Denis Howell MP, Minister for Sport in the Labour administrations of the late 1970s) that eventually ushered some Federation officers into the (official) presence of senior football administrators for the first time. The football authorities have, in recent times, often been accused of poor leadership and bad management; at no level of their operations has their past failure been as complete as at that which involved their potential relations with the supporters of the game they administered. In truth, they did their best to ignore them, offering scant concern either for their safety or for their enthusiasm. In this, the FA and FL both continuously reflected the class divisions and particular social history that informed their earliest days. They remained (for their separate reasons) as it were preserved in a late Victorian jar on the shelf of history – fearful, suspicious and, perhaps most of all, embarrassed by the passion that football fired in the hearts of its multitudes of fans.

But why were those fans never able – or moved – to organise themselves effectively, so as to demand more involvement in the game? At local levels, supporters of course did organise to good (fund-raising) effect but they were led largely by those whose vision of the supporters' role was limited to that thought 'appropriate' by football club boards. Despite the facts that a club's supporters were not bound together like co-workers in a factory or as co-investors in a financial enterprise, there were none the less strong ties of locality, tradition and shared commitment upon which they could build organisations. Somehow, it seems, the *personalities* required to inspire and co-ordinate football's supporters towards the independent (and forceful) representation of their views did not appear. Perhaps (as I have argued elsewhere[6]) those who might have performed such roles were engaged in more direct, political activities and organisations, seeing football as 'boss' sport with no future.

At the national level, the only organisation to emerge prior to 1985 was the Federation of Supporters' Clubs. In its beginnings, and for many decades thereafter, it was organised as a 'respectable' Supporters' Club writ large. It too saw its role almost entirely within the parameters defined by the 'parent' bodies – the football clubs. It was hardly a vehicle designed to crash through the archaic barriers and ideas which persisted around the football authorities. It never saw itself as such – rather the opposite. Under the banner headline of its monthly newspaper, *The Supporter* in 1935, which read: 'What We Really Stand For', the Federation pronounced its particular role:

> . . . it differs entirely from the usual type of 'Association' movement, in that it is not formed primarily for redressing grievances, nor has for its object the interference with any established practices or the changing of any laws.[7]

As a voluntary organisation, the Federation was 'expressive' rather than 'instrumental'.[8] It embodied the shared commitment of busy chaps who ran Supporters' Clubs, expressing their whole-hearted support of their football clubs, and their desire to raise the 'esteem' in which supporters were held. In such an organisation, it is *the members themselves* (in this case, the Supporters' Clubs) who are the raison d'être for its existence, rather than any public policies or campaigning objectives. Providing a service to those members – helping them to help their 'parent' clubs – was what the Federation actually did. It neither sought actively to represent the views of ordinary supporters to the football clubs or to the football authorities; nor did it wish, in reality, to campaign on behalf of the crowds or the Supporters' Clubs. As Federation Chairman, Ray Sonin, put it in 1956, when some member clubs wanted to establish a Legal Aid Fund, 'We're not so much a fighting organisation as a helpful organisation.'[9]

With some irony, the Federation's most energetic and successful campaign was fought (as it turned out) *for the benefit of the football clubs*, when it worked assiduously for a new 'Lotteries Bill' in 1956. This legislation, once allied to the FA's de-restriction of football clubs' involvement in 'gambling' schemes a few years later, set the stage for a massive collapse of the Supporters' Club network, under the impact of wholesale take-overs by their child-devouring 'parent' bodies.

Yet the Federation was able to provide real assistance to many supporters' clubs within its sphere. It encouraged and assisted in the formation of new clubs where supporters could gain access to organised travel to games, social and fund-raising activities. From the mid-1950s onwards, it has offered various insurance schemes to member clubs seeking to protect their individual members on journeys to or from football matches or whilst attending them. These schemes have additionally, particularly over recent years, provided a valuable source of steady income to the Federation. For the current Chairman (himself an insurance salesman), these schemes represent some of the finest achievements of the organisation.[10] The Federation also offered a useful pool of experience, information and advice about the various matters that concerned many Supporters' Clubs – the legal complications of owning property, organising transport, and staffing tea-bars and clubs. It successfully liaised, on a number of occasions over decades, with transport authorities presenting difficulties to particular clubs. It also offered, at least until the early 1960s, free advice about specific legal and tax matters which concerned its members. The Federation was able, too, to provide some information and advice to Governments from the mid-1960s onwards about the range of activities supporters engaged in through their clubs, making a significant contribution to Norman Chester's far-sighted report (1968). Its members also worked hard to run youth '5-a-side' competitions and leagues of Supporters' Clubs teams.

But the Federation failed where it could, arguably, have achieved most: it failed to provide supporters in general, and Supporters' Clubs in particular, with either a high public profile or a demanding presence in any football debate. Though the Federation's primary aim may have been 'To Help and Not To Hinder' the football clubs, it also aimed initially to 'have more weight within the football world' on behalf of supporters.[11] In this quest it significantly fell short of the goal. The organisation's chronically poor management of the media (one of the few arenas, especially in recent decades, that has proved a potentially powerful territory for organised supporters) proved a major impediment to advancement in the public domain. For the Federation, the time to strike was probably in the late 1940s to the mid-1950s. It was then, with a nominal membership of anything up to one million fans – and members raising regularly the crucial funds to sustain many clubs – that the Federation might have turned the screw to gain an official presence in the oak-panelled rooms of football administrators.

Most of the active members of the Federation appeared to have neither the heart nor the vigour for such an attack upon the status quo of the football authorities. As an 'expressive' organisation, its members were not drawn together with much by way of 'shared objectives' in policy-making and campaigning. Often the members of individual Supporters' Clubs knew little if anything of the Federation's activities (precisely because these largely involved the servicing of the committees that ran Supporters' Clubs), and even less did they 'mandate' the Federation to act on their behalf. The Federation's officers and active members have remained, from the organisation's earliest days, almost entirely drawn from the middle-aged or older age bracket; ill-equipped in recent times to excite media attention as 'representatives' of football's fans, they appeared more like (and sometimes actually were) the directors of football clubs. In addition, the Federation sometimes appeared as if it wished to be *like* the Football Association (and its preliminary attempts to officially 'affiliate' with the FA in the 1950s were a logical consequence of that desire, not just hopeful routes to an allocation of Cup Final tickets [12]). The organisation also looked (perhaps unfortunately) not unlike some of the Football League's more recent management committees: an unnecessary tier of administration, spending money that could be better used in other ways, and utterly incapable of reflecting the interests of the wide range of clubs it purported to represent. In its poorest light, the Federation seemed to combine the worst of both worlds: all the impotence of the Football League in alliance with the ageing, bumbling respectability of the FA Council.

The most remarkable feature of Federation discussions in the post-war period was what was not included for debate. Whilst great time and energy was spent talking about the 'Football Queen Competition', the steep deterioration in the conditions and facilities for ordinary supporters at football grounds was virtually unmentioned. The physical *safety* of supporters was never once a topic for debate prior to the 1980s, yet the Federation reconstituted itself with great expectations and a huge membership in the years after the war, immediately following the tragic deaths of dozens of fans at Burnden Park, Bolton, in 1946. There is no mention of this disaster in the AGM Minutes from 1948 onwards, nor does the Ibrox tragedy in 1971 appear to ripple the surface of Federation discussions. Basic issues – like toilet facilities at grounds – do not provoke concern or a desire to campaign publicly to improve them. Such matters even appear to embarrass the Federation officers. When the subject of women's toilets at football grounds (usually poor; sometimes non-existent) was attemptedly raised at conference in 1961, the Federation Chairman cut discussions short by claiming it was 'not a pleasant matter' and advised supporters' clubs concerned about such problems to 'buy them yourselves for the (football) club'.

Along with basic provisions for supporters, there was no debate prior to the 1980s about facilities for disabled fans, nor does there appear any recognition of the rise of racism amongst football crowds. This is not to say that individual Supporters' Clubs did not seek to tackle those and other issues. Some did, vigorously and to good effect. But one suspects that such positive efforts by organised supporters at local levels would have happened anyway, with or without the Federation's existence. Much the same is true of the practical efforts made by some Supporters' Clubs in recent decades to deal with the rising crisis of hooliganism at home and abroad. The innovations – pre-match visits to hosts, liaison with foreign police forces, etc. – were made by individual Supporters' Clubs (and attemptedly funded by themselves or in combination with their football clubs).

Even after the Federation had achieved financial stability in the early 1980s – indeed, with around £30,000 on deposit for most of that decade, with cash in hand – there was no inclination towards spending some money on national campaigns to promote better supporter relations and conditions. Instead, the organisation preferred to live off the interest the money generated.

The Federation's major opportunity to develop a clear public profile (and take part in a national debate) emerged with the rising tide of crowd disorders in the 1970s. But the Federation failed to provide a *distinctive* voice for the concerns of many 'ordinary' supporters. Rather, it largely reflected the opinions of the football clubs and administrators. It accepted without demur the 'law and order' agenda that dominated strategies to deal with hooliganism, and even (so it seems) *initiated* the proposal for compulsory identity cards for football supporters as early as 1974. As late as 1988, current Chairman, Tony Kershaw, could still be heard calling for the return of corporal punishment and national service.[13]

Despite its weaknesses, and the vicissitudes of the football world over the last thirty years, the Federation has shown great 'stickability' simply to survive. It is an accolade to the Supporters' Clubs involved and the voluntary work of their officers. The world of supporters' organisations has changed radically since 1985, with the emergence of the Football

Supporters Association (FSA); dozens of 'independent' Supporters' Clubs and associations, and literally hundreds of fanzines appearing. Rather than disabling the Federation, the effect has been to concentrate it much more on attempting to deal with issues of the day which affect all supporters. The current representation of supporters to Government, football authorities and various other bodies – though hardly satisfactory – is more frequent and serious than ever before. But all that, as they say, is another story.

In 1985, at the end of a century of professional football, the potential relations between fans and the game remained largely an undiscovered territory. No significant attempt had been made on the part of the football authorities to unpack the possibilities inherent in that relationship. Discovering the 'appropriate', institutional expression of the bond between supporters and their football was (and remains) a complex task. It is complicated by the very nature of that experience of identification and enthusiasm which is characteristic of the game's crowds. This complex emotional cargo tends to burst the vessels that would contain or define it. It is not just about spectators witnessing a spectacle; nor just consumers purchasing a leisure product; nor is it even only the close ranks of a particular community supporting an emblematic representation of their solidarity. All these descriptions can be true, but there is something else, more difficult to rope down, which can make football's fans appear more like temple-goers of a localised religious sect with international affiliations. There are the ritualised events at the regular gatherings; the singing and shuffling in unison; the high dramatic possibilities risking victory or defeat; the powerful identification between those who attend the rite and those who perform it. Individually, too, there are, for some who witness, private peaks of intense emotional surges which mark their lives like signposts on a journey or stages of a pilgrimage. Yet football's congregation includes not only those who watch but also those who *care* for the game, for a particular club or a team. It was this original 'congregation' that provided the enthusiasm the game required for its growth and proliferation; it also physically helped build (or provided the funds to build) many of the 'temples' where the games are played.

Football owes the particular place it occupies in British life to this deep and broad purchase it gained on people's hearts. It was football's *fans* that marked the professional sport out from a crowd of other spectator sports, and they who gave it both a local particularity and an almost global popularity. For those not directly involved in supporting the game, the most remarkable and gripping feature of football has always been its supporters, with their outlandish garb, fierce enthusiasm and idealistic investments of time, energy and money.

The problem of developing the appropriate expression of this intense relationship between fans and the game was never seriously approached. Supporters themselves have been too apathetic and unsure of their ground;

too slow to realise the power they might have exercised before the 1960s –
and too inappropriately organised since then to represent their real interests. The football clubs and administrators at the League and the FA
sought only short-term advantages. It was, in reality, not only in their own
interests but also for the long-term benefit of the game that relations with
supporters should be deepened and widened. It was the *duty* of the football
administrators as 'custodians' of football's good health to develop those
relations for the good of the game, if necessary with direct encouragement
– and, perhaps more importantly, with some financial assistance – to
enable supporters to take a proper part in the game's affairs. Without such
encouragement, the bulk of supporters were always likely to remain on the
fringe of the 'real-politik' of football.

Without the help of football's administrators, supporters might still have
advanced their cause through links with the players. If the various versions
of the Players Union had succeeded earlier in organising its members more
powerfully – and an *alliance* between professional players and supporters
had emerged – then the history of the game off the park might have proved
quite different. That potential alliance between those who play and those
who 'support' – the *primary* alliance in the early formation of so many
football clubs – is the natural counterweight to the 'alliance between clerks
and self made businessmen' who came to run the game. Yet that natural
partnership has yet to re-emerge, and when the players' PFA finally
succeeded in the early 1960s in throwing off the shackles of the Victorian
employer-employee relationship, one effect was to unleash a strain of
commercialism in modern football clubs that did more to destroy any
existing contacts with organised fans than anything previously. Only recently, under the leadership of Gordon Taylor, has the PFA sought to
deepen its relations with supporters' organisations and offered financial as
well as moral support for various campaigns.

The history of supporters' involvement with football – their willingness
to organise and fund-raise; their infectious enthusiasm and bizarre dedi-
cation; even their *misbehaviour* as unruly crowds – all point towards and
demand a much greater role at local and national levels of the game.
Indeed, there is some evidence in that history which supports some of Ian
Taylor's speculations about the relationship between the process of commercialisation and 'bourgoisification' of football, and the rise of modern
forms of hooliganism.[14] It is, for example, unmistakably the case that, at
precisely the time when crowd disorder, fighting and pitch-invasions were
rising in the 1960s, the game was busily engaged in dismembering the
(already weak) links between fans and their clubs that had centred around
fund-raising and other activities. The emergence of the 'commercial de-
partments' and 'development associations' at football clubs was paralleled
by the rise of hooligan 'firms'. The *context* of this resurgence of crowd
disorder must also include, as at least one significant element, a recognition

of the chronically failed relationship between fans and football over the previous sixty or seventy years. This context does not preclude other factors involving a complex web of social trends that impinged on the groups of (often) young men engaged in serious disorders; it informs and substantiates them. It gives at least a part of the answer to the oft-posed question about hooliganism: why *football*?

It may be that the way to begin the process of building football supporters into the game's political structures will involve some democratisation at local and national levels of the game's administration. Despite the inappropriate (and, some argued, plainly dangerous) implications of the compulsory identity card proposals included in the Football Spectators Act (1990), there is the germ of an idea in there which makes sense in the context of the history of football and its fans. It is the idea of *membership*, but not of the restrictive, involuntary kind described (though now dropped) in the recent legislation. Supporters need a kind of membership that works both at local and national levels to involve them more deeply in football's fabric. It was, after all, the membership of local football clubs – the 'enthusiasts' in every sense of the term – who drove football forward over a century ago from its public school, amateur 'Corinthian' origins, through its professionalisation to become the only game to claim a worldwide audience. The season-ticket holders and those who join the supporters' organisations are an immediate, identifiable membership-body of English football (as Norman Chester far-sightedly argued nearly twenty-five years ago). That body might form the basis of an organisation intent on including *all* the supporters who regularly attend. Football's fans have an historical and cultural right – and a right in commonsense justice – to take a real part in the running of the game. It is also in the game's best interests. But it is unlikely to happen without the moral and financial support of football's administrative bodies. There are signs in the FA's *Blueprint for the Future of Football* of perhaps some readiness to stimulate the organic development of more effective supporter-networks.[15] But these latter must develop *independently* amongst the fans themselves, with the assistance, but not under the control of, the football authorities. On the evidence of past history, such a possibility looks thin.

There are some who believe that the supporters' days are numbered, and others who think the game can be sold almost entirely to television. It is undoubtedly true that the 'televisualising' of football over the last quarter century has been the single, most powerful contextual change to effect the game.[16] But Margaret Thatcher's reported vision of football played in empty stadia run on TV and associated sponsorship alone was ill-judged and uninformed. Even in televisual terms, the supporters may prove as essential as ever they were to the creation of the intensely dramatic encounters the television producers require. No amount of dubbed soundtrack of crowds roaring would cover their absence or the draining of their enthusiasm. In the end, the crowd is the supreme authority without which the golden core of the game has no currency. Without the particularity of its fans, football makes no magic so that materialises only within and through those who are there to witness it.

NOTES

1. 'Make the fans feel wanted', *F.A. News*, vol. XIII, no. 12, July 1964.
2. See E. Dunning, *Aspects of the Dynamics of Sports Consumption: A Figurational/Developmental Analysis*, 1991, A Paper available from the Centre for Football Research, Leicester University.
3. Dunning, ibid.
4. This is not to say that there were not local businessmen keen to make a profit from their connections with football clubs. Brewers and builders were prominent on many football club boards.
5. See Chapter 2.
6. See 'Walking alone together', in J. Williams and S. Wagg (eds), *British Football and Social Change*, Leicester, 1991.
7. *The Supporter*, vol. 2, no. 3, November 1935, p. 5.
8. I have borrowed these terms from an unpublished paper entitled 'Voluntary organisations and their membership' by Dr John Lansley at Liverpool University's Department of Continuing Education, 1990.
9. Nat. Fed. AGM Minutes, 1956, p. 40.
10. When asked at interview for the single achievement of the Federation that he was most proud of, current Chairman, Tony Kershaw, replied: 'I can't think of a *single* achievement . . . I would like to have been able to say that all 95 who died at Hillsborough were covered by our insurance scheme, but only one supporter was . . . It would have been something to be proud of if all those fans had. been covered by the insurance scheme' (personal interview, 13 February 1990).
11. *The Supporter*, vol. 1, no. 1, September 1934, p. 2.
12. See Chapter 6.
13. In a speech at the 'Football into the 1990's' conference, at Leicester University, 1988.
14. See 'Football mad: a speculative sociology of football hooliganism', in E. Dunning (ed.), *Sociology of Sport*, London, 1971.
15. See principally, Section Three of the FA's *Blueprint*, published in April, 1991.
16. As Stephen Wagg has argued in *The Football World*, Brighton, 1984.

FINAL WHISTLE

13

FINAL WHISTLE

There may be some readers surprised that this book ends its account of supporters' organisations and their relations with the game in 1985, and includes little mention of subsequent developments. Given my own direct involvement with the Football Supporters Association (FSA), perhaps those readers will have expected a much more detailed account of the new 'alternative' supporters' movement, which includes the FSA, independent associations and the fanzines.

In response, I would say firstly that the period 1885–1985 is a convenient time-block. It starts with the rapid rise of the professional game to mass popularity and ends with, arguably, English football's worst year of all. It is also (though I hope less so now) a period of football supporting without a history to its name. It was a story that needed a telling, if only to help us understand better the developments, that have flowed from 1985. As football supporters, if we don't know where we have come from, how can we know where we are?

Before 1985, I had simply watched football from the terraces, occasionally complaining to whoever stood within earshot about what was wrong with the game from the punter's viewpoint. I had little idea how intricately complicated the web of professional football really is – as complex a game off the park as it is simple on it. I became naively involved in the beginnings of the FSA, without any previous knowledge or experience of supporters' organisations. I knew nothing of the existence of the Federation for example, at all.

Since then I have learnt something. The pace of events in the football world seemed, after Heysel, to quicken to a permanent sprint. As Chair of the FSA for the first four years of its life, I found myself almost continuously involved in issues of real importance to hundreds of thousands of people. Just consider a few of the items on that agenda – the aftermath of Heysel; the establishment of a national organisation; the media groundwork; the 1986 Cup Final debacle (outside Wembley, that is); the Cup tickets petition to the FA; the League's 'fifty per cent' membership scheme; the attempted club-mergers; the 1988 Championships in Europe; the Government's ID Card Scheme; Hillsborough; Lord Justice Taylor. All that was from a standing start. There was hardly time to draw breath and look back at the person I was before some of those particular and awesome football events bent my life away at a tangent. I am deeply grateful for the *time* given me to write up this account of fans and their relations with football before 1985. Having witnessed such momentous events, I needed to go back and catch up their roots.

There can be little doubt that the last half of the past decade has witnessed a great turning of the gyre in football's history. Events still move ahead quickly. The re-structuring of the Football League (largely behind closed doors without reference to either players or supporters of the game) looks like so much *perestroika* without even a dash of *glasnost* – and recent history illustrates that the one doesn't work without the other (though, in Gorbachev's case, it was vice versa). Football appears prepared to blunder into its future – as it has largely lived its past – without either the sanction or the wisdom of, to my mind, the two most significant parties in the game: those who watch and those who play. Football, as it has existed throughout most of the pages of this book, *is* dying – but only to be born again. It is the new character and form of the professional game that is currently gestating. There are forces and voices that seem to require the new creation to be utterly cut off from its traditional inheritance, its traditional audience. The plans outlined in parts of the FA's 'Blueprint for the Future of Football', which include converting 'going to a match' on a Saturday into having 'integrated leisure experiences' (p. 11), ring an ominous bell. They reflect the ambitions of those who eye covetously the commercial American sports format.

They want to move British football 'up-market' to attract a higher spending, growing middle class audience. It is a philosophy which invites the marketing strategist into the driving seat. In such a circumstance, if traditional customs clash with the marketing plan, the latter will prevail. Already in America, the National Baseball League (representing the American game with social roots most like football in Britain) has already organised the playing of League matches in Japan, denying the teams' supporters their time honoured 'right' to watch their home team play. If this harbinges Manchester Utd v Arsenal playing for League points in some Sheik's back garden in the Near East, then there will be trouble ahead.

There are other powerful forces – which include the media and the market place – which might successfully constrain such ambitions. Football has drawn deeply from a reservoir of affection among 'ordinary' British folk for over a century. The alternative sources of enthusiasm for the game, particularly those 'up-market', may briefly shimmer in the commercial sunlight, yet dry up almost overnight. Football may be moved out of its water so traumatically that it loses its viability. It is true that British supporters have traditionally had their football 'cheap' compared with their continental counterparts (though, as this book illustrates, they have paid additional cash in other ways). But some of the big clubs in London and elsewhere may soon price themselves out of the market. How many can expect their fans to pay up to £20 for either a match or an 'integrated leisure experience'?

Football Clubs big and small face the most serious financial crisis that has ever threatened the game. The implications of modernising the nation's football grounds to the standards required by Lord Justice Taylor are legion; the costs enormous. The annual funds available through the Football Trust from Littlewood's, Vernon's and Zetters' 'Spotting the Ball' competitions (currently around £13 million) plus the Pool's Betting Levy reduction of 2.5 per cent (around £20 million a year) sounds like a lot of money to be dispensed annually within the game. But the truth is that it hardly touches the sides of football's thirsty requirements. The real costs (if most of our clubs are to survive) may be in the region of £700 million and rising. The game will not be able to bridge the gap. Even our biggest football clubs are the financial equivalents of corner shops when compared to the giants in Italy and Spain. Britain's biggest club, Rangers, only turns over around £15 million a year – roughly one tenth of AC Milan. Yet Rangers is (financially) nearly twice the size of Manchester United, Arsenal, Liverpool or Everton. The big clubs as well as the smaller ones face very genuine financial difficulties which will have to be resolved for them to survive. Consider Liverpool's current situation: the redevelopment of the Kemlyn Road Stand will cost around £8.5 million. One quarter of this will be met by a Football Trust grant; perhaps another £1.5 million can be raised by leasing (for three years in advance) the new executive boxes. Only 4,500 extra seats will be gained, yet the borrowing of perhaps £4 million will have to be financed by a Club which only turns over around £8.5 million a year. And there is the Kop to seat by 1994. For smaller clubs the problems are equally if not more acute, and of a different order. How will a second division club like, say, Barnsley FC raise the money to be able to attract the maximum grants from the Football Trust? If a club must raise £3 million to attract £1 million in grants, how will it manage? Who will lend Barnsley the £3 million?

Only the Government of the day can realistically deal with the threat to our football clubs great and small. Only the voters can convince the Government that football *counts* that much. To date none of the main political parties in Britain is committed to seeking a realistic solution to football's fiscal nightmare; yet we all saw in Italy how a Government that recognises the cultural significance and power that the game encompasses can find the money if it wishes.

The future of football in Britain is unfolding before us. I am convinced that there will be opportunities for supporters – in conjunction with the media and in partnership with the players – to influence the shape of things to come. It would have been possible, of course to include a further chapter or two in this volume, and attempt to discuss the latest developments but, inevitably, it would have appeared tacked on to a story which stands well on its own. To my mind, the events in the football world since 1985 represent the beginnings of a new stage in the history of the game; one which includes the rise of the FSA, the 'independents' and the fanzines, Hillsborough, ID Cards, Italy' 90, League re-structuring, TV influence, the return to Europe and future cross-cultural developments between supporters. These subjects are all part of the 'football revolution' through which we are now living. They deserve a book to themselves.

INDEX